Entrepreneurship:
Back to Basics

Entrepreneurship: Back to Basics

Gordon B. Baty
and
Michael S. Blake

BeardBooks
Washington, DC

Library of Congress Cataloging-in-Publication Data

Baty, Gordon B. 1938-
    Entrepreneurship--back to basics / Gordon B. Baty, Michael Blake.
        p. cm.
    Previously published: Entrepreneurship for the nineties, Englewood Cliffs, N. J. :
    Prentice Hall, 1990. With new introd.
    Includes index.
    ISBN 1-58798-140-8
        1. New business enterprises. 2. Entrepreneurship. I. Blake, Michael. II. Title.

HD62.5 B378 2002
658.4'21--dc21

                                                                        2002028226

Printed in the United States of America

To
Robert Oaklund
engineer, entrepreneur,
and a very tough guy
1941–1974

Other Beard Books on Business

Beard Books

Dangerous Dreamers: The Financial Innovators
from Charles Merrill to Michael Milkin
Robert Sobel

Distressed Securities: Analyzing and Evaluating
Market Potential and Investment
Edward I. Altman

Getting It to the Bottom Line: Management by
Incremental Gains
Richard S. Sloma

Inside Wall Street
Robert Sobel

Merger: The Exclusive Inside Story of the
Bendix-Martin Marietta Takeover War
Peter F. Hartz

No-Nonsense Planning
Richard S. Sloma

Takeover: The New Wall Street Warriors: The Men,
the Money, the Impact
Moira Johnston

The Luckiest Guy in the World
Boone Pickens

The Rise and Fall of the Conglomerate Kings
Robert Sobel

For more information on these titles and for a complete listing of
available Beard Books titles, see www.beardbooks.com

Contents

Preface

"We are not here to sell a parcel of boilers and vats, but
the potentiality of growing rich beyond the dreams of
avarice." .. Samuel Johnson, presiding at the sale
of Thule's Brewery, London

This book, like its predecessor, *Entrepreneurship for the Nineties*, was written as a resource for the entrepreneur and the would-be entrepreneur. As observed in the preface to that work, entrepreneurship is one vocational calling for which there is really no apprenticeship. Working in other companies, even small ones, cannot prepare one for the responsibilities, the incessant demands, the highs, the lows, and for the loneliness of running your own company.

These things remain as true as they were a decade ago. Also unchanged are the long hours, domestic sacrifices, and financial commitment of the career. In addition, many of the fundamentals of managing people, promoting products, and negotiating and dealing with customers are still valid and will remain so for a long time.

What has changed, however, is the environment in which the entrepreneur must operate today. It is, it seems to us, a very different world from that of the decade from which we are now emerging and recovering. Or perhaps *World* is not the right astronomical metaphor. Today, the venture business seems more like a dwarf star, the leftovers from the entrepreneurial supernova that was the late nineties. Or another metaphor: we are all recovering from a mega-hangover from a really huge party. But like all hangovers, this will end, and we will all get back to business.

The party was characterized by the most egregious overinvestment in companies, public and private, that the world has ever seen. As the bubble grew,

- Entrepreneurship came to seem like the easiest game in town.
- Every self-respecting engineering or MBA student has a business plan to promote.
- Deals were started to be flipped. The real product was stock.
- Starting and financing deals had to be done in 'internet time". Since deals were expected to move from startup to IPO in a few months, there was no time for investor evaluation, no time to build a proper team, no time to form a real board, no time to talk to real customers. No time to build a company.
- Not only was there often little prospect of earnings, and certainly none to match the capitalizations — often there was not even a coherent plan for how earnings might one day be achieved.
- Investors were asked to forget traditional metrics, and to concentrate instead on share of "market", earliness of entry, market capitalization achieved in financing, number of site hits per week, number of "eyeballs", and numerous other ingenious measures of merit.

Everyone wanted to be an entrepreneur. It was better than being a rock star, because it did not require much talent or very much work. Just one successful performance was enough.

Other hung-over occupants of our dwarf star include the investment banking community, the public accounting profession, the venture capitalists, a good many future corporate superstars, and investors of all sorts. It also includes quite a few entrepreneurs.

Does all of this spell the end of the new-venture industry? Well, hardly. The pool of invested venture capital is, at time of writing, at a record high. The rumblings of economic recovery are being heard throughout the land. A new crop of entrepreneurs is surfacing, each one looking for the next big thing. But whatever the next wave looks like, one thing is certain: investors, customers and employees will all be looking for the same things: genuine customer value, sustainable competitive advantage, believable earnings potential, and a team dedicated to building a company, not flipping one. These are hardly new ideas; they are in fact the bedrock ideas that have historically driven the venture-creation process.

It might appear then that we have come full-circle, back to basics. However, the authors believe that life proceeds not in a circle but in a helix: we have learned some useful lessons on the last trip around that can serve us well on the next cycle. Moreover, the opportunities, resources and ideas are better each time around. Compared to a decade ago, there is much more venture capital under management now; there are many more skilled lawyers, accountants, bankers and consultants who understand the process now; there is much broader acceptance of entrepreneurship as a legitimate business career than ever before (indeed, it is hard to find a university that does not offer a course or two in new ventures). Yet, to exploit these factors fully, a grasp of the old-economy basics is needed. That is the purpose of this book.

We do not intend this book to be a complete reference manual of everything you need to know to start your company. Such a book would be so long that no entrepreneur would read it. Excellent sources exist for information on every functional business area (e.g., finance, accounting, project management). The web is a wonderful source of resource sites for entrepreneurship and small business management.

Our focus throughout is on the growth-oriented (gazelle) venture, as opposed to "small business" although of course many of the same management ideas apply to both. We are interested in the problems of the person who is attempting to build a rapid-growth company by exploiting some new technological or marketing idea — a company with the potential for multinational marketing, the potential for exponential growth, and the prospect of making its founders millionaires in an interestingly short time.

This book is not offered as an academic, or even a balanced, view of Entrepreneurship. It is written from a definite and pragmatic point of view, which, roughly, is this: Neither innovative genius nor business school training, not hard work, nor even luck is in itself a guarantee of entrepreneurial success. Assuming all these are present in some degree, the missing catalytic element often seems to be what we might call the entrepreneurial mindset. It can be characterized as a degree of tough-mindedness that stops short of truculence; a confidence in one's intuitive as well as rational faculties; a capacity to think on one's feet, as well as to plan in the business-school strategic sense; an attitude that stresses timely action based upon usually inadequate facts, ahead of prolonged fact-finding; a mental set stressing integration of many facts of action into action plans, rather than endless analysis. It is an attitude that says, in short: "I didn't just come to play the game — I came to win".

We hope this book will help you become one of the winners. We hope it will sit on your desk and become a friendly resource to be opened, reread and underlined — to stimulate your thinking, to get you talking to the right sorts of people, and concentrating on the right things. We hope it will save you some calendar time, some costly mistakes, some needless worry, and some precious entrepreneurial energy. We hope it offers the prospective entrepreneur some idea of how to go about collecting your building blocks, and offers the up-and-running entrepreneur some glue to hold them all together.

Gordon B. Baty
Michael S. Blake

Acknowledgements

The people who have provided ideas and encouragement for this project over the years are far too many to acknowledge individually. We are especially grateful to our friends in the academic, business and financial communities, many of whose thoughts and ideas have profoundly influenced our own. We also owe a sincere debt of gratitude to the hundreds of entrepreneurs whose search for capital has brought them to our respective venture capital firms, and from each of whom we never fail to learn something new. Finally, as is customary and proper, we accept full responsibility for the final product, warts and all.

Note to the Educator

This book is quite properly placed in the category that one academic has dubbed "normative folk wisdom", as opposed to "knowledge" (research findings). It relies heavily on our many years of experience in starting, managing, building, financing, and directing companies (perhaps fifty), as well as several collective years of teaching entrepreneurship, mainly at the MBA level, both here and abroad. Based on these experiences, we believe that students will be distinctly shortchanged if they are *not* exposed to a lot of folk wisdom, in writing and in person, in their attempt to understand entrepreneurship, by working in small companies, by project work in consulting, and by reading.

The messy real-worldliness of entrepreneurship teaching is not always comfortable to the professional educator/researcher, the best of whom are always superb analysts. However, you are trying here to train and to motivate a synthesist, because that is what entrepreneurs really are. It is of course a mistake simply to think of the startup as a miniature General Motors. Intensive analysis of cases, of research findings, of markets and strategies is without a doubt necessary — but it is not sufficient. An integral part of the student's experience should be exposure to some entrepreneurial points of view, some synthetical superstructures, to help the student form his/her own perspective.

This book was not designed as a textbook. There are some excellent textbooks out there for entrpreneurship courses. Our book is intended for use with other sources; it is deliberately brief, easily read in a long evening. We hope it is motivational and fun, as well as informative.

Finally, although not a scholarly offering, this book is intended as an offering to the serious scholar attempting to innovate educational methods to teach what seems to us to be the ultimate synthesis of business subjects: entrepreneurship. Good luck.

I
FORMATION

1

Why Start a Company?

The reasonable man adapts himself to the world; the unreasonable man attempts to adapt the world to himself. Therefore all progress depends upon the unreasonable man. . . George Bernard Shaw

It should not be astonishing that entrepreneurs have been studied, as individuals and as groups, to a rather extensive degree. Psychologists are interested in finding out what motivates them. Investors are interested in finding some saliva test that will tell them in advance which entrepreneurs are going to make them rich. Business school professors are interested in the questions of whether and how entrepreneurial behavior pattern and skills can be taught. Legions of people in government have begun seeking ways to engage entrepreneurs in programs of regional development, minority enterprise, leadership training, export promotion, and "technology transfer"—all in the name of the commonweal.

Needless to say, all of this activity has produced, not one, but several disparate literatures on entrepreneurial motivation and behavior. Books are being written, reports filed, symposia convened, theses and learned papers ground out. Some interesting specimens of this genus are listed at the end of this chapter, and are recommended reading. From a practical standpoint,

1

however, it does the individual very little good to know that statistical chances of success are relatively poor for an entrepreneur if he or she (a) is a Gentile; (b) does not have a businessman or self-employed professional for a father; (c) has a PhD level education; (d) is not 32.2 years of age.

While it may be interesting to know this sort of average or modal information, much of it totally misses the point of entrepreneurship: it's a diversity (or if you will, statistical variance) of traits that has historically characterized successful entrepreneurs. If your traits don't seem to fit neatly into the profile of "successful entrepreneurs," you may take comfort from the fact that Edison, Ford, Land, and most of our other entrepreneurial geniuses probably wouldn't have, either.

The germinal question to ask at the outset is somewhat existential: Why should I start a company? The range of possible answers to this question includes the following:

1. To make a lot more money than I could with some other application of my energies during a comparable period of time.
2. To get out of a professional rut—to see ideas through to completion, to gain professional recognition, to accept responsibility for the full consequences of my ideas.
3. To be my own boss, control my own destiny, set my own hours, etc.
4. To prove to myself (my spouse, my father, my ex-boss, etc.) that I can do it.
5. To advance technology, society, etc.
6. To develop and deploy talents I feel that I have outside my area of specialization.
7. To show up somebody with whom I intend to compete.

This list could be greatly extended.

None of these motives is without some subjective validity, and no doubt examples of companies founded on the basis of each could be shown. In real life, however, human motives are never unmixed. Your own answer will be a weighted sum of several of these, plus some additional twists resulting from your own unique outlook and experience. The question is, does the sum of all these motives justify the cost, sacrifice, and risk of becoming an entrepreneur? The sum should be reckoned, but the yes-no answer should be held in abeyance, at least until you can more clearly evaluate some of the probable costs. Such evaluation is the subject of the next chapter.

From our list of possible motives, it may appear that all are of equal merit, since all are of some subjective validity. Nothing could be further from the case. It appears that the most successful firms are started by people who are predominantly motivated by #1 on the list, and, to a lesser degree, by #2. To the extent that you are concerned with rebelling against your employer, proving yourself to your spouse, advancing social causes, etc., you are, from a statistical point of view, allying yourself with less successful entrepreneurs.

The central objective of the business enterprise is to make money for its owners. To the extent that you are seeking to maximize a number of other effects, you will inevitably be diluting your energies from the central objective. When the business dies, *all* objectives are lost. And it will take most of your energy just to keep it alive.

"Why start a company?" is a question that can be answered on yet a different level. During the last decade, a variety of factors have turned many talented and capable people away from business enterprise as a means of self-fulfillment and social contribution. In the 1960s Charles Reich in *The Greening of America* epitomized this mentality: "We as a people have abandoned Consciousness I (the ruthless entrepreneurial spirit) in favor of Consciousness II (the gray organization man) but through enlightenment we should evolve soon to Consciousness III (the socially concerned man) to achieve the long-awaited Greening." How ironic it must seem to Mr. Reich that significant numbers of talented and educated young people appear to have gone full circle, abandoning the beatitudes of Consciousness III for some sense of purpose and accomplishment of socially useful tasks through starting new enterprises—a return, it might seem, to Consciousness I!

In the eighties we had a new ethic: that of the yuppy (young urban professional, for those of you who spent the decade on Mars). Work hard, get into a big-name college, go to law school or better yet, to Harvard Business School, get into arbitrage, LBOs, corporate law (whatever pays top dollar), and cash in. Lead the good life, buy the best of everything. But alas, all good things must end. The yuppy ethic ended around October 1987, with major Wall Street layoffs, massive restructurings in financial and industrial firms, and a number of heros of the age ending up under criminal indictment. Yes, there are still lots of young professionals, many of them urban. But a remarkable number are now seeking very different career paths, starting or acquiring small companies, becoming involved in independent professional practices, and, in some instances, entering public service.

In all, it seems to me the emphasis is shifting back toward the creation of value, rather than its manipulation.

In all of this, one finds a growing search for independence through entrepreneurship.

The point of all the foregoing pop sociology is this: there is no inherent relation between the possession of a social conscience and the possession of entrepreneurial drive. Without talented and unique individuals who possess both qualities, little of significant value would be accomplished. Not only are most of our successful businesses started by such people, but these same people also start and operate our clinics, laboratories, dance companies, consumer-action groups, museums, alternative schools, and most of the other new initiatives that contribute to what we consider our civilization.

This is in no way to say that there are no entrepreneurs motivated by cupidity and greed; nor is it to say that most or even many new enterprises are initiated with the intention, let alone the prospect, of accomplishing any significant social end. However, some successful new enterprises *are* organized to accomplish specific social goals, and there exists no inherent conflict between such goals and profit. Additionally, social ends are often served even in the absence of conscious social goals. One hears, for example, that the purpose of our society has shifted from the creation of material goods to the creation of jobs. To the extent that even a mundane new enterprise creates jobs, incomes, payroll taxes, taxed welfare costs, and human dignity that might not otherwise evolve, it is *inadvertently* playing a very desirable and constructive role in society. A similar case could be made for the creation of important products, desirable services, and much-needed exports.

There is another set of reasons why more talented and ambitious people should consider entering into a new business enterprise.

1. Going into business is not as difficult as is often supposed. "Sacrifices," while you must be prepared to make them, are not always, in fact, made. Enormous talent is not necessary. As a matter of fact, it is sometimes a liability. Engineering, sales, and "business" people usually can be hired when needed. There is enough professional help available, both on a part- and full-time basis.

2. At no time and in no place on earth have the conditions ever been more propitious for starting a new business. Hundreds of venture capitalists exist in the U.S., in a form still rare in other countries. Banks, accounting firms, investment bankers, and other institutions have acquired an understanding of new enterprise unmatched in any time or any place. The whole essence of capitalism and the Protestant ethic (whether or not you take it neat) is at work, to the benefit of the new enterprise.

3. There are hundreds of companies who will design, manufacture, and package your product to your specifications. There are inventors, consultants, lawyers, and vendors who will work with you, advise you, and sell you their goods and services on very liberal terms, perhaps for

stock. Maybe these people hope to develop a major new customer, or, more likely, to share in the excitement of your venture.

4. In America innumerable ready-made channels of distribution exist for nearly any class of product. In an open, mixed economy of our type, there are commission representatives, distributors, wholesalers, house-brand buyers, and jobbers of every description—all waiting for the new product that will really "click" for them.

5. At no time and in no place have skilled people been more accessible to the new enterprise. There are several reasons for this: (a) At any given moment, many people are dissatisfied with bureaucracy, lack of recognition, and dead-end careers in large firms. Many would seriously consider a stimulating, if less secure, position in a small new enterprise. (b) Unlike many other industrial societies, ours does not stigmatize the job-changer. You can hire away the best salesperson from your competitor without incurring the moral wrath of the entire community. (c) People are more mobile than ever. It is common practice to recruit top people across town or across an entire continent—and top people expect to change employers when opportunity and growth dictate. (d) Due to tax and emotional preferences, many professionals will work as hard for stock as they will for cash. Having a "piece of the action" is as much in the American tradition as winning the Rose Bowl.

6. It is more difficult to fail than is often imagined. The business failure statistics collected by Dun and Bradstreet and mournfully recited by the press are compilations that include every type of venture from the doomed "ma and pa" grocery to moribund used car lots, gas stations, small jobbers, wholesalers, needle trades firms, and every other conceivable form of enterprise. When you begin to bear the lugubrious chant about the 80 percent rate of business failures, tune out. This is data, not information. A more interesting analysis was put forth by Professor Edward Roberts of MIT, who estimated that only about 20 percent of the large number of MIT spinoff firms ever fail completely. And, should disaster impend, the extraordinary bankruptcy laws of our land (discussed in a later chapter) provide still another mechanism to protect the struggling new enterprise.

7. In federal and local governments a populist political bias toward small business exists (A similar romantic bias exists toward the small farm). The declared purpose, of course, is to permit small firms to compete on fair terms with large firms. The effect, however, is to produce a positive bias in some areas favoring small business. This bias shows itself in the small business set-asides in federal procurement, in the existence of the

Small Business Administration and the Small Business Investment Corporations, in the existence of a variety of regional development authorities, as well as in other ways. Our tax structure—with differential capital gains, what used to be "Subchapter S" corporations, tax-loss carry forwards and carrybacks, and "Section 1244" corporations—also tends to create a desirable climate in which to raise capital for a new venture. It is debatable how effective these various measures have been in actually promoting the small business sector, but surely no one can doubt the intent behind such legislation and appropriations. No government official wants to be considered anti-small-business.

8. **The personal and professional risks of a new enterprise are rather less than might be imagined.**

To be sure, you may be giving up a $50,000 job for a $20,000 job for a couple of years; you may miss some vacations and some professional meetings. Yet, assuming the worst, you lose your savings and go back to a $50,000 job having become a broader and more valuable person than you were when you left.

None of this is to say that the process is risk-free; nothing worth doing ever is. It merely says that the downside risks are not unthinkable and may be a lot less than you would imagine.

9. Starting a business doesn't require as much experience as you might think. Naturally, business experience and contacts are usually assets. However, the person who goes to work for a large company to get ten or fifteen years of solid experience before starting out independently may be taking the wrong approach. With a few notable exceptions, most big companies provide the poorest sort of background for the would-be entrepreneur. Most employees find themselves working upward through a functional specialty, such as manufacturing, accounting, research, or sales, gaining experience that is negotiable only in that or a similar company. Moreover, experience teaches us our limitations all too well, and makes us pessimistic about the ability of new ideas to get anywhere. Some real-world experience is, of course, essential; more essential, however, is the enthusiastic damn-the-torpedoes spirit that one expects from youth (but which one is sometimes pleasantly surprised to find in the not-so-young). Enthusiasm, vigor, energy, and the skin of a rhinoceros are far more valuable assets than the "many years of experience" which are all too often the same year repeated many times.

10. Finally, we reach the consideration that is probably more significant than the rest together: starting a new business is more fun than almost

anything else. *Of course*, you're going to have to work long hours. But all professionals worth their salt, no matter what the field, work long hours, nights, weekends, holidays, sixty and seventy hour weeks. *Of course*, there are going to be headaches—and maybe stomach aches, too. But how do you expect to avoid them in any other significant professional job? The big difference is this: instead of immersing yourself in someone else's organization and struggling with *its* problems, in a new enterprise you create your own organization (with its own problems) and run it as you think it should be run. You stand or fall on the result. And that's about as much fun as most of us can handle.

Perhaps at this juncture, we can step back from the question "Why start a new business?" and turn toward "Why *not* start a new business?" The remaining chapters of this book are dedicated to those inclined to say, "Let's get on with it!"

REFERENCES

1. McClelland, D. C. *The Achieving Society.* New York: D. Van Nostrand Co., 1961.

    This is the classic, a fascinating study of entrepreneurs and what motivates them.

2. McClelland, D. C. "Achievement Motivation Can be Developed." *Harvard Business Review*, November–December, 1965.

    Discusses the philosophy, methods, and limitations of efforts to develop entrepreneurial drive.

3. Timmons, Jeffry A. *The Entrepreneurial Mind.* Andover, Mass.: Brick House Publishing Co., 1989.

    One of the leading academics in entrepreneurship distills a career's worth of findings on what makes entrepreneurs tick. Outstanding.

4. Collins, O. V., and Moore, D. G. "The Enterprising Man." *Michigan State University Business Studies*, 1964.

    This is a unique work in which 100 entrepreneurs from all different types of industries were studied, with regard to personality traits. Entrepreneurs turn out to be a rather grubby and generally unlikeable bunch of social outcasts. The book even includes a sort of psychoanalysis of the typical entrepreneurial type, examining childhood deprivations. Message: Nice guys don't win.

5. Roberts, E. B. "How to Succeed in a New Technology Enterprise." *Technology Review*, December, 1970.

    All you need is the right parents, the right age, the right religion, etc. Based on studies of about 300 MIT spinoff technology ventures.

6. Baumback, Clifford M. and Mancusco, J.R. *Entrepreneurship and Venture Management.* Englewood Cliffs, N.J.: Prentice Hall, 1975.

    This is a book of readings by some 35 contributors, giving research findings, normative advice, descriptions of the venture capital market, and other perspective building materials, in an easy-to-digest form.

7. Myers, Gustavius. *History of the Great American Fortunes.* New York: Modern Library, 1907.

    If you *really* want to know how the old rich got that way, read this first bit of muckraking, written before Nader's grandfather was born.

2

Risks and Rewards

*It is only by risking our persons from hour to hour that
we live at all.   .. William James*

APPARENT VERSUS REAL RISKS

The decision to become an entrepreneur has two basic components: (a) Am I
an entrepreneur? Do I have the abilities, the attitudes, the motivation? and
(b) Are the potential rewards commensurate with the risks? Each of these
questions has a number of components that should be explored before any
decision is reached. The world is full of examples of successful and wealthy
entrepreneurs. (Indeed, it is difficult to find examples of first-generation
wealth made by people not in business for themselves.) In accounts of their
experience, however, one seldom gets an accurate picture of the risks that
confronted them or how they evaluated these risks at the outset. It is questionable whether these people even recognized many of the risks when they
started their businesses, or the role played by luck.

It all looks too easy. The unsuccessful entrepreneurs are seldom heard from. They are hard to find, since they don't usually identify themselves, and often give self-serving accounts of the failure mode—for example, "Our product was too advanced for its time," "We did not have enough capital."

In these cases it is very hard to separate the effects of bad timing, bad management, and back luck—even for the founder.

FINANCIAL RISKS

Usually the financial risks involved in starting a new enterprise are numerically low, but of great importance to the entrepreneur. They involve savings, house equity perhaps, and some temporary reduction in income. Maybe the spouse will have to go to work. Many people are unwilling even to consider a reduction in their standard of living or in their financial security, in order to start a new company. They are not entrepreneurs at heart.

However—and here is the crucial point—while you must be *prepared* to make financial sacrifices, there is a very good chance that you will never actually *have* to make them. It is much more important to *appear* willing to put your hand in the fire. To illustrate: Several years ago a businessman in Massachusetts decided to start a company in specialty food packaging. His personal assets consisted of equity in a house, the cash value of his insurance, and a few thousand dollars in savings. When the time came, at last, to leave his job with a food broker and set out on his own, he sat down with his boss and showed him the business plan. The boss, himself an entrepreneur, was impressed by the idea. He was, however, more impressed by the fact that the young man's business plan involved many months of deferred salary, as well as most of his savings and a second mortgage on his house. This guy had to be crazy, the boss thought, or else onto a sure bet. He decided it was the latter, and volunteered the necessary seed money in exchange for a minority equity position. As a result, both made a great deal of money, and a successful, growing company exists today. Note: Our entrepreneur never missed a paycheck, never refinanced his house, and never put over 25 percent of his savings into the venture!

So, when considering the financial risks, remember the following:

1. The real risks may be less than the apparent risks.
2. You can always get another job if the company folds.
3. You can rebuild your savings account.
4. Corporation law prevents you from being liable for more than you have invested in the company.

CAREER RISKS

This is an important area, which is seldom discussed by business writers. Yet it may be even more significant than the financial risks confronting the new enterprise. Simply stated, it is the risk that, having stepped outside your profession for a few years, re-entry may be difficult. Certain professions, such as law, are structured to permit an interruption in one's career for a few years without excessive penalty. This is one reason why so many politicians and "public servants" are lawyers. Some other professional careers are not as easily turned off and on at will, however. A professor leaving his post may miss an opportunity to achieve tenure. A scientist starting a small company may discover that the time demands are so heavy that he or she loses touch with colleagues, funding sources, and the broader front of research progress in a particular field. A very senior executive may relinquish seniority, vested savings, stock options, or retirement benefits. A skilled machinist may relinquish seniority in a union, a nice thing to have when layoffs hit.

However, there is another side to the story. A take-charge person who has evidenced the courage to leave and start a new business, will, if the new business should fail, return to the former employer as a broader, tougher person. At least some organizations seem to believe this—and if your old one doesn't, its competitor probably will. Moreover, those who start new companies are probably more inclined than others to find new and different uses for their talents, and thus are among the least likely candidates to sit wondering if their old desks are still waiting empty at Titanic Industries.

PERSONAL RISKS

The level of personal risk is the most difficult of all to analyze. It is difficult because it involves one's own family members, social friends, and other human beings whose reactions may be very hard to predict. Unlike financial cost, which may be avoided under some circumstances, the commitment of almost all one's leisure time and energies is usually inescapable in starting a new company. Many marriages simply cannot survive the long absences of a spouse. Vacations have a way of getting postponed indefinitely. Meals get cold. Weekend outings vanish from the calendar. Social invitations go unaccepted and unrepeated. Reduced family cash flow may dictate fewer dinners out, less entertaining, etc. These factors put a strain upon any household. Whether they might wrench yours is a question that deserves some sober reflection.

On the asset side, however, are the following considerations:

1. Your absence from the hearth may create the opportunity, necessity, or excuse for your spouse's going back to work full- or part-time. Depending upon this person's abilities and psychological makeup, this may be the best thing to happen, not only to him or her, but to your marriage.

2. The necessity of constant absence from home diminishes with time. Let your new sales manager make some of those trips to Cincinnati. Let your accountant prepare those draft budgets for your review. Let your VP deliver that paper at the association meeting. Eventually you will be able to find more time to devote to your domestic life. Whether you exercise that ability is, of course, your choice. The company often provides a convenient excuse for staying *away* from home.

3. You must ask yourself what the time demands of your present job are going to be, if you are to be successful. Many people, as they scale the professional ladder, find that their broadened responsibilities keep them away from home more, rather than less. The reasons are many: attending meetings with the West Coast subsidiary, troubleshooting the new plant in Kuwait, attending sales meetings, visiting the consulting client in Boise, delivering a paper to the Society in London, plus expanding one's social and civic responsibilities to fit the perceived desires of the firm, all at the expense of one's private life.

The important thing is to compare your future life as an entrepreneur with your *future* life on your present trajectory.

In summary, of all the risks—those to your financial, career, and personal life—the last usually proves to be the most important, primarily because the costs are the least escapable, and secondly because its total impact is the hardest to predict. A demolished home life is a high price to pay for business success, and can ultimately undermine the company itself.

Here are some ways in which entrepreneurs have dealt with this problem:

1. Set aside a sacred day—Sunday is often best—and make it an inviolable rule always to be home and never to schedule work or meetings. This is harder than it sounds.

2. Make sure your secretary reminds you of social engagements, your spouse's and your kid's birthdays, anniversaries, and the like, so that something happens, to acknowledge the occasion, even if you're not home.

3. Substitute the three-day weekend for vacations. Four or five short trips a year will go far in refreshing mind and spirit if time and finances don't permit a regular vacation.

4. Occasionally, conduct business over breakfast, and meet your spouse in town for lunch. Stay in touch.

5. Put your spouse to work on specific company problems. As time and interests permit, involve him or her in a full- or part-time professional capacity as a partner, employee, or consultant. This is good for the family exchequer as well as the family morale.

6. Keep your spouse informed. Even if your spouse can't fully appreciate the breakthrough you're aiming towards in the laboratory, or the big contract you're hoping to sew up, your sharing your hopes and problems and making him or her a part of your big adventure *will* be appreciated.

In addition to helping, your spouse will gain insights into your problems, and a sense of sharing in the venture. But be sure that the company pays him or her whatever the going rate is for such work—even if it's in IOUs! Don't hesitate to use your spouse as a sounding board when you're thinking aloud about a problem.

You can imagine at least a dozen more ways in which to ease the strain upon your domestic life—and perhaps turn your venture into something of an adventure for your family as well as for yourself.

REWARDS

The rewards of successful entrepreneurship are legendary. There are few other ways in which wealth can be accumulated in this age, and fewer still that provide the sort of satisfaction that can be provided by the use of all of one's talents and energies in building a successful company of one's own. In a society such as ours, which exalts commercial success above inherited status, cultural attainments, or even intellectual accomplishment, the successful entrepreneur is probably assured a disproportionately high return on his or her investment of energy and time, relative to other equally talented, hard-working people.

An anonymous sage once observed, "Money isn't everything, but it's sure better than whatever's in second place."

Among the second place contenders, excluding things that money can buy, we must list a sense of social contribution, professional satisfaction, esteem of peers, community status, and perhaps even a sense of power.

Sometimes even "not-too successful" companies provide these rewards to their founders to a substantial degree.

BALANCING RISKS AND REWARDS

It may be that the accounting model can provide a useful way to structure your thinking about risks and rewards. Try making up a balance sheet along the following lines, to pull your thinking into focus in evaluating the "net worth" of your venture.

Rewards (Assets) Results	Maximum Value	Probability	Expected
Rewards			
a. Significant wealth	9	50%	4.5
b. Professional satisfactions—sense of achievement	8	80%	6.4
c. Community status	4	20%	0.8
d. Power being boss	3	100%	3.0
e. Control over own life	8	70%	5.6
TOTAL ASSETS			20.3
Risk (Liabilities)			
a. Loss of savings	10	20%	2.0
b. Reduction in professional status	7	30%	2.1
c. Diminished leisure	6	80%	4.8
d. Increased marital stress	10	40%	4.0
e. Health risk	5	20%	1.0
f. Psychological cost of "failure"	5	20%	1.0
TOTAL LIABILITIES			14.9
	NET WORTH OF VENTURE=		5.4
	ASSETS MINUS LIABILITIES=		
LIABILITIES PLUS NET WORTH			20.3

Notes:
[1]Your own asset and liability lists may be quite different from those shown.
[2]The maximum value attached can be any number, zero through ten.
[3]The probability is your estimate of the likelihood of attaining the maximum value.
[4]The expected result is then the product of maximum value times probability.

This sort of model is certain to seem excessively formal to some and hopelessly naive to others of a more scholarly bent. My own experience in advising entrepreneurs has shown it to be useful, if only as a way of documenting some very crude a priori estimates for later review.

HOW TO TELL IF YOU'RE AN ENTREPRENEUR

You're an entrepreneur if:

1. Your analysis of risk and reward shows that the probable gains outweigh the probable net costs by a substantial margin, and,
2. Your personal profile is not outrageously at odds with the known facts about successful entrepreneurs.

WHAT KIND OF ENTREPRENEUR TO BE?

There are innumerable patterns of entrepreneurship. Many people start out as one kind and end up as another. Karl Vesper offers this list of entrepreneurial styles. (See References at end of chapter)

1. *Solo, self-employed individuals.* "Ma and pa" stores, dentists, doctors, consultants, accountants.
2. *Team builders.* One-person shows that build up teams of helpers—for example, Ford, Coca-Cola, John Deere.
3. *Independent inventors.* Bell, Edison, Kettering.
4. *Pattern multipliers.* J.C. Penney, McDonalds, Colonel Sanders, Stretch n'Sew.
5. *Economy-of-scale exploiters.* Discount merchandisers.
6. *Capital aggregators.* Banks, savings and loans, money-market funds, mutual funds.
7. *Acquirers.* Buyers of existing businesses, who try to regenerate and improve them.
8. *Buy-sell artists.* The realm of corporate raiders who turn around, sell, and liquidate.
9. *Conglomerators.* Those who buy earnings with stock.
10. *Speculators.* Those who buy and sell land, war surplus, antiques, timber leases, without adding value.

11. *Apparent value manipulators.* Those who acquire assets at a discount, representing them for a new use or market, and who restructure balance sheet to improve current ratio.

Each of these entrepreneurial types implies individual differences in talents, commitment, circumstances, and interest of involvement. Any one of them may characterize you at some stage of your venture.

CONVENTIONAL WISDOM: The risks and costs of failure are almost unthinkably high for a person starting a new company today.

REALITY: Not only are the risks much less than is commonly assumed, but by planning, they can often be reduced, if not altogether eliminated. Your financial backers may be taking a lot more risk than you are.

REFERENCES

1. Vesper, Karl. *New Venture Strategies.* Englewood Cliffs, N.J.: Prentice Hall, 1980.
      This unusual book explores the various ways in which people get into business, and discusses the usual ingredients needed for success. Plenty of anecdotes and mini case histories. Excellent.
2. Timmons, Jeffry A., Smollen, Leonard E., and Dingee, Alexander L.M. *New Venture Creation—A guide to Entrepreneurship.* 2nd ed. Homewood, Ill.: Richard D. Irwin, Inc., 1985.
      This has become the backbone of many MBA-level entrepreneurship courses, and for good reason. Its thoroughness makes it an invaluable resource for the entrepreneur, and its war stories make it fun. Excellent contributions on team formation, ethics, and personal career strategy.
3. Ronstadt, Robert C. *Entrepreneurship—Text, Cases and Notes.* Dover, Mass.: Lord Publishing Co., 1984.
4. Liles, Patrick R. *New Business Ventures and the Entrepreneur.* Homewood, Ill.: Richard D. Irwin, Inc., 1975.
      Basically a case text. This book nonetheless offers several excellent sections on venture risk, evaluation of going companies, raising venture capital, and the nuts and bolts of securities regulations.

3

What Kind of Company?

*The man with a new idea is a crank—until the idea
succeeds.   . . Mark Twain*

A cynic might divide all new ventures into two groups: (1) those companies
organized to profit from the sale of products and services, and (2) those organized to profit from the sale of stock. To draw this distinction is not to say that
the two are necessarily mutually exclusive. However, some companies with
excellent earnings may not sell for much (i.e., for a low price-earnings ratio),
while other companies with negligible earnings or even large losses may sell for
a lot of money (i.e., infinite or negative price earnings). The reasons are not
hard to understand. A company with good earnings may sell cheaply because

1. It is in a static or declining industry.
2. Impending events may cloud the future. Examples: maturing market,
   patent expirations, growing competition, antitrust actions.
3. Its growth is limited by such factors as its local character (for example, a
   dry cleaning plant), a saturated market, and scarcity of raw material (for
   example, fish processing).

4. Its product or technology may be simply out of style in the investment community (for example, electronic capital equipment firms and nursing home chains—as of the time of this writing).

5. Investors may just have lost a bundle in similar companies.

Conversely, a company with a terrible earnings record may sell for a lot of money because

1. It owns substantial net assets (i.e., high liquidation value).

2. It has a tax-loss status of value to the buyer.

3. It has a product or service that has tremendous potential.

4. It has excellent distribution channels.

5. It is in style.

The trick in deciding what kind of company you're going to start lies, of course, in finding a combination that will make money from product sales *and* from equity sales. Elementary, you say. But, as experience will verify, it is much harder actually to make money in a rapidly growing firm than is generally supposed. It is incredible how rising materials costs, expanding sales organizations, product design, product delays, and collection problems can devour that marvelous projected gross margin. The obvious hedge is this: make every conceivable effort to be in one of the areas in which companies with less-than-zero earnings can be sold profitably, *or* be in a dead-end situation where the profits that can be milked are so great that you don't care if you have to throw your stock away in five years. Generally, one should avoid the middle of the intervening spectrum. As a matter of practical experience, it is probably true that the stylish company is the better choice for the first-time entrepreneur, while the turnaround or liquidation project is the province for more experienced venturers.

Most entrepreneurs like to think in terms of building a company that can eventually go public, thus allowing them to cash out via the founders' stock. Yet, many successful ventures are acquired by bigger companies, and some can be said to have been developed and groomed with that disposition in mind.

A third, somewhat dated, philosophy is to build a solid company to own, operate, and pass on to one's children. There is nothing wrong with that. Generally speaking, however, if you build a company that meets the tests of the capital markets in order to go public, the chances are that either of the other two routes will still be open to you, should you change your mind. The reverse is not always true.

SERVICE VERSUS MANUFACTURING

It may be that there once was a bias within the capital markets toward companies whose product was hardware rather than services. It is apparent, however, that today an innovative idea in service or in service delivery can be quite capable of attracting both capital and investor interest. A roster of currently stylish areas would include examples of both types of company. Service industries which have attracted investor interest in the last few years include computer retailing, health service delivery (e.g., nursing homes), medical monitoring, fast food merchandising, on-line database services, tax-preparation services, and parcel delivery services. In the gradual shift of our economy toward more service industries, entrepreneurs and investors alike should become increasingly sophisticated in judging the risks and returns of new service ventures. Both hardware and software offer opportunity for the entrepreneur with an innovative concept.

FASHIONS IN TECHNOLOGIES AND MARKETS

Although it is true that definite fashion trends may be found in capital markets, it is a bit unfair to use the word "fashion" when referring to the venture capitalist—unfair in that it connotes an irrational preoccupation with trivia (such as hemlines and lapel widths). In fact, most venture capitalists and investment bankers are engaged in a rational, cold-blooded analysis of what will sell.

Changing fashions come about in new ventures not because someone wants to make the shares of stock that his customer purchased last year obsolete, but because new and exciting ideas and technologies are constantly being created. Innovative marketing ideas are emerging and new market needs are developing. At the same time, as the glamour industries of yesterday mature and consolidate, competition reduces opportunities for large profits, and fewer new ventures come forth for capital from those industries. Moreover, some new technologies (such as artificial intelligence) and some new markets (such as factory automation) are oversold, yield disappointing returns to their early investors, and are pushed aside in the venture capital market in the next wave of changing fashions. For these and other reasons, discernible trends do exist in the market. It is up to the pragmatic entrepreneur to discern them.

The best way to discover the current trend is to find out what's being financed. A look at the annual reports of some of the major public venture capital firms will indicate what kinds of businesses have been added to and deleted from their portfolios. The brochures of private VC funds can often yield similar information. One useful source for such data is the *Going Public—The IPO Reporter* (2 World Trade Center, New York, NY), which gives summary information on most new ventures presently in registration with the SEC, as well as rundowns on the product and stock performance of many over-the-counter companies. A still better source, if you can get your hands on it, is the monthly *Venture Capital Journal*, published by Venture Publishing Co., Wellesley, Massachusetts. Reading such a publication over a period of time can also give one a very good sense of the investment patterns of different financial institutions and underwriters. One, for example, may specialize in computer companies, while another seems to follow medical firms, and so on. The reason for this pattern of specialization is fairly obvious: a firm simply gains experience in evaluating ideas and entrepreneurs of a particular sort, thereby reducing both cost and risk. *Venture* and *Inc.* magazines are also good information sources.

Once you have tentatively identified your general area of interest or have confirmed that your initial idea is sufficiently fashionable, you would do well to approach whatever underwriters are active in that area and have a long talk with them. You'll learn a great deal about who the present and future leaders are in your particular field and what's going on in the industry, and will get at least some idea of how much longer that industry will stay in the top ten. The editors of the industry magazines are another good source of this sort of information. It is their business to be alert to new trends and to evaluate the viability of new developments. They are generally interesting, interested people, and such acquaintances can be extremely valuable to you in terms of publicity and contacts, once your business is off the ground. Take an editor to lunch today. Or better yet, an editor and a broker. To paraphrase a cliché, "If you're going to sell steak, just be damned sure it's still sizzling."

WHERE TO LOOK FOR IDEAS

Despite the myth to the contrary,

---

most new companies are *not* started on the basis of totally new or original ideas. Most are simply based on old ideas that have been updated:

---

current ideas repackaged for a new market; straightforward extensions of existing products; products that are designed to fit into a niche between existing larger competitors. This is one of the reasons why ordinary people can start extraordinarily successful businesses. It is not necessary to be an innovative genius to come up with a suitable idea. Many of the most profitable and hence fundable, low-risk ventures are merely mundane-looking extensions of existing products (such as a cheaper laptop computer, a higher-performance servo motor, a fancier motor home). One of the best places to look for specific first-product ideas is right under your nose: in the development direction of product lines already being marketed in your target area.

What is required? What will sell? What will the market demand next year? This approach may pit you against established competition, but at least you don't have the enormous investment and lead-time required for the development of a new market. Investors look with favor upon this approach.

Here are some of the other idea sources that you might also look into, in rough order of descending effectiveness:

Present job environment
Successful entrepreneurs
Trade shows
Trade publications
Editors
Commerce Business Daily
Management consultants
Idea brokers and patent brokers
Venture capital firms
Technology transfer agencies
Regional development agencies
Official Gazette, U.S. Patent Office

Once you have picked a general product there are, of course, many ways in which to focus more closely upon such concerns as alternative design approaches, existing and abandoned state of the art, probable research efforts by competitors. Agencies such as the Library of Congress National Referral Center, the Smithsonian Institute's Science Information Exchange, and the National Technical Information Service of the United States Department of Commerce, are good places in which to find specific information, but aren't much good for browsing.

Once you get into it, you may find in your idea search that there are many people with ideas that seem better than yours—ideas just sitting there, waiting for the right person to match them up with the people and resources needed to exploit them. So don't lock yourself in a closet and try to think of the ideal product. It's probably sitting out there in the world, just waiting for you.

CRITERIA FOR FIRST PRODUCTS

It is important to remember that the product that is one firm's home-run may be another firm's disaster. Success and failure are determined by the nature of the organization and the people who will exploit the product. The criteria for a beginning company's first product are particularly stringent, due to the organization's extreme limitations in terms of staff, experience, market contact, capital, and every other factor needed to make a new product sell.

The following table offers one general way of classifying your first product candidates. The examples in the boxes are illustrative.

	Existing Product	Modification of Existing Product	Totally New Product
Existing Market	"New" shaving cream	Disposable hospital bedding	Laser surgical instruments
Identifiable Market	Children's cosmetics	Laptop computers	Spanish language news-only TV station
Unknown Market	One-person submarines	Computerized home intrusion alarm	Internal combustion pogo stick

Try placing your first product ideas into these pigeonholes. Then consider the following:

1. The closer you are to the northwest corner, the safer and easier-to-finance your product will be. This is often a winning combination for the first product, even though the potential payoff may be higher for future products.
2. The further toward the southeast corner you get, the harder it will be to find financing and develop a profitable enterprise.
3. In general, a new company is better off in the northeast corner, where the market is at least *known*, than in the southwest where it may never make the first sale. This is true because new companies usually have less marketing competence than product development ability.

4. Since high rates of return nearly always involve higher risk, you ought to consider reserving riskier, higher-potential ideas for second or third products. By then you'll have a company going and, hopefully, some modest first-product success.

Here are some of the additional criteria to which first-product candidates must be subjected:

1. *Is it proprietary?* This is the first question an investor will ask. It doesn't have to be patented (although patents are great window-dressing), but it should be sufficiently proprietary to permit a long head start against competitors and a period of extraordinary profits early in the venture to offset startup costs.

2. *Are the initial production costs realistic?* If your first product is plastic canoes, perhaps they are. If it is seagoing LPG tankers, perhaps they aren't.

3. *Are the initial marketing costs realistic?* A specialized scientific instrument may, measured in this way, be a better first product than a new razor.

4. *Does it have potential for very high gross margins?* This is almost a necessity for a fledgling company. By this measure a "new" cosmetic product might be less of a risk than a new machine tool. Note that gross margin is one thing that the financial community *really* understands.

5. *Is the time required to get to market and break even realistic?* If you have no idea how long it will take to get there, then you can't even estimate how much money you'll need. In most cases, the faster the better. You can always hold your new product in reserve, announcing it to the stockholders immediately after you announce your first profitable quarter.

6. *Is the potential market big enough?* By potential market, look ahead three to five years. By this gage, specialized instrumentation for student laboratories might be a better product than specialized instrumentation for metallurgical laboratories.

7. *Is your product the first member of a growing family?* If so, it's a better first product than a solo virtuoso. If it requires a lot of high-margin accessories or supplies, so much the better. Most of the best growth companies have products with large doses of this characteristic. Again, due to the enormous costs, delays, and uncertainties of market development, a stream of products aimed at the same market is a safer investment than trying to develop entirely new markets for your old product.

8. *Do you have some ready-made initial customers?* It is certainly impressive to financial backers when you can list your first ten customers by name.

9. *Are the development cost and calendar time realistic?* Preferably, they are zero. A ready-to-go product, with the development already paid for (by your old company, the government, an offshore manufacturer, or anybody else) gives you a big leg up over other small companies who dissipate their initial stake in seemingly endless product development. Save your jazzy product-development efforts for your second, third, or fourth products.

10. *Are you in a growing industry?* This is not absolutely essential if the profits and company growth are there, but there's less room for mistakes. A growing company in a growing market can survive a lot more management blunders and bad luck than a company in a stable market and still succeed.

11. *Do you understand the buying cycle?* Do you know who the decision maker is? How long does it take to get an order? Why does this person buy? Who else must approve the customer's decision?

12. *Can your product and the need for it be understood by the financial community?* If the product is super-technical, investors can always get a consultant to evaluate its merits. But if they can "evaluate" it themselves, you're golden. One of the best products that I ever saw in this respect was a tiny, portable, heart-monitoring system for post-coronary use. Half the people who heard the presentation had had coronaries themselves.

The list of criteria could be extended ad nauseam, but by now you have the idea of what kinds of questions to ask yourself. If you can answer "yes" to at least seven of these, go see your Aunt Hattie about some start-up money. If you ace all twelve, go see Goldman, Sachs.

VENTURE ARCHITECTURE

For any given business opportunity (new market or product) there are generally multiple modes of exploitation by the entrepreneur. For example, an incipient entrepreneur discovers that lawfirms are both numerous and poorly managed in a business sense. He realizes that a small computer for lawyers could process both their text and their business data. His primitive entrepreneurial instincts tell him, therefore, that he should raise money, set up a company, design the computer and software, set up a sales service organization, and revolutionize the legal industry—or should he? Let's consider some alternative ways of exploiting this same opportunity. He could

1. Design a computer, have someone else build it, and concentrate on marketing it to the lawyers.
2. Buy out and turn around an existing firm in this field.
3. Buy computers, write some software, and resell the package to lawfirms (the so-called value added reseller or turnkey service strategy).
4. Set up a service bureau and process information for lawfirms.
5. Set up a facilities-management company to operate lawfirms' computer operations on an in-house basis.
6. Offer consulting and seminar services to lawyers, advising them on setting up their own information systems.
7. Become a salesman for some firm already marketing a suitable product to lawyers.
8. Become an agent or distributor for such a firm, possibly adding other complementary products as well, such as supplies, books, and accessories.
9. Set up a leasing company to finance the acquisition of such equipment by lawyers.
10. Start and operate a *really* efficient lawfirm.

The true entrepreneur probably adds more creativity and value to the venture at this stage then at any other—the venture architecture stage that must occur before the preparation of formal business plans can even begin.

Venture architecture is the process of designing the new company. Therefore, not only must issues of product source and sales methods be addressed, but many others as well:

1. *Form:* Will it be a partnership, single proprietorship, corporation, cooperative, real estate trust, or some other legal entity?
2. *Financial structure:* How should it be financed? Some ventures such as risky R&D efforts will be largely financed by equity (i.e., stock) sales. Others, such as garment manufacturing can be financed by bank debt and receivables factoring. Agricultural and real estate ventures are most often debt-financed, with the land securing the notes and mortgages. And so there is generally a "best" financial structure for a given type of venture.

3. *Organization:* Will the company be steeply hierarchical, as a typical manufacturing firm might be, or will it be collegial, as might befit a consulting firm? How will the structure fit your management style? Will it be a holding company with specialized subsidiaries? Will it be acquiring other companies?

4. *Marketing structure:* Should the product be sold by a company sales force, or by representatives, dealers, agents and other nonemployees? What form of field support organization will be required? Will you start in one mode, with the intent of changing later?

5. *Product supply:* Will you make or buy? Will you specify a product of your own design, or will you simply sell something already manufactured, tooled, and available? Will you buy something standard and modify it to meet our customers' needs (for example, adding our software to a purchased computer)? Will you start out one way with the plan of switching over later as volume grows?

6. *Technology:* Will you develop on your own, or license the technology of others? How large an engineering department do you really need? Can you retain a contract engineering firm?

7. *Location:* Not all locations are equally suitable for sales, R&D, and marketing. Your location may *be* your business.

8. *Distribution of ownership.* How many financial and operating partners are needed? How should each be compensated? Who will be needed in the future?

Obviously, a great many issues must be addressed in the architectural stage. A number of possible solutions should be explored for each issue, rather than just jumping on the obvious or the customary. Moreover, many of the solutions are certain to be interdependent. For example, if debt-financing is seen to be the optimal financial structure, the corporation is likely to be the preferred form to insulate shareholders against losses in excess of their investment.

WHAT CHARACTERIZES GOOD ARCHITECTURE?

As in selection of a first product, the entrepreneur selecting an architecture for a first venture must deal with more constraints than a more experienced venturer. When you have enumerated some alternative architectures for your new venture, you should then subject each to the following tests:

1. Does it provide a way of getting into business earlier than other strategies? (Time is still money.)

2. Does it provide a low-risk market entry opportunity? For example, a dealership for a proven product may be less risky than designing, building, and marketing a new product.

3. Does it build on your personal strengths? Can you make maximum use of your technical skills, selling abilities, industry contacts, and personal capital?

4. Does it provide a growth path if it succeeds? For example, Tussey Computer began life as a branded-software discounter, operating out of the founder's apartment, via direct mail response to small ads in the computer press. Three years later, the firm passed $30 million, marketing discount software and IBM-compatible PCs via the same channel. In this case, the marketing channel and a reputation for service provided the growth path.

5. Does it make maximum use of other resources in the environment? Manufacturing might *in principle* be the best architecture but without a local infrastructure of vendors, trained workers, and engineers, it might be a very poor architecture for your particular venture.

6. Does the architecture provide built-in hedges against failure? A consulting practice might be easy to reorient if the opportunity doesn't pan out, whereas a manufacturing plant may not be so easy to redeploy.

7. Can it result in the kind of company you want to own? Will it make a good living for you but be unsaleable—like many agencies and consulting firms—or will it be a high profile product venture that will later be saleable to a larger company?

8. Does it provide access to capital that might not be available otherwise? For example, if your make-or-buy decision is to manufacture, you may have access to financial and tax incentives to create jobs in particular locations of high unemployment.

9. Will it be consistent with the kind of life you want to lead? Though they may not admit or realize it, many entrepreneurs would be miserable as manager of their own big companies. Day-to-day operations, hiring and firing people, dealing with auditors, government agencies, stock analysts, and other "nonproductive" tasks can make life an agony for the free spirit who loves to design, manufacture, or just sell things. Does the architecture, if the venture succeeds, really suit your life?

Some High-Growth Opportunities for the 1990's

I. *Low Technology*

Service chains: medical, dental, optometric, physical therapy, funeral

Translation services

Courier services

Computer and software retailing

Sportswear and sports equipment manufacturing and marketing

Buyer protection: home and auto inspection, etc.

Word processing and rapid print bureaus

Health/beauty/fat farms and salons

Local airlines and other common carriers

Contract training services

Specialty foods (organic, low cal, Kosher)

Specialty restaurants

Telemarketing services

Services/products aimed at affluent elderly

Economic uses of waste streams (municipal waste, sewage sludge, tires)

Support systems for working women (health care, shopping, child care)

II *Medium Technology*

Third party maintenance of computers, office equipment, and instrumentation

Computer software: standard packages for mass market

Computer software: customized packages and services

TV retailing

Program material for home video consumption

Domestic security systems

Municipal waste management, recycling, energy recovery

Computer-aided design services

Specialized job shops (laser machining, micro-inspection)

Recycling services for motor oil, asphalt waste, industrial solvent, etc.

Medical monitoring: clinical and ambulatory

Toxic waste cleanup: services and products

Laser disk data base publishing

Radon monitoring/removal

Secondary oilfield recovery

III. *High Technology*

Personal computer applications: all kinds

Value-added datacom networks: retailing satellite and fibreoptic channels

Specialized computer peripherals: voice recognition, debit cards

PC-video interfaces, miniature, and color displays, etc.

Imaging systems for science, medicine, military

Paperwork automation systems: image management, fax, laser printers

Hazardous waste management

Data security/encryption systems
Computer-aided design/manufacturing/testing systems
Energy storage (exotic batteries, for example)
Efficient electric motors: conventional and superconducting
Exotic composite materials
Bio sensors
New diagnosis techniques
Bio-engineered therapeutic drugs
High-definition video
Flat-panel video and computer displays
High-tech prosthetics
Broad-band networks and devices
Propellant alternatives to freon
Fast ASIC fabrication systems
Drug-detection systems
Explosives and firearms detection systems
Personal security devices and systems
Diamond and other hard coatings
Hardy crop plants (resisting drought, salty soil, etc.)
Superconductor applications

REFERENCES

1. Karger, D. W., and Murdick, R. G. *New Product Venture Management.* New York: Gordon & Breach, 1972

   This is the best all-round book on new product development. It starts with evaluation of market needs and goes right through to public offering. The section on marketing and promotion is particularly good.

2. Vesper, Karl. *New Venture Strategies.* Englewood Cliffs, N.J.: Prentice Hall, 1980.

   Excellent section on new venture ideas and criteria.

3. Timmons, Jeffry A., Smollen, Leonard E., and Dingee, Alexander L.M. *New Venture Creation—A Guide to Entrepreneurship.* 2nd ed. Homewood, Ill.: Richard D. Irwin, Inc., 1985.

   The sections on new venture opportunities and the venture opportunity screening guide are both worth some serious time.

4

Measuring the Need

*Market demand for a product is the total volume that
would be bought by a defined customer group in a
defined geographic area in a defined time period under
a defined marketing program.* . . *Philip Kotler*

It is probably true that entrepreneurs are worse at selling their own products
than they are in any other area of endeavor within the business structure. Yet
selling is the most *critical* area of activity in most companies. Its importance
cannot be overemphasized, especially in the case of a new venture.

There are many ways of obtaining a product to sell: it can be designed,
manufactured to order, imported, or assembled. The one thing that you
yourself must do is sell it. Your merchandising methods may, in some cases,
be the major "product" of your company (as with Colonel Sanders, Avon, and
Savings Bank Life Insurance).

Finally, an amateurish or unrealistic marketing program is one of the
major "weak spots" for which prospective investors watch. This chapter attempts to point out some of the major pitfalls present in the planning and
execution of a market analysis program.

When you begin to develop a marketing program, the first step is the identification, measurement, and documentation of the *need* for your *product*. The focus placed upon *need* and *product* is intentional.

Many entrepreneurs, if they do any market analysis at all, simply take the top-down approach. That is, go to the library and find some statistics (usually outdated) on the historic and projected growth rate of some large superset of the market they hope to penetrate. Then, in a heroic leap of faith, it is stated: "If we reach only 2% of this huge market by 1995, we will have a $50 million dollar company." This is a worthwhile exercise, especially if several sets of independent projections can be compared. At least it may tell you if your potential market is measured in millions or billions. However, the top-down analysis is not the end of the process—it's only the beginning.

Here are some questions which you should ask yourself:

1. Will you be serving your customers' real needs? What are these needs? How much will your customer be willing to spend for your product? What is different about your product that will cause the customer to choose it over that of your competitor? What are the quantifiable benefits? Would they even consider buying from a startup company?

2. To what industry will your sales efforts be directed? What is its size now, and at what rate is it growing? Who will your principal customers be? For what purposes will they use your product? How significant a competitor can you be in your industry? What else can you sell into this market?

3. How are selling and distribution usually handled by your competitors? What are the buying habits of your prospective customers? What will be the selling and distribution costs?

4. How many industries can you serve? Some entrepreneurs see so many potential applications for their product that they are unable to focus their initial energies upon developing *one major initial class of customer.* They try to reach all classes simultaneously, possibly with different distribution methods needed for each class. The results of such a practice can be disastrous!

5. What are the principal market segments that are reachable, and on which one will you concentrate? (For example, if you're selling electronic controls to machine tool builders, you will want to concentrate your sales efforts upon those companies that do not have in-house electronics capability.) Who will the principal customers be within your chosen segment? How much will each customer buy? At what price? What product is the customer presently using that will be replaced by your product? What is its cost? What will it cost you to make the cus-

tomer switch to your product, in terms of design change, tooling costs, changes in methods, etc.? How long will it take? What market segments do you wish to reach later on in your endeavor and in what order?

6. What are the major representative, distributor, and dealer firms within the industry who now call on your prospective customers? Which ones would be most suitable for you to use in your sales effort?

7. Who are your present competitors? Who will they be in three years? What are the major characteristics of their products and their marketing methods, and what are the strengths and weaknesses of each? Are they planning the introduction of a new product in the near future, which would endanger your business? How large and how profitable are they? Are they making any money in areas that would compete with yours?

8. What will it cost you to sell to your proposed market segment over the next few years? How much money should you allocate for such concerns as salespersons' salaries, regional office expenses, representatives, commissions, field service organizations, applications engineering, customer training, warranty repairs, documentation, advertising, and promotion. Must you rent the product?

9. How long will it take to get your sales effort into full swing? Does the customer require a long cycle of need-evaluation, funds approval, and vendor selection? Is a long period of training on a unique new product required? Is intensive advertising over long periods of time necessary? Will use of your product force major changes in the way your customer runs his or her organization?

10. What are the names of the ten major customers who will be buying your product? (Note: General Electric Company is not a customer—Joe Snodgrass, equipment buyer for the General Electric Missile and Toaster Division, may be.)

The final distillate of this information-gathering process is the top line of your *pro forma* profit and loss statement: dollar shipments per month. This is the great leap, the key assumption, the base of your entire business plan, the yardstick against which you and your business will be measured.

In general, it is easier to explain away the absence of profits than the absence of sales. If sales are materializing on schedule, investors tend to be more patient about profits that are below your stated target. Therefore, your chances of successfully financing and operating your business are increased by your knowing as much as possible about your product's users and your ability to present massive documented evidence regarding your market.

WHERE DO YOU LOOK FOR INFORMATION?

Once you have a business opportunity for which there appears to be good potential, your immediate aim should be researching and documenting that opportunity. In this way you will be able to convince others, as well as yourself, of its validity. There are many sources of data for any new product.

Your first task in the research process will be listing those sources to be investigated in their order of use to you. Some data sources, such as direct mail surveys, take a long time to complete and therefore should be begun at once. Others, such as searches of literature, telephone interviews, and personal interviews, will produce almost immediate results and therefore can be scheduled on an *ad hoc* basis. In order to make the best use of your time, it is advisable to schedule them around other activities.

Some forms of research, such as library research, can be accomplished with little or no cost to you; others, such as hiring Dun and Bradstreet to analyze their market data base are so costly that you may rule them out altogether. It is important to be sure that you proceed by exhausting those sources that will be least costly and most helpful at the outset of your research.

Some of the most common sources of information on potential markets for new products are as follows, in approximate order of descending cost-effectiveness:

1. *Library research.* This can be initiated in a university or large public library, and can be extended into technically oriented libraries or to the Library of Congress, National Technical Clearing House, and so on. You will make use of all the conventional methods and reference materials used in library research—abstracting services, specialized bibliographies, *Reader's Guide to Periodicals,* technical digest services, and, in some libraries, computer data-retrieval services.

   Your research tools will, to a large extent, depend upon the field that you are researching. For example, if you are interested in a use for integrated circuits in automobiles, you could include such references as the electronics trade press and the end-user press (e.g., *Road and Track*), government automotive research standards and patent documentation might also be useful to you.

   If this form of research sounds endless to you, you might consider engaging the help of a diligent graduate student to aid in conducting the actual library research, under your close supervision.

2. *Questionnaire surveys.* The questionnaire survey is the mainstay of market research, whether it is conducted by mail, telephone, or personal

interview. You are reaching your prospective customer *directly*, learning about his or her needs, problems, quantity requirements, and opinions regarding your proposed product. No form of indirect or inferential information is as up-to-date, helpful to you, or convincing to others. The questionnaire is always used (even if it's memorized) to ensure that the results are as comparable and uniform as possible.

There are perils, of course. A poorly-structured questionnaire or an interview conducted with a weak format can result in your information being false or misleading. It is difficult, for example, for a customer to imagine using a product that he or she has never seen, that may be the first of its kind, and that is possibly still nonexistent. Books have been written on survey techniques, questionnaire design, and interview psychology. By consulting some of these references, you may be able to avoid some of these problems and make your survey far more efficient and effective.

3. *Existing research reports.* If the market you wish to reach is growing, it has probably been studied by someone in the recent past. The task is to discover who has done it and where to find the study. Many investment banking firms do such research or have it done by consultants for limited distribution to their customers. Various investment advisory services, such as Arthur D. Little's Service to Investors, do much the same thing. Consulting firms' livelihoods depend upon private studies of products and markets, both those that are potential in nature and those that already exist. It is difficult, however to obtain these reports unless you are in some way connected to the firm that commissioned them.

Some large studies, however, are syndicated by research firms as well as other agencies, such as Stanford Research Institute or Batelle Memorial Institute. In such studies, which are directed towards many different clients, many copies may be available and your chances of obtaining one are better. In order to find out if any current study or report exists, ask your prospective customers, prospective competitors, and trade association personnel, as well as consulting/research firms themselves. Reference libraries can often be helpful also. When you discover one, you may also discover that it is costly to buy. Your best bet is to borrow them from buyers.

4. *Published market statistics.* There are two important sources of published market statistics: the U.S. Department of Commerce and trade associations. The economic time series of the USDC are often criticized because of the tendency towards aggregation of figures, as well as slow reporting, smallness of samples, and out-of-date SIC classifications. However, in some industries you will find the data to be quite current

and detailed. Moreover, you can always contact the USDC directly and tell them the information you need. They have much data at their disposal (some already published and some not) and they may be able to provide you with information that is more detailed and current than you would expect. There may be a charge, or they may do it for free, depending upon the complexity of your needs.

Trade associations usually publish gross industry sales, which are broken down into major product categories. Get in touch with those associations relevant to you, and find out what they publish. If you are able to get to know someone on their staff at a national level, you may be able to obtain the information that they have but don't publish. Such information is not necessarily secret, but simply may not be in demand. Your ultimate objective, of course, is to find out *who* is shipping *how much* to *whom*. Finding such information may require some persistence on your part.

5. *Trade association meetings and trade shows.* It is possible to obtain a lot of valuable information by attending the appropriate association meetings and trade shows. You'll find out who your liveliest competitors and customers are, who is spending the most money on promotion (or at least on booths), and what their newest products look like. You will be able to discover their major trends, what their literature and product documentation are like, and perhaps who their best sales people are. If you go to the technical sessions, you will find out about your competitors' *future* products, or at least about the technology they will embody. You may also hear something about what is happening in your field overseas. You might meet some potential offshore product sources, licensors, or distributors for your product. All this information can be yours for the price of a ticket to the annual meeting.

6. *"Experts."* Much valuable information may be gained from talking to experts in your field, such as trade magazine editors, consultants, university researchers, analysts in investment banking firms, and trade association staff members. Aside from industry gossip and rumors, they can tell you about new technology that may soon revolutionize your field, some of your potential competitors who may be in trouble, which products are good and which are bad, and so forth. Aside from sharing information, these people are generally interested in getting to know *you*, as an entrepreneur who is about to enter their world. Many of them will be happy to help you in any way they can, including paying for lunch occasionally.

7. *Phantom products.* One method that is often used to obtain market data is the press announcement of a nonexistent or prototype product. Then

sit back and see who responds. This is sometimes done rather elabo-rately, with heavily airbrushed photographs of a mockup product, or with artist's cutaways. A press release may be distributed to major jour-nals, sometimes even using an assumed company name. When the di-rect mail results are analyzed and certain respondents contacted, you may find this to be a rather effective method of gathering information. Poorly handled, it may also backfire, and of course the ethical aspects may be considered somewhat questionable by some.

8. *Business and credit services.* Firms such as Dun and Bradstreet, NCO, the American Bankers Association, and Corp Tech maintain extensive files of information on industries and companies. They can be excellent although costly sources of data. From them, one can gain knowledge of the size and geographical location of potential competitors, and specific classes of customers with whom they deal. Chilton Publishing Company and McGraw-Hill, for example, maintain files on several different indus-tries. McGraw-Hill's *American Machinist* marketing service can tell you the location, type, and age of nearly every machine tool of the U.S.A. Other business publishers also offer market data services, again at a price.

9. *Professional market surveys.* The value of a report from a prestigious market research firm should not be underestimated as a tool in selling your proposal to investors. The length of such a report does not matter. The chances are slight that you will learn anything new by contracting for a market survey, if you have done tasks number one through eight of this section thoroughly. However, a corroborating report from a third party might be a source of extra confidence for you as well as for investors.

You will also learn simply from the process of negotiating questions of capability, scope, and cost with the market research firm. They must convince you of their experience and ability to deal with the question you present. Therefore, you will have to meet their "expert" in your field, and they may well show you some nonclassified reports that they have done for other clients in your field, or in similar fields. It is entirely possible that they will suggest an "in-depth" study that will cost you $10,000 to $20,000. What you really need from them, however, is a study costing between somewhere between $1,000 and $2,000, with you "helping" the researcher to understand what it is you need and want to know, and sharing your present information with this person.

If done thoroughly, your market analysis will be beneficial to you in several different ways. It will provide you with quantification and documenta-tion of the demand for your product. It will aid you in redefining the product (if redefinition is needed) and in modifying its specifications to fit the market more closely. You will be made more aware of what your competitors are doing, and of trends in distribution and promotion. Your analysis will give you a list of your first customers and perhaps even yield one or two "letters of intent to purchase." On the other hand, your research may show that your technology is obsolete; that you will only have one tenth of the market you originally expected; that there is already overcapacity in the business, forcing down profit margins; that there is some built-in reason why no one would buy your product, even it if was better than that of your competitor. (For example, for many years, the slogan "Buy American" has had an extremely powerful influence on the use of imported parts and equipment, even though foreign-made products have often been cheaper and frequently of better quality.) Avoiding just one massive blunder can more than justify the cost of the research.

CONVENTIONAL WISDOM: The true entrepreneur will not be able to afford the time and money for fancy "market research"—and probably won't need it anyway.

REALITY: A little effort may yield enormous returns of information and increase credibility—both scarce commodities in most new ventures.

REFERENCES

1. Gumpert, David E. and Timmons, Jeffry A. *The Insider's Guide to Small Business Resources.* Garden City, NY: Doubleday & Co., 1982.
    This is an indispensable shelf-book, offering extensive access to market research data sources and lists of everything from courses to money sources.
2. Dible, D.M. *Up Your Own Organization.* Santa Clara, Calif.: Entrepreneur Press, 1971.
3. Aacker, David A. and Day, George S. *Market Research.* New York: John Wiley & Sons, 1980.
    One of the best references on all phases of market analysis.
4. Erdos, P. L. *Professional Market Surveys.* New York: McGraw-Hill Co., 1970.
    This is a very practical treatment of the design, execution, and interpretation of mail surveys—the principal tool available to entrepreneurs.
5. Smith, J. F. *Interviewing in Market and Social Research.* New York: Bosh, Routledge, & K. Paul, 1972.
    Useful guidance to the techniques of interviewing.
6. Breen, George F. *Do-It-Yourself Market Research.* New York: McGraw Hill, 1977.
    Breezy, practical; 80 percent of all you'll ever need to conduct shirt-sleeves market analysis. Good section on questionnaire design.

5

Selection of Cohorts

*". . . I'm not too bright myself but I have a lot of very
bright people working for me."*   *—Anonymous*

Companies are groups of people. Skillful management is fundamentally the
ability to attract, train, motivate, and retain good, experienced people. However, your reasons for starting a new business may or may not include an
exhibition of your superb managerial skills. The main objective should be to
make money. This implies the retention of a maximum amount of equity for
yourself as you raise the funds necessary for each ensuing stage of your
company's growth.

Backers have a powerful and statistically well-founded preference for the
"founding *team*," as opposed to the individual founder. Both academic studies
and venture capitalists' experience seem to confirm that a team effort is more
likely to succeed than an individual effort. The team, theoretically, should not
be one-sided in its area of expertise but should rather be a complementary
group of people whose specialized skills cover the major, functional needs of a
company at your stage of development.

IS A TEAM REALLY NECESSARY?

The question of the desirability and size of a team deserves some scrutiny, since there is an obvious conflict between having partners and retaining the majority of the stock for yourself. Whether a team is really necessary depends upon two major factors:

1. *The character of the venture.* Do you require a top-notch performer for every role, or can satisfactory people be hired later for the key roles?
2. *Your own personality, energy, and ability.* Are you the kind of person who is equally comfortable making technical, marketing, and business judgments? Or do you feel that it is essential to have a strong partner in one or more of these areas? Will you be comfortable in allowing your associates to tend the business while you're away, or is a real alter-ego necessary to your peace of mind? Will you need a partner to share the day-to-day burdens, or would a partner just be in the way?

The indications are that small founding teams work better than big ones. Despite the prevailing conventional wisdom of having teams share entrepreneurial efforts, it is the author's belief that the burden of proof is definitely on the larger team. A classic team structure is the two-person model: the technologist and the peddler.

COMMON TEAM PROBLEMS

Teams, especially democratic ones, can create as many problems as they solve. This is especially true in cases in which team members have not known one another before, or have not worked together in stress situations. On the other hand, people who *have* worked together tend either to be personal friends or to be in the same specialty. Personal or non-complementary relationships may tend greatly to dilute the alleged benefits of a team.

There also exist a number of potential sources of team conflict that are hard, if not impossible, to evaluate before the business is launched. People vary widely in their ways of handling pressure, willingness to work long hours, ability to deal with ambiguity, ethical standards, sense of humor, and innate intelligence. Serious mismatches in any of these areas can create conflicts that can easily destroy a fragile young company.

Certain of these risks might be avoided by applying modern methods of psychological testing. Much is known about complementary and conflicting personalities. As a practical matter, however, it is unlikely that your team will consider it necessary to hire an agency for this purpose, however desirable the process may seem. Many will say "That's just for other people." And, of course, each person's sense of privacy may surface. Don't forget Oscar Wilde's bleak observation: "To be understood is to be found out."

THE QUESTION OF STOCK

A more important consideration at the outset will be:

Who should have how much *stock?* Or, more bluntly, *why should I part with any of it?*

This is not a decision to be made lightly over a few beers with friends. It will have much to do with the future of the company. This decision greatly influences the direction the company takes, how swiftly it can respond to changes in its environment, and how effectively its plans can be formulated and executed. Moreover, there is a tendency among teams to think of equal partnership as being not only fair but also the proper way of doing things. After all, if the company hasn't even gotten off the ground, why should anyone doubt that each partner will make an equal contribution?

In thinking about equity distribution, keep the following considerations in mind:

1. Partners need not be equal partners. Common stock makes unequal partnership both feasible and easily quantified.
2. Do not take on a partner if you can hire a person for the same role.
3. Do not take on partners because you think having a "balanced team" will impress financial backers. Responsible backers will be much more interested in knowing that the people who are actually responsible for the company's progress are the ones who hold the motivating stock.
4. Do not allow your innate sense of democracy to cause you to part with more stock than is needed to give your partner the motivation to use his or her full energies. Try to view the situation from this person's standpoint. What is your partner doing now? What are his or her prospects? Does your partner have a better opportunity?

5. Do not allow the immediacy of your present need, whatever it might be, to bias judgment in favor of a partner versus an employee.

6. Stay flexible in terms of compensation and motivation. Consider stock options, or, preferably, bonus plans. Don't use stock when cash or IOUs will work as effectively. And don't make vague promises about stock when hiring.

7. Do not approach potential partners with tentative offers in order to elicit their help in shaping your ideas, until you have gone as far as you can go without them. Get your initial business plan in order, incorporate, get an office, stationery, and phone, and find a part-time accountant. In short, make sure that you have established the company as *yours,* so that anyone joining you will do so on *your* terms.

8. If your analysis shows that you can do it alone, don't be afraid to try it. If you discover, as things progress, that you really *do* need a couple of partners, it's easier to get them later than it is doing it the other way around.

If the above seems to some to be rather Machiavellian, it will seem to others to be nothing more than obvious common sense. It may be that the team idea has been greatly overemphasized. One or two carefully selected and functioning partners can greatly smooth the road to success, but a team for team's sake is simply a source of more problems for the entrepreneur at a time when there are certainly enough problems already. Contrary to the widely-held view, the stock of a new company, rather than having zero value, is the only thing it has of value. Do not use it to compensate the janitor!

In presenting a business plan to potential backers, you will, of course, be expected to indicate the two or three key people who will be working with or for you. You should be able either to state who will fill the roles or to demonstrate convincingly that you understand the job requirements and possess the managerial competence to recruit and utilize people, when and if they are needed.

Ideally, the people you choose will have functioned in small-company roles before. Even an unsuccessful former entrepreneur may be a better bet than someone who has had no entrepreneurial experience whatsoever. If you need someone who has been a project manager from Colossus Aerospace Co., who has a brilliant record, but who has normally had three assistants and 100 engineers under him, consider making this person a director or a consultant. The same is true for the marketing manager who functions only "first class," with huge advertising budgets, big staffs, and a nationwide direct sales force, replete with pep rallies in Bermuda. You will be better off with a bright junior person who knows his or her way around your industry, but whose mistakes are not going to destroy your company by sheer magnitude. If this person has had some entrepreneurial or bottom line management experience, perhaps as a rep or a division manager, so much the better. This is the person who will get out of bed in the mornings and make four sales calls and twenty phone calls. This is the person you need.

Hire the people with the qualifications you need *now*. With luck, the person will grow with the job. If not, you can replace this employee at some later time. But don't make the error of hiring overqualified people, thinking that the company will fully utilize their skills when sales reach $10 million. Your job is to be sure those sales get to $6 million at all.

Offers made to prospective partners and employees before the company is on its feet have a somewhat surrealistic quality. The company has no money, no customers—in short, it is not a functioning company—yet. Realizing this, the prospective employee will expect some stock. But he or she will also expect market-rate compensation, even if it comes in the form of IOUs. Don't make the mistake of hiring someone who is worth $60,000 for $30,000 and a lot of stock. Pay this employee his or her worth, even if it is partially deferred. Make the question of stock contingent upon performance, not time.

The proper function of founders' stock is not compensation for past deeds. It is, rather, to provide motivation for deeds yet to come. The deferral of ownership vesting privileges for a couple of years should not be viewed by the employee as the withholding of just compensation for two years of service. The two years should properly be considered as a probationary period, during which time the company must decide whether the person is worth having around for a longer time. During that period, the employee should receive full compensation so that if for any reason relationship doesn't work out, he or she will have no basis for complaint and will not walk away with a lot of stock. Your attorney will be able to help you in evaluating the various combinations of present and deferred salary and stock rights that are appropriate in different stages of corporate growth.

EQUITY DISTRIBUTION: ONE APPROACH

There exist alternatives to the atavistic, keep-it-all philosophy of equity distribution. One such formula, for which Richard White reports good results (see References at end of Chapter), is essentially an earn-in system. Under this plan, each founding member of the team agrees in advance to a schedule of values to be placed upon each major task to be completed during the initial one to two years. For example

Team Member	Task	Value (In Shares)
President	Write busines plan	500
	Raise $100,000 seed Capital	500
	Find facility	100
VP Marketing	Recruit 50 dealers	250
	Recruit and train three regional managers	200
	Write and print literature	100
	Obtain three letters of intent	300
Chief Engineer	Complete prototype development	400
	Complete production tooling	200
	Complete production documentation	100
	Complete *User's Manual*	100
	Hire software manager	100

As each task is completed on time, the shares are credited or distributed. Late or over-budget completion may be penalized. And, as tasks are added to the list, the founding team meets and agrees upon their value to the enterprise.

There are a number of obvious benefits to such a contractual approach to equity distribution.

1. It eliminates the arbitrariness and potential unfairness of simply giving most of the stock to the first one or two people in the boat.
2. By relating distribution to actual accomplished tasks, each individual partner has special motivation to perform.
3. Since completed tasks trigger stock distribution, the nonperformer can be dumped more easily than if he or she held a negotiated share of the company's equity.

Despite its appeal to sweet reason, however, the formula approach may contain the seeds of serious later problems for the company. This is because

1. It is very hard to gauge correctly the relative difficulty and worth of accomplishing specific goals. While we can easily estimate the effort needed to write a business plan, for example, it can be very hard to estimate what's required to raise capital—especially in a tight market.
2. The completion of a task is not necessarily the same as brilliant completion. Although the Chief Engineer has finished the working prototype,

the design may be costly, inefficient, inflexible, or unmanufacturable. As always, quality of work is more elusive to measure than quantity.

3. It is likely that the future abilities and contributions of individual team members will be quite unequal. The person who was very good at getting start-up tasks done may prove later to be of much less value than a more managerial partner—yet they may both hold equal amounts of founders' stock.

Despite these pitfalls, the formal approach to equity distribution has some appeal and should certainly be considered by a founding team as an approach to solving this always-sticky problem.

HOUSECLEANING

In the very early stages of forming a company, you are likely to discover that you have already made some mistakes in choosing your partners or employees. It's possible that your marketing manager will disappear to Cape Cod on the weekend he or she was supposed to finish your marketing plan. Your chief engineer may anguish for days over details that should be resolved within a few minutes. In short, for any number of reasons you may decide that you have hired the wrong person. What do you do? Your employee knows your plans. You've given this person stock. You've told your prospective backers that he or she is nothing short of indispensable. This employee quit his old job and already has new business cards. What can be done? Well, maybe you should go ahead, raise the money, and keep the lid on. This problem can be dealt with later. Right? Wrong. Get rid of this person now. Even though funding is in prospect, the stock has no "value," and it will take much longer than you expected to get your money in the bank. Now is the time to level with this person, making an offer he or she can't refuse. Give IOUs bearing interest for the estimated work-hours the employee has put in. Offer to buy back his or her stock at a substantially higher price than was originally paid. Offer to reimburse this person's placement fees if another job search is in order. Offer to retain him or her as a director or consultant. Pay this person's price in "consulting fees" if necessary. But *get this person out.*

However friendly, forthright, and rational you try to be, you may expect the person to be hostile, irrational, and ungrateful. You have challenged this individual's professional competence, trampled his or her self-esteem, and left the person on a financial limb. If you were in that position you, too, would be upset. Expect some ugliness. Should it develop, your lawyer can suggest various alternatives. Hopefully it will not come to legal action, and it will be evident to both parties that the partnership just won't work. But if things do get worse, fight it out and remember that it's easier now, when the numbers are small, than it ever will be in the future. As far as your backers are concerned, they probably will not be dismayed by the disorder in your house. They halfway expected it anyway, and it will give them a good chance to size you up under pressure. After all, you were *supposed* to be tough.

The initial stages, before you even reach the starting gate are a lot of fun. This is the idea stage, when the really creative architecture of your venture takes place. Seeds of eventual success or failure are planted. The real entrepreneur, however, is not swept along by the prevailing euphoria. He or she has the guts to correct early mistakes before it is too late.

CONVENTIONAL WISDOM: Every venture needs a balanced team of people with complementary skills in marketing, production, engineering, and operations.

REALITY: Every venture needs a founder who understands the need for supporting skills and knows where to find them when needed.

REFERENCES

1. White, Richard M. *Entrepreneur's Manual: Business Startups, Spinoffs, and Innovative Management.* Radnor, Penn. Chilton Book Co., 1977.

    The author spells out his model for founder's equity distribution among team members.
2. Timmons, Jeffry A., Smollen, Leonard E., and Dingee, Alexander L.M. *New Venture Creation—A Guide to Entrepreneurship.* 2nd ed., Homewood, Ill.: Richard D. Irwin, Inc., 1985.

    Chapter 7, "The New Venture Team" is an insightful contribution based on the authors' experience in building startup teams.

6

The Zero Stage:
Form versus Substance

*Analysis and criticism are of no interest to me unless
they are a path to constructive, action-bent thinking.
Critical type of intelligence is boring and destructive
and only satisfactory to those who indulge in it. Most
new projects—I can even say every one of them—can be
analyzed to destruction. . . Georges Doriot*

Let us define the zero stage of the enterprise as the time that lies between the
fun of conception and the agonies of the birth of a corporation. This is by far
the most fluid stage of the development of a new enterprise. Things may
change radically in any direction during this period. You have your basic idea
for a product, perhaps even a prototype. You have—or think you have—
commitments from key people who will help you get off the ground. One or
two of you is probably spending substantial time on the venture by now, even
though you're still holding down a full-time job. The crude outline of a
business plan exists, but you still don't know enough about the market to
make any defensible sales projections or *pro forma* profitability estimates.
You think you know a couple of investors who might be able to provide seed
money, but you're not sure how to approach them. You're wondering whether
to incorporate, how fast to move in product development, where to go for
legal help.

In short you're asking yourself the question, hour by hour, "What do I do next?"

During the zero stage everything is fluid. Nothing has jelled yet, and this fact amplifies every form of perturbation upon the incipient corporate baby. It is at this stage, for example, that you might discover that, instead of manufacturing, it would make a lot more sense to set up a sales or leasing company. Or, you might discover that your chief technologist is a terrible engineer, and that the prototype he has created doesn't work. Finally, you might discover that you can't enjoy the ambiguities of the new enterprise and that the lack of a structured work day is unbearable to you—and decide to give the whole thing up.

These are all radical influences, to say the least. It seems as though a million things need to be done, and a million questions must be resolved, all at the same time. Among these are:

WHAT FORM SHOULD THE COMPANY TAKE?

Should it be a corporation, single proprietorship, partnership, syndicate, or what? Each of these possibilities has its specific legal, tax, and debt liability consequences, which any attorney can help you to understand. However, unless some special circumstances dictate otherwise, you might as well incorporate right away. It is not an expensive process, and you do not need to have your permanent attorney selected at this point. Moreover, the very act of drawing up your corporate charter may help you in solidifying your vision of what you want your company to become and the possible ranges of its activities. Other benefits include the following:

1. Incorporation forces you to choose a name and research it for prior claimants, thus eliminating the possible awkwardness of having to change the name six months after the inception of the company.

2. Being incorporated gives your venture, if nothing else, the *illusion* of permanence. This is a great help in recruiting partners on *your terms* as well as persuading suppliers, bankers, and customers that you're serious, and plan to be around for a while.

3. In a corporation, ownership is more readily divisible than in the common forms of partnership. This makes "uneven partnershps" more easily quantifiable.

4. It permits you to go ahead with a logo and permanent quality stationery and to have literature designed and produced without risking the possibility of having to do the whole job twice.

Having decided to incorporate, you may ask yourself whether you should (as many big companies have) incorporate in a place like Delaware. The answer is probably no. By the time you face the problems that incorporation in Delaware is supposed to solve you will be able to afford to *re*incorporate there.

Secondly, you must decide what kind of corporation you want to have. There are some forms of incorporation in which special tax features are inherent. A "Subchapter S" incorporation will allow your financial backers to take as an ordinary loss any operating loss incurred by the corporation. A "Section 1244" incorporation permits them to take an ordinary loss on their individual tax returns from the sale of the company's stock, rather than a capital loss. Both these features operate in a similar way. They are intended to induce individuals with high incomes or a large net-worth to invest in risky new ventures. These privileges are, however, limited to companies that fall below specified limits of total capital, number of investors, and so forth. Therefore, the principal benefits are available to the smallest and/or newest ventures. Since these features of corporate law exist, there is very little reason not to take advantage of them. Your attorney, however, should examine the particulars of your situation and make a firm recommendation.

WHAT KIND OF FACILITIES?

There are several reasons why it is desirable to have different addresses for your home and your business. In addition to having a place to which deliveries can be sent, where the phone can ring, and where prototypes can be developed, it is a clear signal to prospective partners that this is *your* turf, and that any agreement made with them will be subject to *your* terms.

You will probably be better off with an office of at least reasonable dignity. The want-ad section of the newspaper often contains information about space to share, along with secretarial help, office equipment, and the like. This can be a better solution than renting space immediately and hiring a secretary yourself. It can, however, be a bit costly. An alternative solution to this problem is to find a friend with an office or plant with the necessary overhead and ask if you can share it, if not for free then on a deferred-rent basis. This might give you access to other desirable facilities, such as a shop, conference room, telephone board—maybe even a purchasing agent—all of which would help you materially as well as enhance your appearance.

You may also have the opportunity to set up shop in a small-business "incubator." These are being set up in many parts of the country to simplify the logistical problems of entrepreneurs like yourself. As a minimum they provide office space and equipment. They can be much more elaborate, including secretarial support, conference rooms, fax and telex services, production space, and even wet labs. Such space is usually priced well below market, and may be just fine for the initial year or so.

Remember: Appearances count, especially in the beginning, when there is so little real substance with which to back it up. You must not, on the other hand, become one of those entrepreneurs who are so preoccupied with the form of the business and the high of being CEO that you forget all about its substance.

DIRECTORS, PRO AND CON

Every corporation needs a board of directors, according to law. Such a board may be comprised of your spouse and yourself or of any number of other people. In theory, the board sets overall corporation policy and the executives execute it.

In the small business venture, however, the board usually serves a somewhat different function. Many entrepreneurs use it as a kind of totem pole, made up of a maximum number of influential and imposing figures whose function is to impress investors. This is, in all probability, the major function of outside directors during the zero stage of a company.

On the other hand, you should not allow the recruitment of important figures to become an obsession—you have other, more important things to do. Important people tend to be busy and are therefore reluctant to become board members—especially if they perceive their function as being mainly one of decoration. As your plans and prospects develop, it will become somewhat easier to find outside directors. Until then, however, too many outsiders may hamper your flexibility and become an encumbrance to your efforts. If you feel the need to have an "outside" officer, your attorney will probably be willing to be clerk. He or she has to do all the work, anyway.

Often an outside venture advisor, or "godparent," can be extremely helpful in starting a new venture, especially if this is an experienced person, perhaps a retired executive who has had first-hand entrepreneurial experience. Your advisor can serve as a sounding board for new ideas, as a reference for banks and attorneys, and, just as important, as a source of guidance and encouragement when you feel as though everything is falling apart.

The venture advisor will often spend half a day to a day per week working as a member of your team and can have a wide range of assignments, depending upon the problem mix of the company and his or her particular talents. Your advisor may chair the design review, conduct the search for a bank, lead the strategic planning process, mediate disputes among the founders, and almost certainly become your confidant—a friendly and fully-informed sounding board with whom to discuss ideas and problems that cannot be readily discussed with partners, subordinates, or investors. The venture advisor is likely someone who has seen every problem in the book, and will be someone to turn to for help when real problems arise.

Your venture advisor probably will not need nor expect to be paid for his or her time. However, you should plan to compensate this person with stock or options, at least annually. Do not be surprised, however, if your advisor gets enthusiastic enough about your venture to volunteer investing some of his or her own money. Finding a good advisor is not necessarily easy. One good source of leads is venture capitalists. They are likely to understand very clearly what you want, and have some good suggestions among their contacts and former CEOs.

PROTOTYPES AND PLAUSIBILITY

You don't need a book to tell you that the more fully developed your product is, the more easily you will be able to raise seed money for it and get the project off the ground. There is, of course, a succession of stages in product development, which runs from idea, to design, to prototype, to pre-production prototype, to tooled production models, to sales of the actual product. You can show your product at any of these stages. It goes without saying, however, that the closer you are to the finished product the better.

In most instances the prototype stage is the earliest point at which you should seek investors. This is the point at which the venture begins to acquire momentum. Products that cannot be explained to prospective backers in technical terms *can* be demonstrated. The functioning entity can give your designers something concrete with which to work, as they begin actually to *see* ways in which the product can be radically improved while reducing the production costs. Most of all, the prototype is the first real evidence that your company *has* a product. Your statements about its marketability and profit-making potential increase in plausibility. In short, you'll probably be better off with a lower profile while the prototype is being built, bootstrapping with whatever resources can be scrounged.

WHERE DOES SEED MONEY COME FROM?

Seed money—sometimes called *adventure* capital—must be clearly differentiated from *venture* capital. Seed money is the money that goes into the company before it is actually functioning as such. Its purpose is to get the company from conception to newborn status, and as much further as possible before outside financing and its accompanying ownership dilution occurs.

The seed capital of the venture, regardless of whether it is from the founders or the outsiders, is highly leveraged money—that is, a great deal of value is usually created for a fairly small amount of money. During the seed, or "zero" stage you will be finishing your prototype, getting your market data, recruiting key team members, further refining your business plan, making some initial customer and dealer calls, perhaps lining up vendors, lawyers, and accountants. You may be working on employment, nondisclosure, and invention assignment agreements for your team. You will be incorporating, working out founders' stock distribution, and, ideally, you will be recruiting and working with your venture advisor (who may in fact become a source of seed capital).

Seed money is most likely to come from the entrepreneur and his or her partners—at least the first few thousand dollars of it. If more money is needed, the search widens. Studies over the last twenty-five years show that

---

almost all seed money for startup comes from wealthy individuals—often entrepreneurs themselves.

In every community there are a few wealthy individuals with an interest in investing in new ventures. They can often be identified through your banker, lawyer, realtor, or other active professionals. Through successive referrals, you will eventually find your way to the right doors. Whether you walk away with money will depend on your sales skills, the excitement of the deal, and the current appetite for the prospect.

The typical private investor can best be thought of as a recreational investor. This person doesn't *need* the winnings from the investment, but gets personal satisfaction and excitement from being involved with a startup and helping others get started. The private investor is normally quite busy with other professional and investment pursuits, so you can expect him or her to spend only nominal effort in evaluating your deal. One of this person's wonderful qualities is that he or she is likely to accept something close to the price you set on the stock, without too much argument. Maybe this is why these people are often called "angels."

In the Northeast there exists an interesting service, called the Venture Capital Network, started by Professor William Wetzel at the University of New Hampshire. The VCN runs a data base or "dating bureau," to match up the needs of entrepreneurs with the investing interests of angels. It is a model which is now being replicated in other parts of the country.

A third source of seed capital has begun to emerge during the past few years: the seed capital funds. These are small pools of money specifically targeted at seed and early-stage companies. Although generally under private management, these funds sometimes get some or all of their money from state or local agencies anxious to promote local economic development. Functionally, these funds are similar to other venture funds, and are intended for similarly large upside potential. However, since they invest at the earliest stage, they expect to work with incomplete teams, unfinished prototypes, and unpolished or nonexistent business plans. In addition to money, these organizations expend a lot of effort in helping to get the venture together and to set the stage for a larger first-stage investment by others. Unlike the angel-type investor, however, the seed funds are motivated principally by financial return. One such seed fund is Zero Stage Capital, of which the author is cofounder; it has regional offices in Cambridge, MA, State College, PA, and Baltimore, MD—each a center of research and academic excellence. There are a number of other funds, some regionally focused, and a few focused exclusively on the needs of a specific research institution.

In sum, there has always been a scarcity of seed money, and it has always been hard to raise. Once your savings are gone and the house is mortgaged, it may be a little late to start searching for outside seed money.

Another caveat: *Don't accept more seed capital than you need.* It is always flattering to have a high valuation placed on your company by even an unsophisticated outsider. However, the more you can achieve on a small amount of seed capital, the more impressive your results will be. It will also be healthier for your company in the long run. In the next round, money will be easier to find and will cost you a whole lot less stock ownership. Hold on to that stock!

WHAT TO DO UNTIL THE MONEY ARRIVES?

Whether or not you have reached your desired minimum level of seed capital, there are certain things that must be done immediately. Some are major, some minor, but all are important.

1. *Make sure that people are able to get in touch with you.* If there are times when the phone cannot be covered, get an answering service or at least a machine.

2. *Begin market research immediately.* This is essential if your information is to be of any value in shaping the product or the company. Since such research usually takes a good deal of calendar time, the sooner you begin it, the better. Be prepared to spend some time traveling, because much of it will probably take the form of personal interviews. Questionnaire surveys can take a lot of time, too, and should probably be the first form of market research undertaken.

3. *Have a logo and letterhead designed.* Don't have your printer do it. Get an ad agency that specializes in that kind of work. It may cost you more money, but it is an investment in image and self-esteem. Then get your letterhead and cards printed, not sacrificing quality for cost.

4. *Get the formal business plan moving,* even if there are large blank spaces to be filled in later. Try to get a feel for the figures, as well as for the sensitivity of your *pro forma* financial statements to variations in sales rates, price, material costs, and so forth.

5. *Write some reasonable descriptions and specification sheets,* and have them set in type and neatly printed. You cannot afford to have sloppy literature, even if it is temporary. Have all line drawings, graphs, and cutaways done professionally, if at all possible. If you can afford it, use more than two colors in your literature. If you can find a free-lance professional artist to work with you, it is better than going to an ad agency. If you went to one it would probably send the job out to the free-lancer anyway. Remember, your printed materials *are* your company to your prospective customers. The more you look like IBM the better.

6. *Give your team enough work to do.* Maintain their level of enthusiasm. Get together with them at least twice a week to check results and keep everyone up to date. Don't forget that, as president of your venture, you are a combination of press agent, errand boy, cheerleader, and ass-kicker—it all depends upon what needs doing when.

7. *Don't stop meeting people.* Keep widening your circle of contacts. Meet with bankers' investors, customers, consultants, other entrepreneurs, editors, professors, employees, and vendors. Try to have lunch with someone useful every day. Tap into their networks. Build that rolodex.

8. *Write some articles for the trade press.* Describe your product, discuss possible applications, work jointly with a user on a story, or, perhaps do a comparative survey of existing products in your field. You'll discover that editors are willing and eager to find a source of new and fresh material, and that the by-line will aid you in spreading your fame and that of your company. Also, reprints make impressive-looking product literature and appendices for financial presentations.

9. *Set up a definite compensation schedule for all your employees.* Make sure that everyone's work hours are recorded and that the rate for each person's work has been agreed upon. Even if you have to issue IOUs, it is infinitely better than trying, a year from now, to distribute stock in proportion to services rendered. Or, even worse, trying to distribute it in proportion to "value contributed."

10. *Stay loose.* During the zero stage, you should try to keep your ideas about your company and yourself as flexible as possible. You may discover a better opportunity. At the same time, you may come up against a complete roadblock that was invisible at an earlier stage. You are certain to learn things you never knew about yourself, as well as discovering new facets of your partners' personalities. You may discover new markets or meet people with better ideas than yours, with which you would prefer to work. The seed stage is immensely valuable, in that it allows things like this to happen without the danger of losing a lot of someone else's money or a great deal of personal credibility with the business and financial communities. Give it all you've got, but at the same time try to maintain a slightly Olympian viewpoint.

CONVENTIONAL WISDOM: Get a million-dollar idea, find some venture capital, and *go.*

REALITY: Venture capital companies are not interested in ideas. Get some seed money, make sure your prototype and your company are "debugged," and *then* go.

REFERENCES

1. Bartlett, Joseph W. *Venture Capital—Law, Business Strategies and Investment Planning.* New York: John Wiley & Sons, 1988

Written for the professional VC, this book contains plenty of substance for the entrepreneur. See especially Chapter 3, "Selecting the Form of Organization."

2. Vesper, Karl. *New Venture Strategies*. Englewood Cliffs, N.J.: Prentice Hall, 1980.

Vesper's description of various venture startup processes is required reading.

3. Mancuso, Joseph R. *How to Start, Finance, and Manage Your Own Small Business*. Englewood Cliffs, N.J.: Prentice Hall, 1970.

Contains an excellent section on the role of directors.

7

Leaving the Womb

Companies are like babies—fun to conceive, but hell to deliver. .. Anonymous

Gestation has run its course, and you feel that the time has come to cut the cord. You have a team, a product, a little capital (at least enough to make a start), and now you must make your first real commitment to the new company's future by devoting your full energies to it. How best to proceed?

The first step is to read (perhaps for the first time) the nondisclosure agreement you signed upon joining your present organization. You may not think that your new product competes with those of your present company. It may be inconceivable to you that it infringes upon your employer's patents, or makes use of its trade secrets, or that it will be sold to the same customers. But take a hard look. It is just possible that your present employer might decide not to agree with you. Consult your lawyer, just to make sure. Courts are more and more frequently deciding in favor of firms holding such agreements, and the form that such agreements take is becoming more sophisticated and enforceable.

Should you decide that there is a possibility of your being challenged, take it seriously. Even if the challenge were frivolous, its mere possibility and the prospect of an impending court fight is enough to send prospective investors into permanent hibernation. Unfortunately, there is no sure way of discovering ahead of time how an employer might view such a matter without your letting him or her know that you are about to quit, and revealing rather fully the details of your venture. You might get some idea of this person's probable reaction from similar situations within the company, but this is far from a firm guide for action.

In addition to meeting your legal obligations to your employer (avoiding prosecution), you should reflect upon your professional obligations as well. These can include the following:

1. Tying up the loose ends of projects on which you've been working.
2. Spending some time helping to orient and to train your replacement.
3. Taking whatever steps are necessary to ensure that your departure causes the minimum possible disruption in the company's business.

Remember, you're going to need all the friends you can get in your new role as entrepreneur. Your old company might be a future supplier, customer, or (God forbid) employer. In any case,

---

it will be among the first sources to which bankers, financial backers, and prospective creditors will turn when checking on your personal integrity. Be sure that what they hear is good news.

NONCOMPETITION AGREEMENTS

Such agreements are most often found in conjunction with employment contracts, and if you have signed one, go at once to your lawyer and have a long talk. While some agreements have defined "competition" so broadly as to be nonenforceable, the merits of the case would determine your actual exposure. If you are, in fact, going to compete with your ex-employer, you may have little choice but to accept the calculated risk of breaking the agreement. The law allows him or her to prevent you from competing. However, your former employer *cannot* prevent you from making a living within your field of expertise. If yours is a borderline case, as many are, proceed—but with caution.

WHEN TO SPLIT

From both a practical and a legal standpoint, it is time to resign when you find that you are spending significant amounts of time on the new venture. This will forestall the appearance of having worked on the project on company time, as well as the question of whether you have recruited company employees or customers while still employed at your old firm. All of these are causes for possible legal action against you.

If (as is likely) your proposed business is something in which your employer has a legitimate interest, you should consider discussing your plan with him or her. The benefits of such a course of action will probably outweigh the risks. If there are problems of proprietary products, patents, or trade secrets, they can be aired at the same time. Possible methods of circumventing problems can also be discussed (e.g., patent licensing, contract manufacture, or outright purchase of company design rights for cash or stock).

The very fact of your giving up the security of your job to start your own company will change your employer's perception of you. You are no longer a hired hand, and your boss must decide whether to say goodbye and good luck, or goodbye, see you in court; or whether to attempt to enlist your newly-revealed entrepreneurial talents to the benefit of the company. The first two cases require no further comment. The third, however, could be interesting in that you might unexpectedly find yourself confronted with yet another career choice.

If your employer likes you or your idea a lot, the reaction to your proffered resignation could be one of several:

1. An offer of a fat pay increase to keep you doing what you've been doing.
2. An offer to create a new subsidiary company to do what your own company is planning to do, with some possibility of equity for you, as president.
3. An offer to take an equity position in *your* venture, supplying capital and perhaps other resources. Your employer could insist on a buy-out option, exclusive marketing rights, exclusive manufacturing contracts, and so forth.
4. An offer of facilities, manufacturing time, marketing capability, or other resources—for a price—in return for design rights, patent rights, manufacturing contracts, etc.

A counter-proposition, depending upon its form and content, may turn out to be a better opportunity than your own company would be; or, it could be that you would just be selling out your chance to build your own company in exchange for a little security.

You must realize that your interests and those of your employer are very different. You want eventual growth in your personal net worth, together with maximum flexibility to go public, merge, or sell out. Products or technology aside, your employer wants maximum earnings per share, plus whatever boost your hot little venture would give to his or her price-earnings ratio (assuming your employer's stock is public). If, after reviewing all of these factors, the proposition seems to make more sense to you than your own, take it. After a year or two, if the new situation proves to be less than you had expected, you may be in a stronger position than you are now to start your own company. *Caveat:* Don't discuss your plans with your employer in such a way that you seem to be expecting a counter-proposal. This situation puts you in an extremely unfavorable light, regardless of the income. Announce your departure and the formation of your new venture as a concrete *fait accompli.*

WHAT TO TAKE WITH YOU

What you take with you to your new venture should be limited to that which is in your head. What you should not take with you is any property of your employer, broadly construed: plans, blueprints, customer lists, vendor lists, research reports, market studies, competitive analyses, or any other documents which cost your employer time and money to acquire—even if you did them yourself, and even if you believe them to be of little value to your employer. Appropriation of such proprietary materials, even if it runs no risk of prosecution, places the formation of your new venture in a very poor ethical light, particularly in the view of your own people. However, it greatly strengthens the case your employer might bring against you sometime in the future.

RAIDING

As long as you are no longer employed by a firm, there is no legal constraint against recruiting its employees. Practically speaking, it may be very difficult to get a firm started *without* recruiting some of your former working associates. The financial community's preference for a team whose members have worked together previously is not without sound basis. (Of course, you, too, will prefer to have had direct experience with the first few employees of your company, whether they are your chief scientist or your secretary.)

Since raiding, however necessary, is not likely to enhance your popularity with your old employer, weigh the benefits carefully against the possible penalties. And under no circumstances should you begin recruiting until *after* you resign.

PARTING SHOT: Try to make your break with your employer as clean as possible, in every sense of the word. Then you'll have no reason to regret it.

CONVENTIONAL WISDOM: Your old employer is a resource to be exploited.

REALITY: Your old employer is a resource to be exploited at your peril.

REFERENCES

1. Vesper, Karl. *New Venture Strategies.* Englewood Cliffs, N.J.: Prentice Hall, 1980.

    Contains excellent section on exit strategy.

2. Goldscheider, Robert. *Technology Management Handbook.* 1982 ed. New York: Clark Boardman Co., Ltd., 1982.

    There may be later editions. This will tell you all you need to know about technology rights, technology transfer patents, and licensing. Sample legal forms included.

3. Navin, W. J. *Patents.* New York: Practicing Law Institute, 1966.

    A very good text, written in lay language. An excellent background book for any engineer-entrepreneur.

4. Lieberstein, Stanley H. *Who Owns What in Your Head?* New York: Hawthorne Books, Inc., 1979.

    A good reference on the ownership and enforceability of trade secrets. Read this before you resign.

5. Neumeyer, Frederick and Stedman, John C. *The Employed Inventor in the United States: R&D Policies, Law and Practice.* Cambridge, Mass.: The MIT Press, 1971.

    Readable, competent, complete. This will tell you more than you want to know about your obligations to your employer.

II
FINANCING AND FINANCES

8

Initial Financing

*Money is the seed of money, and the first guinea is
sometimes more difficult to acquire than the second
million.   . . Jean Jacques Rousseau*

Distinct schools of thought exist regarding initial financing. The first maintains that the more money you can get into the venture at the beginning, the better. The arguments for this point of view are not without merit, and go as follows:[1]

1. Additional money permits you to survive unexpected setbacks, delays, and false starts in getting your product on the market.

[1]H. A. Cohen, *Spin-off Organizations: A Study of Enterprises Spun-off from the MIT Community*, (S.M. Thesis, Sloan School of Management, MIT, Cambridge, Mass., January, 1970). Cohen presents evidence that in a large sample of MIT spinoff firms, those with larger amounts of capital were statistically more successful. However, he also shows that those with large founder teams were also the most likely to raise substantial initial capital (i.e., the principal founder's equity was already spread thin at the start). It would be interesting to know how the *founders* in the sample fared financially in the companies with substantial versus less initial capital. It is also possible, of course, that some of the less successful companies sampled did not have *enough* capital for the venture—an extreme also to be avoided.

2. It allows you additional flexibility in taking advantage of new opportunities, should they arise.
3. Visible working capital eases the problem of obtaining credit from suppliers, banks, and so forth.
4. It makes the entrepreneur feel secure early in the game to see that his or her net worth on paper is substantial.

The second school of thought maintains that in the case of early financing, less is more. That is,

---

you should raise only the amount of money absolutely essential for the operation of the company at each stage of growth.

The following arguments support this point of view:

1. Limited capitalization prevents major losses and the loss of long-term credibility with the financial community, even though it increases the risk of failure should a significant setback occur.
2. Close funding keeps attention and energies focused on the principal objectives and timetables of the company, rather than dissipating them by looking for better opportunities, further product refinements before introduction, etc.
3. Tight funding allows the first-time entrepreneur to gain some experience in cash management, operating on negative working capital, living off vendors, putting pressure on slow paying customers—experience that will stand the entrepreneur in good stead in the future. Whether the company is very successful or very unsuccessful, it will be short of cash. Only mediocre or non-growing companies have no cash shortages.
4. Finally, and most important: If you sell more stock than you need to sell, you are selling it too cheaply. You should consider the amount of money you will be able to make by selling the stock at future, higher prices. Be sure that you need every dollar you raise. "Reserve for Contingency" is a prudent-sounding budget item for your business plan, but don't lose sight of what it may actually cost you personally in the long run.

Selling stock in a brand new company is a little like cutting down a newly-planted forest for lumber. It's worth far more left growing than it would be if it were used for wood now.

A secondary but important aspect of the issue is this: the type of person from whom one is able to raise initial capital may not be the kind of person you want to have heavy voting power, when and if the company gets off the ground. However, by the time financial institutions are ready to put major funding into your venture, it will cost too much to buy a such a person out. Backers do not like to put money into a venture simply to buy out other stockholders. They want their money to go into the company treasury for product completion, market development, and working capital.

WHAT IS THE WORTH OF VALUELESS STOCK?

This is neither a riddle nor a Zen conundrum. Practically speaking, the questions confronting the entrepreneur when raising initial capital are: (a) How much money do we need to get by? and (b) How much control do I want to part with in order to get that money?

These questions are related only remotely to asset values, net worth tests, or capitalized earnings streams. They are not at all sophisticated. Simply stated, you have no tangible assets, no net worth, no earnings. All you can present is your *pro forma* earnings projection, and investors do not credit such projections unduly. How, then, can you calculate and defend a price for your company's stock?

The answer is, of course, that you can't. Pricing a new company's stock is much like pricing any other glamour item (such as perfume, paintings, rare coins) where appeal is based on emotional, as well as analytical considerations. You must try to figure out what the market will pay, independent of analyzable worth. Your considerations include

1. For what price has stock in similar ventures sold recently?
2. To what kinds of people do I hope to sell? What and how strong are their tax and other nonemotional incentives?
3. How glamorous will the offer appear? Is it presented in such a way as to take full advantage of a hot market, new technology, and proprietary product?
4. If things go as planned, what will the payoff be to initial investors? They will be looking for something between ten-fold and fifty-fold appreciation, over three to five years. Knowing this, you can bracket the amount of ownership they will want for their money.

This issue is not worth too many sleepless nights. Your "price" will turn out to be merely the opening shot in what is ultimately a negotiation. After you have tried actually to *sell* your stock, you will have a good idea of the extent to which it is overpriced. On the other hand, should you get your money without earnest negotiation, you will never know to what extent it was *underpriced!*

VENTURE CAPITAL: WHAT IT IS AND ISN'T

In Chapter 6 we drew the distinction between venture and *ad*venture (or seed) capital. Venture capital, despite its connotation, is most generally not available to the startup company. It is, rather, a term that is normally reserved for the first major outside financing. It is normally available only when (a) the company is off the ground, (b) the team is functioning, (c) the product is on the market with demonstrated acceptance, and, (d) the company has demonstrated its potential for orderly growth and responsible management of other people's money.

If you make the rounds with the Venture Capital Directory in one hand and your business plan in the other, you are wasting credibility, calendar time, and entrepreneurial energy. You should, instead, be talking to a few, carefully selected, affluent individuals (see Chapter 6). The principal share of your energy, however, should at this stage be put into the details of actually getting operations off the ground, many of which do not require much or any money.

WHY NOT GET A LOAN?

In order to finance a new venture while keeping all the stock possible, a loan would seem to be the most logical route. The major problem is that you probably won't be able to get one—at least from a bank. Banks require assets that can be used as collateral, together with the visible means of paying off the loan at a reasonable point in the future. They also want clear evidence that you will be able to produce the cash flow required to meet interest payments. Since few seed-stage ventures meet any, let alone all, of these conditions, the bank loan as a means of starting up a business will almost certainly not work.

However, this does not mean that you should not talk to bankers. Your principal criterion for choosing a bank should be their relative willingness to lend you money at some early point in the growth of your company. Some banks, for example, are willing to lend money to companies whose balance sheets are weak, on the basis of pledged accounts receivable. So, if you have made a big shipment, by all means talk with the banker about a loan.

Banks *have* been known to waive orthodox lending standards and lend substantial amounts of money to beginning ventures on the basis of contracts (not accounts receivable) in hand or even on the founder's signature alone. Other banks have Small Business Investment Companies (SBICs), through which they try to work with new ventures. It is to your advantage to associate yourself with a good bank as soon as possible. The sooner you do it, the sooner you will be able to find out how much credit is actually available to you.

Of course, there are other sources of loans, besides lending institutions. Perhaps you will be able to borrow seed money from a relative or friend who does not want to become a stockholder in your company. In this case you, not the company, are borrowing the money and are fully responsible for its repayment. (However, a bank also will want your personal signature on any early loans it makes to your company.) In any case, you may prefer to have a relative as a creditor rather than as a vocal stockholder.

Other sources of seed money loans may include regional development agencies, mortgage brokers (using your house equity as security), credit unions, the Small Business Administration, suppliers, and, in some cases, customers. Do not overlook the possibility of negotiation for advance payment, progress payments, or other advances from your customers. Depending on the industry, this may be the orthodox way of doing business, and they will expect such requests. Capital cost is, of course, included in the negotiated price of the products or services you are supplying, despite the fact that interest is seldom charged on such prepayments.

Your particular situation may permit you to function either partially or entirely on borrowed funds from the beginning, even though it is usually necessary to sell at least some equity in order to raise seed capital. Naturally, the feasibility and desirability of following such a course should be carefully analyzed.

OPERATING WITHOUT CAPITAL

As suggested above, there are many substitutes for permanent equity capital available to the beginning venture. All of these possibilities should be exercised, not only because of the effects of early dilution discussed earlier, but also because there will, sooner or later, come a cash crunch when you'll need to use them anyway. Every tightly-run company reaches this point.

Earlier in this chapter, we listed some sources of cash loans. Other sources of borrowed value exist, however, to an extent that is not readily appreciated by the new entrepreneur. These sources include

1. *Your vendors.* A new venture's suppliers can be among its most valuable friends. If such a relationship is not excessively abused, one's suppliers can be among the most important sources of short-term capital. Most firms will offer thirty days credit to even a new company, with a penalty for running over thirty days. Other companies charge the penalty indirectly, by denying an early-payment discount to thirty-day accounts. Even if such an arrangement costs you money, at least the credit and the materials are available to you. You will discover, practically speaking, that you can *occasionally* run considerably over the thirty-day limit as long as you reach a current status again, as quickly as possible.

2. *Your capital equipment suppliers.* In their desire to sell equipment, suppliers will often make very favorable terms available even to new companies. This is possible because the equipment itself secures the loan. The contract may be a lease, held by the seller or a leasing company, or a conditional sales agreement (usually cheaper) whereby the seller retains a lien or title until the last installment payment is made and received. Generally, capital equipment and plant facilities are easier to finance than ordinary working capital requirements.

3. *Your employees.* Nobody has a greater stake in the health of your firm than your own employees. For the more mature firm the Employees Stock Ownership Plan (ESOP) may provide an investment vehicle for the employees. For the smaller firm struggling for survival, however, the employees may be an obvious source of aid. The financing can come in the form of loans (interest-bearing debentures), stock purchases, or even deferred compensation, backed by interest-bearing notes. Your employees may be your best possible investors since you can pay them substantially higher interest than they could get elsewhere and, in the case of stock purchase, they acquire a whole new stake in the success of the firm.

4. *Export banks.* If your company either imports or exports significant amounts of a product, you should know of the existence of export banks. Every industrial company has some such organization designed to promote the export of its products. Such export banks, including the US Export-Import Bank, are empowered to offer attractive credit terms to domestic manufacturers and foreign buyers of their goods. This function is also performed to a degree by the large trading companies of Japan and the East Bloc nations. They all represent a source of capital over and above that available from normal financial institutions.

5. *Leasing companies.* Such companies can, as noted previously, make it possible for you to buy capital equipment. This arrangement can, however, work the other way around if you make capital equipment. In such a case, your capital equipment suppliers can make it possible for your customer to buy the equipment, on a prepaid basis, before it is even built, especially if it is custom-designed, one-of-a-kind equipment.

6. *Receivables factors.* Certain institutions, instead of lending money against accounts receivable, buy the receivables outright, at a discount. Thus you are relieved of the delay and cost of collection efforts. However, factors are usually geared to specialized customers and typically serve firms that have a seasonal or cyclic business pattern. Unless your venture falls into this category, you may find it either difficult or excessively expensive to work through factors.

7. *Deferral of payables in general.* When money is tight, most companies (including very large ones) lag behind in their payment of bills. There will be times when you must avail yourself of this source of short-term financing. Also, don't overlook the fact that certain of your employees (especially professional employees) might be willing to defer portions of their salary, to take notes, either as a gesture of solidarity, or as a practical measure to avoid being laid off.

One person from whom you should *not* borrow short-term capital is Uncle Sam. Make your withholding payments on time, or you are in for a lot of trouble.

In addition to these possible funding sources, there are ways in which you can save valuable cash while getting your no-capital venture off the ground. These include

1. Sharing office and shop space (and thus overhead) with another company.

2. Doing any carpentry and painting that needs to be done yourself, in order to create offices, a lobby, etc., in low-rent space. (If Digital Equipment Corp. could do it, why can't you?)

3. Using other firms' capital equipment during off hours. This could include their machine shop, printing equipment, test equipment, data processing machines, or anything else that has low incremental cost of operation.

4. Purchase used office and plant equipment wherever possible. Preferably, buy it at auctions or bankruptcy sales. Such a practice can save you 50–90 percent of new equipment costs.

5. Use part-time specialists. Engineers, technical writers, layout artists, technical typists, etc., can all be hired on a part-time, moonlighting

basis often at a much lower cost per hour than their own employer pays, since that company covers their benefits. In some cases, you may be able to avoid withholding taxes—for example, if the person qualifies as a "consultant." Check with your accountant on this point.

6. Begin your sales effort by using reps or agents, rather than hiring a full-time sales force. Although most new companies haven't much of a choice, try to evaluate the use of reps thoroughly before hiring direct salesmen.

7. Have your product manufactured wholly outside your company. This can avoid many headaches and is, in many cases, cheaper, due to the economies of scale inherent in most manufacturing efforts. In some areas, competition among vendors is so great that you might be able to arrange to have your vendor stock your finished goods at no carrying charge. This is, of course, a reversible decision. You can, when you wish, bring prime manufacturing efforts back in-house, while subcontracting any overflow to your (by this time well-debugged) vendor.

8. Make use of free public relations instead of paid advertising. Send out a news release to your trade press at least once a month. Write stories for the trade press, arrange to be interviewed about your product, company, and prospects. Hold a press conference in a decent hotel suite to launch your new product. Avoid ad agencies, and the big advertising budget that goes with them, like the plague.

9. Arrange to buy materials at cost from a larger user who commands a large amount of purchasing power. You will both benefit, since it is possible that your volume will add to this user's clout with vendors.

10. Push your customers hard for prompt payment. Convince them that it is better to pay you on time and let their other creditors wait. Frequent contact with the accounts payable department at your customer's office will, eventually, have its effect. Unfortunately, most entrepreneurs regard the collection of bills as at least uninteresting, if not degrading. They would much rather spend their time and energies in getting a new order or in filling one that already exists, rather than in collecting money for one that is already completed. But unless you get paid on time, all of your other efforts will be in vain. If you can't stand this work, get someone who can. However, make sure that you, personally, keep a sharp eye on the receivables problems.

11. Above all, stay cool. Don't panic, even if ten suppliers have called in the last hour, demanding payment. If you find that it will take ninety days instead of thirty to pay them even after all your planning, go talk to the head of the supplier firm. Work out a schedule of partial payments and

then stick to it. Nothing else you can do will go further in bolstering this person's confidence in you. When all of this gets *too* depressing, go make some sales calls.

THE MAGIC OF INITIAL SALES

On the day that you make your first sale, your baby becomes a business. Up until that point, everything is preparation and hope. Once the first sale is made, you know that you can not only get your product to market, but that there is someone out there who will pay money for it. Symbolically, the importance of the first few initial orders cannot be overstated. It may be the ounce of proof for which outside backers are looking, the signal to backers that a modest loan may be in order, the indication to suppliers that they will probably get paid—sooner or later—and that they might even be justified in increasing your credit limits. It also does fantastic things for your morale and that of your team. You are finally *shipping products!* Put your concentrated efforts into reaching this goal as early as possible, with little or no outside financing. Such an achievement will go far toward ensuring a healthy start and a successful first financing.

CONVENTIONAL WISDOM: The failure of most new companies can be attributed to inadequate initial financing.

REALITY: Many of those companies that fail are adequately, if not overly, financed. Most of these failures can be traced to inept management, of which "inadequate financing" is one symptom.

REFERENCES

1. Freear, John and Wetzel, William E. *Equity Financing for New Technology-based Firms.* Durham, NH: Center for Venture Research, Univ. of New Hampshire, 1988.
       Documents results of a study of the critical role of informal private investors in the entrepreneurial process.
2. Summers, George W. *Financing and Initial Operations of New Firms.* Englewood Cliffs, N.J.: Prentice-Hall, Inc., 1962.
       A good practical guide to getting off the ground, financially and otherwise.
3. Wayne, William. *How to Succeed in Business When the Chips are Down.* New York: McGraw-Hill, 1972.
       This gritty little book is full of suggestions on operating without cash, infighting with the bank, chopping costs, and so forth.

9

Equity Sources: A Range of Motivations

**For the engine that drives enterprise is not Thrift but
Profit. . . John Maynard Keynes**

Your seed money is beginning to sprout. Most of the early problems with your product have been ironed out, and the team has survived the initial stresses inherent in any startup venture. The first few sales have been made. People are beginning to hear about your company and your product, and to get excited about them. The time has come for you to find and use the first serious chunk of outside capital. Where do you go from here?

Unless your company is very unusual, this is the stage at which some equity financing is required. There are several different reasons for this. First, it is extremely difficult to borrow for such purposes as market development, research, and product development. These are investments, but they do not normally appear as assets on your balance sheet. Second, borrowing would place undesirable strain on your cash flow during this critical growth stage, due to interest payments. Third, a layer of long-term equity money will give your company the financial strength required to borrow strategically. And fourth, you don't want to be faced with the necessity of paying back loans just as the company begins to move. This is especially true if you later encounter a tight money market, or if more funds are unavailable for refinancing. Such leverage multiplies the risk of failure.

Your basic need at this point is for *permanent equity capital,* even though the financing may include a component of debt—possibly convertible into stock.

Equity capital sources you can explore probably fall into one of these categories:

1. Private individuals or groups of individuals.
2. Private venture capital partnerships and other venture capital firms.
3. Quasi-public venture capital organizations (for example, Massachusetts Technology Development Corp.).
4. Fiduciary manager (for example, university endowments, foundations, pension funds).
5. Industrial corporations.

All of these are or have been significant sources of venture capital for young companies. All are similar, superficially, in that they invest reasonable amounts of equity monies in risky enterprises, hoping for substantial capital gains. However, each one has its distinct reason for being in the business. Consequently, each has distinct attitudes and policies of operation. It is important that you, as an entrepreneur, have some appreciation of these differences in order to ensure that the capital search is as efficient as possible, and to maximize the chances that the new partnership will work out as hoped.

PRIVATE INDIVIDUALS OR GROUPS OF INDIVIDUALS

The private individual will sometimes be the same one who invests seed money in a startup venture. This individual is likely to be either a self-made, entrepreneurial business person or a member of a high-income profession, such as medicine, law, real estate development, or investment banking. In any case, this individual is likely to act independently, having strong confidence in his or her instincts and ability to size people up. Sometimes, the investor will "syndicate" a larger deal. Even then, however, friends may play a secondary role, depending largely upon this person's judgment.

Aside from large capital gains, this individual has other motives for venture investment that differentiate him or her from institutional sources of capital. First, this investor's principal business probably gives him or her a large taxable income. Therefore a Subchapter S or section 1244 feature may be a significant inducement for the private investor, although seldom, if ever, a deciding one.

More important is the fact that this individual may simply enjoy associations with entrepreneurs and with the business growth process. He or she may see great social usefulness in the product being developed or may feel that the economy of the region will benefit from the new company. This investor may feel some obligation to give something back to the system that allowed him or her to prosper. The private investor has both the funds and the autonomy to pursue personal inclinations, for whatever nonfinancial reasons, and has always been, and undoubtedly always will be, a major source of venture capital, especially at the earliest seed and startup stages.

Such an investor's operating policies often include a willingness to become involved at an early stage of the growth process. Occasionally, the investor will desire to become involved more or less actively in the management of the venture as consultant, director, or godparent.

Usually the private investor will be more willing to accept high risk than will institutions. Often this person also has a lower economic investment size. Both of these facts make him or her a good partner for the beginning entrepreneur. This person is sometimes willing to invest further in the company. Such investment, however, is likely to take the form of nonequity commitments (for example, cosignature on bank loans). His or her preferred waiting period may be somewhat less than that of institutions—perhaps two to four years.

A major benefit to the starting entrepreneur is that the private investor has a very short decision cycle—sometimes measured in days rather than the several weeks or months that it can take a venture capital firm. This individual's requirement for documentation and backup may also be much lower, and he or she will rely on instincts and character judgment much more than on research (called "due-diligence" research by venture capitalists). He will often require a far less formalistic set of investment documents as well, which will keep the legal costs down.

A caveat in dealing with the private investor: you must understand that although he or she is excited about investing in your deal now, it is likely that this investor will not be there for the subsequent financing rounds. This person may have lost patience with the company's rate of development; realized too late that he or she isn't going to get any dividends; hoped for a larger advisory role than what materialized; realized that the fun-to-work ratio is a lot lower than he or she thought; may prefer only to invest in seed-round deals; or may just be out of mad money by then. For whatever reason, you cannot assume that your private investor(s) will be there when you need more money.

It is therefore doubly important to the company's future that you bring competent counsel to the process of structuring this initial investment, even though the costs may seem high to you and your investor. Unless the deal is structured appropriately at this stage, you may be creating a poison pill that will make later investment by others difficult, undesirable, or impossible. Be *sure* the lawyer selected is familiar with the structuring of venture investments, and do not accept the investor's old, reliable personal lawyer. Counsel should represent the *company*. If the investor wants the work reviewed by his or her own lawyer too, that's fine.

Some common errors in structuring private investments include the following:

1. Widespread solicitation. You may inadvertently be violating your state's security laws.
2. Misleading representations. You may be setting yourself up for a shareholder suit if the investor thought the deal was a sure thing, and can show that you misrepresented the risks.
3. Taking debt without enough equity. The company may be under heavy pressure to repay just at the time when it can least afford it.
4. Useless directors. Your brother-in-law or your orthodontist is not likely to be too helpful to your new venture. Press for strong outside directors instead.
5. *De facto* veto power. Giving small early investors a strong say in important matters (as in merger or later finance rounds) can be deadly. Press for non-voting or even redeemable stock instead.
6. Strange deals. Your investor may believe himself to be a financial genius and propose oddball financing that may hobble the future of the company. Examples: royalties on sales, shared-earnings schemes, asset based borrowings (using for example, receivables or patents as collateral), debt service disguised as "consulting services." Avoid any consulting contracts, sole-source supply contracts, or other contracts that may poison future financing efforts. Also avoid anything that smells like a scheme to fool the IRS.

It is not difficult to find prospective investors within the category of the private individual. Your lawyer, banker, and other entrepreneurs are good sources of names, and you will probably be able to turn up a number of prospects through them since your strongest prospect is the person who has already invested in similar ventures. As mentioned in Chapter 6, there also exist agencies that may be helpful in locating private investors (or "angels," as they are sometimes known).

Investment bankers, especially in smaller regional firms, often play a role at this stage, even though your company is not ready to go public. If they think your proposal is feasible, investment bankers may syndicate a private placement of your stock to a small group of sophisticated investors. They get a substantial fee for this work although they do not underwrite the offer, and proceed only on a best-efforts basis. This can be an extremely good way of raising private equity, as well as guaranteeing that there will be an interested underwriter when the time comes to go public.

VENTURE CAPITAL FIRMS

Closed-end investment funds existed even before the term venture capital was invented. Firms such as Venrock (Rockefeller Brothers) and Payson Trask were investing family wealth and operating in the 1930s and 1940s. American Research and Development essentially invented venture capital as we know it, under George Doriot in the 1940s, investing in Boston high-tech companies. Many of the senior venture capitalists today are alumni of these venerable institutions.

From that time until about 1980, the venture capital business was a sort of club, with a few dozen firms and officers who all knew one another well. Today the club has become a large industry; since the revision of the rules governing pension funds during the Carter administration, the industry has gone from about $4 billion under management to over $30 billion, as of time of writing. The recent influx of capital has been about $4 billion per year. There are about five hundred firms with about two thousand professionals—hardly a club any longer.

The motivations of firms in the venture capital industry range from pure return-on-investment (ROI) to nearly pure strategic plays (for example, seeking to advance technologies, employment, economic development). Many funds are a mix of both, determined mainly by the source of their money. Venture capital firms who get most of their money from financial institutions (such as pension funds, insurance companies, and endowment funds) can be relied upon to behave in a very single-minded, ROI-maximizing mode. They will be highly unromantic about the technology, the benefits to mankind, and so forth. On the other hand, firms who get their money from corporations are likely to be seeking investments of particular relevance to their funding source. This may include technologies of interest, specific product areas, or particular markets of strategic importance. Firms that get their money in part from state or regional development agencies, or even from state pension funds, may have a charter to promote employment and economic development, while achieving a more modest ROI. It is for these reasons that you should understand the sources of money well; it may have a lot to do with how tough the investor is on valuation and other terms of the negotiation.

You will quickly discover some other facts about the industry. Many firms tend to focus on one or two technologies, or markets, simply because they have tended to acquire familiarity with them, or because they have had some past successes. Some firms even exist solely to invest in specific types of deals (for example, computer software, consumer products, materials science). Firms are specialized also in terms of stage of investment (such as seed only or leveraged buy-out only, or mezzanine-financing only). Some firms specialize by region, while others don't care where the venture is located. These are all facts that will affect your choice of targets.

The backgrounds of the managers (or general partners) may also affect your chances of getting money. If the partners have technical backgrounds, it may be easier to get them to listen to a highly technical story than others. If they come from investment or commercial banking backgrounds, technology may bore them, and they will focus on marketing, business strategy, and financial alternatives more heavily.

You will also discover that some firms like to be the lead investor, negotiating the terms, rearranging the organization chart, structuring the deal, then bringing in follower investors. Often a VC will tell an entrepreneur, "Your story is interesting but we don't lead. Go find some other investors, then come see us." The VC is not making a commitment, but is merely indicating a precondition to any further consideration.

Another set of motivations may affect your choice of targets. The risk-reward profiles of deals vary radically, of course. One deal might be an "easy double"—that is, the ultimate opportunity may not be huge, but the probability of achieving it is high. An example might be a new "niche" software product, with a total market of $20 million. Another deal may be the "home-run" variety—such as a cure for AIDS, which will take three years and $10 million in R&D even before you can tell if it will work. But if it does work, the potential market may be billions. If yours is a home-run type of proposal, you are likely to find your best audience among the longest established, most successful venture capitalists, who have the self-confidence and the support of their investors essential to the taking of such risks. An easy-double deal is likely to interest them less than it would a younger, perhaps first-fund investor, who will likely stick to lower-risk, smaller-size deals for a number of years.

Finally, one finds increasing numbers of foreign corporations and institutions setting up shop in the US for both ROI and strategic reasons. Sometimes they are "follower funds," just seeking to learn the venture capital business by observing the activities of their co-investors. At other times, however, they can be quite aggressive in initiating projects in markets and technologies of special interest. It is not unusual for the foreign VC to be seeking two-way relationships between the venture and companies in this person's home country. Such an agenda may be a burden to you, but it could also be an opportunity to access distribution, low-cost manufacture, complementary technology, or other resources that would otherwise cost you money, time, and precious equity.

The reception you get from a venture capital fund may also be influenced by a number of variables somewhat external to policy issues. Among these are

1. Liquidity. Did the firm recently raise new funds? Are they doing a lot of deals, or will you just be educating them?

2. The stock market. If there is currently a good market for initial public offerings, the fund may be interested in initiating some new investments. If the IPO market is dead (as it often is), the VC may be reserving capital for future rounds to support his or her present companies, and not be eager to start new deals.

3. The size of the fund and the dollars under management per professional. Recently, many VC firms have raised such large amounts of money that they have neither the staff nor the inclination to do the smaller, early-stage deal. If they do such deals at all, it will be as a follower in a syndicate led by others. If the firm is over $100 million, your chances of getting a hearing are relatively poor.

ADLER'S LAWS

Venture capitalist Fred Adler has condensed his experience into a few epigrams that give some insight into how a VC thinks.

1. The probability of a company's succeeding is inversely proportional to the amount of publicity it receives before it manufactures its first product.

2. An investor's ability to talk about his or her winners is an order of magnitude greater than the ability to remember the losers.

3. If you don't think you have a problem, you have a big problem.

4. Happiness is positive cash flow. Everything else will come later.

5. The probability of success of a small company is inversely proportional to the size of the president's office.

6. Would-be entrepreneurs who pick up the check after luncheon discussions are usually losers.

7. The longer the investment proposal, the shorter the odds of success.

8. There is no such thing as an over-financed company.

9. Managers who worry a lot about voting control usually have nothing worth controlling.

10. There's no limit on what one can do or where one can go if he or she doesn't mind who gets the credit.

So, there is a lot to learn before your start ringing VC doorbells. Where to start? Standard references such as *Pratt's Guide to Venture Capital,* and Silver's *Who's Who in Venture Capital* (available in bookstores and libraries; see References at end of chapter) are both good. Also, a phone call to any venture capital firm will get you a copy of a brochure that will tell you a lot about the firm, its people, its policies, and its current portfolio.

SMALL BUSINESS INVESTMENT COMPANIES (SBICs)

Larger, publicly-held SBICs would include such names as Naragansett Capital Corporation and Greater Washington Investors. However, there are several hundred smaller SBICs, often operating as subsidiaries of banks. Enabled by the Small Business Investment Act of 1958, these companies function, with loans from the US government, on a leveraged capital basis. They most often invest in the form of mixed equity and convertible debt/debt-with-warrants, or on the basis of debt exclusively. Their use of debt is based on several factors—most importantly, on their need for current income to service their government loans as well as their administrative costs. Their stock price is a strong function of current income and only a weak function of asset value, as in other public companies. Although there are about 325 SBICs in operation, it has been asserted that only about two dozen of them are active in the venture capital business; these two dozen are, for the most part, publicly-held. The rest are simply in the business of making orthodox small business loans as subsidiaries of banks.

One nice advantage that the publicly-held SBICs offer to the entrepreneur is that their portfolios and investment records are public information.

One can easily gain access to facts regarding specific case histories of companies in which the firms have invested, thereby simplifying analysis. The ventures in which they have done well and/or poorly are readily visible, and you can contact the entrepreneurs with whom the firm has invested in either category, and find out how they regard the firm.

These firms differ greatly in their desired amount of management involvement with the portfolio company. Some require management consulting revenues to meet current expenses, so it is advisable to ask (in advance) about their policies toward such involvement.

On the average, according to Russel B. Faucett[1], these firms remain invested on an average of 2.7 years. In Faucett's study of thirteen publicly-held SBICs, he discovered that while most of his sample firms did not, as a rule, invest heavily in the earliest stages of company growth, the early investments were statistically more profitable than were the later ones. This finding may foretell a shift in attitude toward early investment or even investment at startup stages, on the part of some SBICs. Faucett also discovered that the firms in which the investments had been primarily of an equity nature fared better than those in which they were mostly debt. One may assume that the case outflow for debt service may have adversely affected performance of the company in at least some cases.

FIDUCIARY FUNDS MANAGERS

This category (although the nomenclature is not completely correct) would include insurance company managers, university endowment funds, pension funds, and other funds held in trust for other people. Venture investment never represents more than a minute sideline for the managers of such funds. The possibility of substantial capital gains compared to other, more orthodox investments, has, however, attracted many such institutions into the direct venture capital investment business, as well as into investing in VC partnerships.

These investors' policies are far from uniform, and it is hard to generalize about them. Some of the larger insurance companies have been involved in venture capital investments for many years, and have developed a professional investment approach. Other institutions who have entered the field more recently may still be experimenting with policy variables such as the deal size, desired markets, time horizon, and level of risk.

[1]Russel B. Faucett, "The Management of Venture Capital Investment Companies," (thesis, Massachusetts Institute of Technology, 1971).

The portfolios and investment records of such institutions are not, for the most part, public knowledge. It is not easy, therefore, for the entrepreneur to have advance knowledge of exactly what he or she is dealing with. Nonetheless, fiduciary funds would appear to continue to be a significant source of risk capital, and the institutions themselves may take further steps to attract better deals for their consideration.

INDUSTRIAL CORPORATIONS

There is some evidence to suggest that industrial corporations are a significant and growing segment of the venture capital scene. Some industrial corporations flirted with the idea of venture capital in the early sixties, both as a source of new subsidiaries and as a "window" through which they could view new technologies not readily developed in their own laboratories. A number of companies later withdrew from venture capitalism, somewhat the poorer for their experience; others withdrew without having made a single investment. Still others, have stayed in the market, presumably with good reason, and others are entering and leaving all the time.

The entrepreneur must realize that the industrial corporations have different objectives from those of other venture capital sources. Their main interest is in building and strengthening their basic business to the maximum degree possible, and venture investing is but one instrument of their corporate development activity. Return on investment is much less important to them, as a rule, than the idea of finding entrepreneurial, highly-motivated people to work on problems of interest to the corporation. If such an investment can lead to a new division for the corporation, so much the better.

Corporations are motivated by other factors, too. Some may be seeking complementary products to push through existing sales channels. Some may be seeking access to new markets, on a low-risk, low-profile basis. Some may be seeking "strategic partnerships" (a buzz-word of the 1980s) to exploit specific products or markets on an accelerated basis. Certain other corporations seem to invest in the hope that the technological glamour of the new enterprise will provide a newsworthy kicker for their own price-earnings ratio. One suspects that the results of this tactic have, at best, been temporary.

For certain types of new ventures, industrial firms may be the best financial partners to be found. Often they can offer management assistance, ready-made marketing or distribution channels, manufacturing services, and, in some cases, a large, built-in demand for your product. Often they understand the business problems you encounter much more fully than would a straight financial investor. Hence they may be more disposed toward patience and calm. Also, they may present a ready market for any or all of the founders' stock, when it's time for the entrepreneurs to cash out.

On the negative side, however, you must keep in mind several factors concerning industrial corporations, which may be more or less important, depending upon your particular case.

1. Industrial corporations are usually not anxious to see the new venture go public. They are more disposed toward the acquisition of new divisions and/or subsidiaries.
2. For this reason, you may find yourself tied in, either with a buy-out formula based upon performance or, at the very least, a right of first refusal to buy any founders' stock. In the first case you may actually end up donating your stock to the corporation, if the performance test is not met.
3. Your affiliation with one major corporation may, in effect, stop you from selling your product to its competitors. This could cut off a major portion of your potential market.
4. If your deal is poorly structured, your business may be required to adopt certain operating policies, banks, accounting conventions, etc., recommended by the investing corporation. You may also be required to share research results in order to use the corporation's facilities (whether or not they are the lowest cost) or to meet other requirements that further reduce your autonomy. Such requirements may run counter to the reasons why you began a company of your own in the first place.
5. It is harder to fool an industrial corporation than it is to fool other financing sources.

Balance the pros against the cons. If the pros win, find the biggest and best firm that might have an interest in your field and approach it.

Table 9-1 provides a quick summary of the principal distinctions among the various categories of venture capitalists. Naturally, large variations exist *within* each category as well, and the table is merely indicative of tendency, in the author's view. Individual sources within the category may be radically different on one or more characteristics from the central tendency of the group.

In summary, you will never be able to find out all you need to know in advance about a particular funding source you may be approaching. But the more you know, the better your negotiating position (in that you will know what concessions are of most value to them), and the better the chances that,

TABLE 9-1 Equity Sources Motivation and Other Characteristics

Motivation	Private Individual or Syndicate	Private VC Partnership	SBIC	Fiduciary Funds Managers	Industrial Corporations
Non-financial: excitement of new venture, regional development, socially desirable product, etc.	H	H	L	L	H
Tax shelter for ordinary income	M	M	L	L	L
Long term capital gains	H	H	H	H	M
Current income from dividends, interest, management fees	L	L	H	L	L
Desire for future subsidiary, technology, new markets	L	L	L	L	H
Other Characteristics					
Desired waiting periods, yrs.	1–3	3–10	1–5	2–7	2–5
Willingness to invest further	H	H	M	M	H
Minimum economic investment	$10,000	$200,000	$100,000	$1,000,000	$100,000
Risk acceptance	H	H	M	M	H
Management involvement	L to H	L	M	L	H
Early investment preference	H	M	L	L	H

Code
H = High Degree
M = Moderate Degree
L = Low Degree

once made, the deal will be comfortable for all concerned over the next several years.

THE ONLY GAME IN TOWN?

Many first-time entrepreneurs focus more or less exclusively on the standard individual and institutional equity-capital sources, while overlooking other, less expensive ways of getting the company off the ground. This focus on the conventional channels is understandable, due to the high visibility of the venture capital firms. However, in a rush to get into their game, the entrepreneur may be overlooking some very good alternatives. A very partial list might include the following:

1. *Internally generated funds.* The possibility exists that the company can generate enough cash and credit to supply its own needs. This is not the usual case, but is common enough to justify some serious analysis of your venture before heading down the venture capital trail. A combination of high margins, fast collections, and intensive use of short-term capital and operating tactics *could* get you to the point where you're ready to go public, with *all* the stock in your possession.

2. *State and regional development agencies.* There are numerous agencies, charged with the responsibility of increasing job opportunities in particular areas. In some areas you can obtain long-term, low-cost loans for plant and equipment—forgivable in some instances. Outright grants of money for each job created in such a way are not unusual. Attractive working capital loans can often be arranged through banks with the guarantee of the public agency. Grants for the training of new employees abound. Other schemes and inducements to entrepreneurs are offered by regional development agencies. If your venture has the potential of employing reasonable numbers of people, be sure to investigate these opportunities in all areas where you would consider locating.

3. *Technology development agencies.* The U.S. and Canada both have a variety of programs aimed at development of commercially-significant technology, to bolster the economy, create jobs, taxes, and export opportunities. In Canada, government programs offer outright grants for the development of new commercial products, processes, and technologies. In the U.S., the emphasis is on technology transfer—getting technology originally developed at government cost into commercial markets. Pilot

programs have been funded in both the National Science Foundation and the Bureau of Standards for this and related purposes. Also, several countries, including Ireland, Taiwan, and Israel, have technology development programs to develop partnerships with U.S. firms.

While such funds are normally not available to startup ventures, once your enterprise is off the ground with proven capability in an appropriate area of product development, you may well qualify for such a grant.

The National Science Foundation's Small Business Innovation Research (SBIR) program was started in 1979 to fund quality research proposals. Their main criterion is that the research, if successful, have "significant public benefit." Secondly, they hope to convert publicly-funded R&D to privately funded commercialization. This program provides up to $25,000 for feasibility research, up to $200,000 to conduct the research, and an open-ended phase-three funding by the private company sponsoring the work.

A large fraction of proposals have been funded with firms of ten or fewer employees. Thus, the chances of the entrepreneur to obtain R&D seed capital from this source may be relatively good.

4. *R&D contracts.* The emphasis on the "Venture Capital Scenario"—garage-to-VC-to-Wall Street—tends to obscure the fact that a large fraction of today's high technology companies got started on the basis of a fat government research or development contract. Usually such contracts originate in the same agency that funded the company founder's work of the time of his or her previous job. The benefits of building a technology company on this basis are

a. You are working at the frontier of the art.

b. You immediately have a cash flow that will permit building up the professional staff and overheads necessary to attract private work or to develop products.

c. Your work will be recognized and you will have a chance to establish your firm as a leader in its field.

d. You may obtain access to expensive government-owned equipment and facilities that would otherwise be inaccessible.

The drawbacks include, of course, all those inherent in any single-customer firm:

a. Slow collections (sometimes).

b. Dependence on contract funding, vicissitudes of such factors as congressional spending.

c. Negotiated or capped profit margins.

   d. Detailed government financial reporting procedures and other red tape.

   e. Lack of pressure to develop a marketing capability.

These perils notwithstanding, government R&D contracts have launched many fine technology companies, providing the base from which commmercial research and product development have grown. It is probably true that this route was easier in the past when defense-oriented contracts were relatively easy to obtain. Nevertheless, there are still many opportunities and will be in the future. However, they are accessible mainly to the entrepreneur who has already been actively engaged in the field, working with his or her former research sponsors.

5. *Consulting.* Often an aggressive professional will decide to start a company on the basis of the ability of the founders to attract consulting contracts, with the ultimate objective of developing products as the company gathers financial momentum. This has worked well in many cases. Consulting provides the cash flow to pay the team, support facilities, and maintain technical prominence. However, this route is not without its perils. Often the necessity of getting a number of successive consulting contracts just to stay alive totally diverts the energy and resources of the firm away from product development, with the result that ten years later the venture is still a small consulting firm hoping to get around to developing some products some day. The product, the staff, and the marketing orientation simply do not seem to develop spontaneously from a consulting environment.

An alternative approach has been adopted by some other consultant entrepreneurs, with some success. This approach envisions the consulting group as the R&D department for a succession of new companies. The reasoning is, that by developing and spinning off a succession of new product-oriented companies, the consulting firm can maintain an equity position in each and still support a much better engineering capability than any of the individual spinoffs. Eventually, in theory, the consulting firm develops a portfolio of new venture stocks not unlike that of a venture capital firm.

The preceding list, then, suggests five ways you can get your company rolling without selling *any* of your stock. There are others. Be sure you investigate a few of the more promising ones before committing yourself to the venture capital scenario.

CONVENTIONAL WISDOM: Every new firm needs equity venture capital to get it through the early growth stages.

REALITY: All new companies need financing from somewhere, but not all have to sell stock in order to get it.

REFERENCES

1. Gladstone, David J. *Venture Capital Handbook—An Entrepreneur's Guide to Obtaining Capital to Start a Business, Buy a Business or Expand an Existing Business.* Englewood Cliffs, N.J.: Prentice Hall, 1983.

    Despite its ponderous title, this is a fun, fast-moving book by a well-known venture capitalist, giving a lot of dos, don'ts and general advice to the funds-seeker.

2. Bartlett, Joseph W. *Venture Capital Law, Business Strategies and Investment Planning.* New York: John Wiley & Sons, 1983.

    This is a sophisticated and thorough book by an outstanding VC lawyer. Though written for the VC, it will give you the story on every aspect of fund raising, including pricing and structuring the deal, and searching for capital and employee compensation.

3. Pratt, Stanley E. and Morris, Jane K. *Pratt's Guide to Venture Capital Sources.* Wellesley, Mass.: Venture Economics Inc., 1987.

    This book, updated annually, is the definitive directory to venture capital firms. However, it also has about 150 pages of outstanding essays on how the process actually works.

4. Silver, A. David. *Who's Who in Venture Capital.* 3rd ed. New York: John Wiley & Sons, 1987.

    Another VC directory, but with the added feature of biographical sketches of most of the VCs, which can be valuable in planning your attack. Also has good sections on marketing and innovation.

5. Burrill, G. Steven and Norback, Craig T. *The Arthur Young Guide to Raising Venture Capital.* Blue Ridge Summit, Penn.: Liberty House, 1988.

    Short, practical, and professional. Includes sample agreements and a brief VC directory.

10

Public or Private:
What's the Difference?

*There are plenty of public companies that should be
trying to go private.   . . V. J. Ryan, Venture Capitalist*

It is impossible to watch the equity markets over a few years without amazement at a phenomenon, the predictability of whose recurrence rivals Haley's Comet. That phenomenon is the *hot new issue market*—the recurrent wave of gullibility and greed that prompts the public to buy the shares of startup or even seed-stage companies. The hot new issue markets usually seem to accelerate in the latter phases of a sustained bull market. One was running in late 1961; it collapsed, along with everything else, in May, 1962. Another was roaring in 1968–69. It collapsed in May, 1970. The most recent hot market was running in the 1983–84 time period. All vestiges of it vanished in the collapse of October, 1987.

As of early 1989, a tiny new issue market has begun to show some evidence of visibility. While it may not rival its predecessor of 1983 in volume or furor, it clearly suggests that there is again an opportunity for at least certain types of young ventures to raise public money.

Without question, there are periods during which it is possible for a totally unseasoned company to go public, to obtain public money, a public market for its stock, and the other (presumed) benefits of public ownership. If that is so, why not sidestep the lengthy venture capital step which, after all, only leads to a public issue anyway? This is a reasonable question.

Hot new issue markets are usually characterized by at least some of the following phenomena:

1. New "underwriting" firms spring up as though by magic. Their disappearance from the market after the inevitable bust is equally magical.
2. Established investment banking houses also get caught up in the excitement and begin to relax their standards a bit to get some of the action.
3. A form of recruiting begins, with representatives of small and not-so-small underwriting firms sitting in the lobbies of small companies, singing the siren song of registered stock, yachts, and homes in the Bahamas.
4. "Deal packagers" roam the back streets of Silicon Valley and the parking lots of Route 128, looking for disgruntled engineers, unhappy division managers, and unappreciated marketing vice presidents, to be set up in business, for the purpose of selling some stock.

The siren song of the fast buck artist is everywhere. Nothing could be more dreary and discordant than the legitimate venture capitalist's carping about sales performance, budgets, meeting profit and cash projections, and all that.

From the venture capitalists you will get a list of reasons for not going public prematurely that goes something like this:

1. It costs too much for a tiny company to go public. Even with a Reg. A (short form) registration, the costs of legal, audit, and placement services can exceed 20 percent of the total issue proceeds.
2. It diverts too much of the young company's energies to establish and maintain the status of a public company. Stockholder relations, SEC relations, and stringent reporting and disclosure requirements all divert entrepreneurial energy from the company's main business.
3. An unseasoned company probably cannot attract a good, reputable investment banking house (whatever *that* may be). It will, instead, be taken public by Blitzkreig Securities, which, as everyone knows, won't even be around two years from now, let alone be able to raise additional capital for you. And, of course, Salomon Brothers isn't going to take over any of Blitzkreig's former deals, are they?

4. If your company doesn't perform as expected—loses too much money, fails to realize sales projections, is unable to debug the product, and so forth—then there is no big brother to turn to for a second, third, or *n*th round of venture capital. The show is over.

5. Everyone knows the record overall of unseasoned public offerings is pretty lousy.

Is this an impressive list of prudent arguments, or merely self-serving screed from the venture capital club? Nobody knows for sure, but one thing *is* sure: this elixir shouldn't be swallowed neat. It does deserve some critical scrutiny before you dismiss the possibility of taking your deal public in the next hot new issue market. Some of the counter-arguments could be posed as follows:

1. A public issue is "expensive," but compared to what? Even after all expenses, companies going public under these circumstances often raise more net cash for less equity than they could ever get from venture capital firms. And don't forget that even a nice dignified private placement by a "reputable" investment banking house can cost you over 15 percent of the gross proceeds, plus warrants.

2. Unquestionably a public company has more overhead and more clients than a private one. However, the overhead costs of working with private backers are not exactly zero, either. They also will require the audits, stockholder and director's meetings, monthly reports, full disclosure, and general good practice that one would expect of a public company. Moreover, if Round One private money is insufficient for all but the initial-stage growth, the entrepreneur will quickly find his or her time being eaten up by further negotiations with the old backers, trying to enlist some new ones, and ultimately parting with perhaps more equity than ever intended.

3. While you *probably* cannot attract a "reputable" investment banking house to handle your deal, *maybe* you can. As noted earlier, a lot of the long-established houses get pretty excited when they see all that action on the street. A look at the registration statements for 1982–83 will verify this. (A review of the brokerage failures and SEC rules violations suggests also that a redefinition of "reputable" may be in order.) Also, a self-underwritten Reg. A offering may not be out of the question.

4. It is almost certainly true that a public company that performs miserably is more or less out of luck—unless, of course, it happens to have an investment banker with sufficient clout and guts to stand by and support

your stock. But it is equally true that a lousy performer—even one with great prospects—also arouses rather limited enthusiasm from the private equity sector. Among the least enthusiastic we may expect to find the backers who have already lost a bundle on the deal. Neither private nor public money is any guarantee of continued largesse for the company whose performance, whether through bad management or bad luck, is poor.

5. It is easier to assert than to prove that unseasoned companies raising public money in hot markets always fare poorly. The author is unaware of any systematic study that shows that they either fare poorly or fare more poorly than their privately-financed counterparts. Many companies have gone public earlier than the conventional wisdom would dictate and have done extremely well.

None of the above can be taken as a conclusive case for or against going public immediately. These arguments are intended merely to show that the case is far from closed, and that there is room for reasonable disagreement with the orthodox cant on the subject.

If you find yourself on the threshold of growth during a hot new issue market, you should definitely weigh the costs and benefits to the company and to yourself of going public. And, if the net benefits seem to exceed those of the private route, go to it.

SIZING UP THE MARKET

Short of actually prancing into Merrill Lynch with your prospectus smoking, you ought to get answers to the following questions:

1. Can you get somebody (anybody) to take you public?
2. Can you get a "reputable" house to take you?
3. Can you raise as much money as you need for as much equity as you're willing to part with?
4. What are the costs of the issue likely to be?
5. Can you get an underwriting or only a "best efforts" deal?

The best way to answer these questions is to take a look at some offerings recently undertaken (so you can see how they sold and later traded) and in registration (so you can see what investment bankers *think* they can sell in the near future). A good starting place is the *Going Public—The IRO Reporter* (2

World Trade Center, New York, NY) which summarizes both. You can then call or write the underwriter or the management of interesting-looking companies, requesting a copy of the prospectus. If you get a prospectus from companies whose scale, markets, and prospects seem comparable to your own, you can get answers, or at least evidence, on the several above-mentioned issues. Some further conversation with the companies' presidents can give you a further feel for the markets, the alternatives that they examined, and the considerations that led to their choice of investment bankers.

If you are encouraged by what you find out and decide to take the next exploratory step, you already have your list of three or four initial contacts to make in the investment banking community. Go at them with a brief (two-page) mini-plan and get their reactions. You'll find out fast if your plan is a salable commodity. And if it isn't, they may make a few friendly referrals—so you can only win. A lawyer knowledgeable in the IPO process can be invaluable here.

THE PUBLIC ROUTE: SOME ADDITIONAL CONSIDERATIONS

Going public is more than merely one of five ways to raise capital for your new venture. It, more than any other financing option, sets the style for your future corporate and personal operations. It may foreclose or encumber certain options that are open to the privately-held venture. These include the following:

1. The possibility of selling out on more favorable terms or cashing out earlier to an industrial corporation or other buyer.
2. The possibility of maintaining the privacy of certain types of information, disclosure of which would be otherwise required by the SEC.
3. The possibility of learning—innovating or making some mistakes at relatively low risk in the early stages. After all, even Polaroid didn't spring on the scene with an instant camera on Day 1. *Your* big winner may be your third or fourth product.
4. The possibility of knowing your backers personally and obtaining nonfinancial assistance from them.
5. The possibility that you discover you aren't the hot-shot you thought you were and that you can't or don't enjoy running a company. It is possible that your exit may be more graceful from a lower-profile enterprise (assuming you're concerned with grace).

The list could be extended, but the point is this: there are many considerations other than feasibility that should determine the desirability of an early public issue. We are not proposing prolonged breast-beating on this question—but merely that all of the important issues get examined before a decision is made for wrong or insufficient reasons.

CONVENTIONAL WISDOM: Before going public, a firm should have net profit after taxes of a million dollars, five years of operating experience, and, above all, a "reputable" investment banker.

REALITY: Before going public, a firm should decide if this route will net the necessary capital on more desirable overall terms than the private route.

REFERENCES

1. Hutchinson, G. S. *Why, When and How to Go Public.* New York: Presidents Publishing House, 1970.

    This is the best thing in print on the practical issues of a public offering. "Must" reading for entrepreneurs.
2. Bartlett, Joseph W. *Venture Capital Law, Business Strategies and Investment Planning*, New York: John Wiley & Sons, 1988.

    See especially the section on IPOs.

11

The Business Plan

*Only one thing is certain about a new venture: it's going
to turn out very different from its business
plan. .. William Congelton, Venture Capitalist*

Your business plan is the essential piece of software that makes your whole machine function. It is your means of communicating your vision to the outside world to help you attract talent and money into the enterprise. It is your internal control mechanism, against which actual performance is measured and to which corrections are made. It is, or ought to be, your regularly-updated battle plan, providing the bridge between distant objectives and present deployment of people and material.

A VARIETY OF PURPOSES

Your business plan is a central and detailed statement of what your business is going to do. A check-list of what business plans should include is provided in Table 11-1. Although the common core of data and assumptions stays the same, there are different uses for business plans. Consequently the form of

TABLE 11-1   What to Put in Your Business Plan

	Fund-raising Plan	Operating Plan
1. Mini-plan: 1-page summary of essential facts. Should be usable alone.	Essential. This is all that many people will read.	Not needed.
2. Background of plan: origins of product, identification of business opportunity, reasons for market need	Essential. One to five pages.	Include for future recollection.
3. The team: description of individual qualifications. Why will it function as a *team?* Present org. chart. Identify directors.	Make it convincing. Some investors will turn here first.	Detailed job description and organization chart.
4. Product description: what it is, what it does, why it's better than competitors, proprietary features. Family-of-products implications. Customer benefits.	This is where the glamour is. Do a good job, illustrated if possible.	Include.
5. Ownership: before proposed financing. Description of any stock options, warrants, other committments.	Include.	Include, with formal criteria for distributing employ stock for options.
6. The market: present documented evidence of market growth, trends in price, need for your product. Include names of key customers, reps and agents. State all assumptions.	Present graphically. Include corroborating opinions of industry leaders, prestigious consulting firms, trade associations, gov't agencies.	Include backup statistics and data, plus segmentation of market.
7. Marketing strategy. Detail sales channels, sales costs, sales calls/salesmen/year. Unique promotional, delivery, other features. Line-item schedules and milestones.	Some detail and evident grasp of costs of marketing is essential.	Present in full detail. Including budgets and schedules.
8. Operations: how to make it, learnings curves, economies of scale; key vendors, make-or-buy decision points. Facilities, inventory costs.	Go lightly. Investors tend to assume you can make things.	Full detail, schedule back-up detail. Project unit costs. State assumptions.

TABLE 11-1   (continued)

	Fund-raising Plan	Operating Plan
9. R&D: Objectives, costs, and schedules.	Stress the D. Investors hate paying for R.	Make sure you can justify. Include all detail.
10. Staffing: time-table, skills needed, availability and cost.	Be brief. Investors are usually willing to assume people can be hired.	Reasonable detail. Try to predict what organization chart will look like in two years.
11. Financial strategy: what cash needed when, for what purposes? Sources of long and short-term financing. Narrative rationale for each. When and why go public? Leasing plans.	Apparent understanding of cash flow *most* desirable. Also present *pro forma* statements in best/expected/worst case forms. Be honest. Have reviewed by CPA.	Full details, including cash flow by month for six months. Graphic format desirable as well as numerical.
12. Contingency plans: outline general plan for dealing with two or three probable crises.	Detail not essential. Evidence of serious consideration adequate.	Include whatever detail is readily available.
13. Concluding summary: Benefits to investor. Identify major risks.	One page, but quantify if possible. How will risks be minimized? Why is this a desirable investment relative to others?	Section on risk most essential.
Appendices		
A. Backup, market analysis data, independent studies etc.	Summarize data, reproduce complete study if feasible.	Include full backup.
B. Biographies of key personnel.	Keep it short. Full resumes are a bit clumsy.	Not needed.
C. Key articles written by personnel.	Include, if feasible, for benefit of outside consultants.	Not needed.
D. Table of competitors and their product specs. Establish sales in relevant products.	Simplifies evaluation of proposal.	Include *all* detail, plus intelligence reports on plans, key personnel.

documentation, the emphasis, the depth of background support, the statistical bounding (best/worst/expected), the line-item detail of financial projections, the sampling rate (weekly, monthly, or yearly) of projections, and other features may vary according to intended use.

The uses of business plans include the following:

1. To raise capital.
2. To provide an internal operating plan upon which to base day-to-day operations.
3. To provide a source of pre-established contingency plans for certain events.
4. To create, through scheduled review and up-dating, a semi-formal mechanism for management planning.
5. To communicate with directors, attorneys, bankers, and prospective employees the plans and progress of the company.

THE FUND-RAISING PLAN

This is usually and unfortunately the first of the two plans put together and is all too often the only one. Logically, the basic work and detail for the operating plan should be done initially, and summarized, extracted, and supplemented to create the fund-raising version.

It is easy to get carried away by the fund-raising plan. Documentary overkill may be responsible for as many fund-raising problems as underdocumentation. Don't forget that those who read such things are people—not information-processing machines. The purpose of the fund-raising plan is *to get people interested*—not fully informed on every last detail of your proposition. Investors want to see evidence that the detail, the backup, and the field work have been done, but if they want the detail, they'll ask you. A concise, attractive twenty-page plan is about fifty times more likely to get read and comprehended than a detailed, gray two-hundred-page job.

Remember your audience. Where possible, tailor the material to the knowledge, interests, and needs of the person whose O.K. is necessary for your deal to move ahead. Is this person an engineer? Then summarize the market data and financial plans in graphs, and beef up technical areas. Is your target reader an SBIC officer? Then show how your cash flow allows for servicing of convertible debt and, possibly, for some management consulting services from you-know-who. Is your audience's background security analysis? Better have a CPA or better, a securities analyst, check your *pro formas* for such problems as out-of-whack ratios.

Don't forget that besides being a specialist of some sort, your reader is also a human being. Business plans by engineers often sound like first attempts at English prose. Keep it readable. Don't make the write-up so interlocking that every preceding page must have been read before the present one makes sense. Include graphs and diagrams. Avoid grandiloquent adjectives when describing your product and market.

Make it attractive. It need not be elaborate, but it must be neat. If diagrams, drawings, and artwork are needed, spend a few bucks and have them done professionally. Get the final version set on a desktop publishing system. Get a first-rate printing job done on good stock, and use GBC or equivalent binding so that the thing will stay open on the reader's desk. Design a decent cover. Where product photos are indicated, consider using half-tones instead of glossies in case your reader wants to copy the publication on an office copier.

Before final typing and printing, pretest the plan on a few knowledge-able friends. Get their comments on such aspects as appearance, content, persuasiveness, form of financials, and believability. They may spot some problems that you can easily correct. Your best critic may be the small-business specialist in a big eight accounting firm.

Above all, try to keep ever before you the picture of your reader: a busy person with twenty other business plans on his or her desk, plus both phones ringing. This person doesn't need vast detail, but rather a fast overall view of what your business is all about, and enough corroborating *outside* evidence (consultants, market data, etc.) to suggest that you know what you're talking about. Don't try to spell out the deal for this reader—just tell how much money is needed. Your goal: Get your plan into this person's briefcase on his or her next airplane trip.

Final note: Write the plan yourself. There are consultants who will offer to write your business plan, stressing that you are an amateur while *they* are professionals. Forget it. Your plan will be better if you do it. Moreover, since you'll know all the assumptions that went into it, you won't get crossed up while discussing specific aspects of it with investors.

HOW MUCH MONEY?

It is a well-known fact that many entrepreneurs simply begin with the amount of money (large) that might possibly be available from the funding source, then back into a business plan that seems to justify this investment. This is a highly refined art, to which this book has nothing to add.

However, if you are a member of the majority of entrepreneurs who are sincerely trying to size their deals optimally, then there will be a definite question as to how much money you should attempt to raise during this round of financing. As General Georges Doriot, founder of American Research & Development, was fond of pointing out, there are two times to raise money: the first (now), when the beautiful dream is almost to be realized—once all the elements are ready to go when the money arrives. The second is eons from now, when the product is proven, the company is healthy, growing, and outrageously profitable. Between those two points in time there will be innumerable problems, refinancings, struggles, reversals of direction, and zero-crossings in the cash balance. These will be times when getting additional money will be difficult, costly, and perhaps impossible. What General Doriot is saying indirectly, then, is get plenty of money the first trip to the well. Or at least get a substantial enough commitment, contingent on performance, so that you don't have to spend the next two years in constant negotiation for capital.

In the zero stage, the shoestring financial philosophy is valid. Now, in the first stage, it is not. Stock sold in the zero stage may be virtually given away; now, it has a demonstrable worth and should bring the company meaningful amounts of capital without parting with control. Adequate funding, a cash reserve of some sort, and a downstream commitment for further funds as warranted are definitely desirable now.

There are several ways to calculate the appropriate magnitude of funding for your company at this stage:

1. *Financial projections.* Your *pro forma* P&L statement, based on the best possible sales forecasts, is the starting point. Developing this into a cash-flow projection will reveal the amount of cash theoretically required at each month of the company's growth. However, a little simulation using your accounting model will show you just how treacherous such cash prediction can be. Your future cash balance is unbelievably sensitive to minor variations in assumed growth rate, seasonality, product cost, overhead costs, and collection and billing times. Trying to develop meaningful best/worst cases from this sort of simulation is mind-blowing. If you vary all factors against you at once, your cash requirements will look like the national debt. About the best you can do is to develop an "expected," a "best," and a "worst" case sales forecast, and work out the cash consequences of each, holding other assumptions roughly constant. However, you should privately realize how slippery these cash requirements projections really are. Don't start believing them too much. For a planning period use the length of time it will take you in the expected case to get to a condition where a public offering is clearly feasible and desirable. This could be when, for example, annual after-tax profits exceed $500,000. Do not be abashed to include a moderate allowance for contingencies. This could be 10 to 20 percent of the total expected requirement.

   From this exercise you will also learn another interesting number: the absolute minimum amount on which your venture can move ahead for, say, one year.

2. *Outside observations.* What sorts of money has your prospective backer been putting into comparable deals, and for how much equity? What have comparable firms been able to command in the recent past from other sources? Other entrepreneurs will often be willing to discuss their experience with you.

3. *What timing of funding is necessary?* Obviously, even if you get all your money tomorrow, it will be some time before it can all be put to use by the company. Therefore, some venture capitalists make it a point to stage the input of funds, often based upon the attainment by management of certain milestones in operations. Your cash flow analysis will help you to develop a schedule of requirements to have in case the negotiations head in this direction. The future funding may take the form of equity, convertible debt, or even a cosigned line of bank credit. Negotiate for a higher price for stock bought by investors at a later date, since the attainment of milestones and operating experience lessens the risk that will be taken by the investing group at that stage.

After you have analyzed the financial projections, the outside factors, and possible deal timing, then think about how hard it's going to be to raise money when and if everything goes wrong in a couple of years. Don't go after too much, but be very sure you're asking for enough, and that you can justify to the investors what you're asking.

THE OPERATING BUSINESS PLAN

In addition to its secondary function as the backup for your fund-raising plan, the operating plan should be the blueprint to running your business. Management consultants and business school professors emphasize the importance of a formal operating plan and, to some extent, they are right. However, the plan must be your servant, not your master. It is not something to be followed slavishly because you think someone expects you to use it. To the extent that it is useful for your management style, you should use it, update it, and modify it in a series of mid-course corrections. File the plan in half a dozen looseleaf binders, and keep it in a place where it's accessible to all the key people in your group, and get them accustomed to using it, too.

Try to think of the plan as a sort of hairy organic creature, not as a tidy finished document. Keep adding your quarterly sales projections to it, but don't throw out the old ones (however great the temptation). Ditto, of course, for budgets. Have a place to plot actual versus planned results. Have a volume for market data, and keep adding to and updating industry projections and shipments. Plan every six months to spend a day or weekend with your key people updating, or at least reviewing, their sections of the plan.

Use the document when briefing directors on progress. Use it to help bring new management personnel up to speed, so they understand not only where you are, but also how you got there, at what rate, and with what mistakes along the way.

Although your plan really won't be much use until you actually have your money and are able to function as planned, you should get it together right away and enlist the aid of your partners in the chore. Then, as you move ahead, the binders become a good place to file reports, idea summaries, acquisition possibilities, and any number of other major concerns bearing on the company's direction.

CONVENTIONAL WISDOM: You only get one whack at the venture capitalist, so you should tell the whole story the first time.

REALITY: If you hand the venture capitalist the complete unabridged edition, this person won't even read the dedication.

REFERENCES

1. McLaughlin, Harold J. *Building Your Business Plan.* New York: John Wiley & Sons, 1985.

    This is a straightforward and thorough nuts-and-bolts book telling you both how and why to do it. A solid, user-friendly guide.

2. Mancuso, Joseph R. *How to Start, Finance, and Manage Your Own Small Business.* Englewood Cliffs, N.J.: Prentice Hall, 1978.

    This book should be called *How to Write a Business Plan.* It is the outstanding reference on the subject. Appendix includes several actual model plans. Mancuso appears to be the only author who has ever asked venture capitalists what they actually do with business plans.

3. Dible, Donald. *Up Your Own Organization.* Santa Clara, Calif.: The Entrepreneur Press, 1971.

    This gives several very useful checklists and general ideas on creating business plans.

12

Shopping and Negotiations

Let every eye negotiate for itself and trust no
agent.   . . William Shakespeare

The moment has come. Your business plan is shaped up, the company is now
able to survive a few afternoons without you, and it's time to raise serious
money. You've evaluated the pros and cons, and the private venture capital
route looks the least bad. How do you proceed?

SIZING UP INVESTORS

First, you should do a little investigation within the class of investors you have
selected (see Chapter 8), and find answers to as many of the following questions as possible:

1. Who likes ventures in your general field? Who will look at anything?
2. Who presently has cash and is looking for deals? Firms who have just

raised a lot of capital or realized large capital gains may be under a bit more pressure to invest than others.

3. What kinds of financing are currently being done by these firms? Is there *any* chance that you will get what you want?

4. What are the operating policies of the more promising firms? Do they want more management participation than you want to give them? Will they want heavy debt? Will they stay in long enough? Will they put in the additional cash needed between first round and public issue? Can their presence attract other investors?

5. What is their track record? Are their portfolio companies happy? Are they competent? Ethical? Reasonable?

It is not easy to answer all these questions before actually contacting the firms. However, one very good source of data on most of them is another entrepreneur who is currently making the rounds or has just finished. If you can find someone who has recently financed a company (or failed to, for that matter), this person will be your most valuable source of current data.

When you feel you know about 80 percent of all you're ever going to know, stop and make up your list of about four top prospects. This is where you'll be concentrating your energy, starting with the *least* likely candidate, so that your story has been tested, modified, and refined by the time you get to the top prospect's door.

A NOTE ON FINDERS

At nearly any stage of a fund-raising effort, someone may emerge from the woodwork, claiming to be a financial consultant. This person thinks your company is fantastic, he or she has some unbelievable (literally) contacts, and, for a reasonable fee (say, 5 percent of the total offering proceeds), will introduce you to some high-level contacts, who will take it from there. This person is known in the trade as a finder, or a packager. He or she may, indeed, have some good contacts, then again, may merely lead you down the street to introduce you to firms you could have found in the yellow pages. Since most legitimate sources of venture capital will make you warrant in the contract that no finder or broker is involved, isn't it a little foolish to start out with one? A finder may have use later in the search, but then only if he or she has been checked out thoroughly, and you understand what this person really is.

FOLKLORE: DON'T SHOP THE DEAL

This is the cant one hears from the financial world. Translated, it means that if investors like your deal they want to be sure they're the only ones who have heard about it, so that competition, or anything resembling it, can be avoided. However, one suspects that very few serious venture capitalists would wish to back a businessperson so naive as to not have gotten at least three bids for the largest purchase he or she will make for some time: the company's operating capital. There are, of course, perils at both extremes. If you do a mailing of your business plan to everybody in the Venture Capital Directory, you will quickly find yourself the butt of some uncharitable jokes. Nobody likes the impression of being shown a "shopworn" deal. The logical strategy, then, is to shop the deal—discreetly. If possible, pick firms whose officers don't eat lunch together—preferably firms in different towns. Try to let each firm know that *it* is the one you really want to get in bed with. If pressed, however, be honest and acknowledge that a couple of other firms have seen your plan. Since many VCs routinely co-invest, your target VC may well suggest one or two others to show the deal to.

YOUR INITIAL APPROACH

Most venture capital firms seem to consider it a bit gauche for a president to march in, unintroduced, business plan in arm. Etiquette aside, there is good reason why an introduction may be helpful at this stage. If you have done your homework well, you will know that in each target firm there is one person you should reach first. This is the one who is interested in your kind of deal, the person who is going to become your champion before, during, and after serious financial negotiations. You should know the name and something about this person before you approach the firm. Your next problem is to find someone who can introduce you and talk you up to your intended backer. You can begin by asking your banker and lawyer if they know anyone in the firm. If not, whom can they suggest? Try some of your "expert" friends, or the president of a portfolio company of the firm. All you really need is a phone call, letting the key person know what your deal is and that you will be contacting him or her in a couple of days to set up an appointment. Then it's up to you. When you phone, the target person may turn you over to somebody else, but at least he or she knows the company is talking to you. This person may ask you to come in, or to send in your business plan, or mini-plan. At this point, you're rolling.

THE PITCH

Assuming your business plan didn't end up in the garbage immediately, you'll be asked to come in and make a presentation of your deal. You'll be selling yourself as well as your enterprise at this meeting, so a little planning is in order. Remember, they will be looking beyond the numbers and the glamour, and will be much more interested in the entrepreneur behind it all. They'll be evaluating your aparent ability to sell, your intelligence, integrity, and capacity for thinking on your feet. They will be trying to decide whether you're going to be the next big winner or just the latest con artist.

Your presentation should be polished to some degree. The typical presentation is twenty to thirty minutes in length, with no more than a dozen transparencies or slides. Some color helps, as do good graphics.

Keep in mind the audience to whom you are making the pitch: intelligent laypersons who have already heard three presentations today.

Yours must stand out. Keep in mind, too, what you are trying to accomplish. You are not trying to get them to invest money now. You are trying to get them to invest their firms' time and energy in conducting a full-scale due duligence investigation of your deal. This is no small commitment. All that a venture capital manager has to sell is time. This person guards it jealously. The purpose, then, of your presentation is not to inform fully or even methodically, but to get people interested enough to move ahead to the next stage with you.

Bring along your operating business plan, too, because they are going to probe your assumptions about market size and customer needs. They are going to want to know where the data came from, how the surveys were conducted. They may want backup schedules for capital equipment budgets, product cost breakdown, or other supporting information. Every question you can field on the spot without having to say "I'll have to send you that later" wins you double points. An effective presentation at this point makes your in-house champion look good, too, and will help move your deal up in the firm's work-order priorities.

RANK YOUR TARGETS

How many parties should you be negotiating with at once? The author's experience suggests that five is about the maximum number. More than that, and you begin to forget what you've told to whom, or what information each is still expecting from you, and for whom that consultant who called you was working. Don't underestimate the strain of doing all this while keeping the company running and the shipments going out the door. However, *do* initiate several discussions close in time to one another, because for any single discussion to come to a conclusion, favorable or unfavorable, can be a matter of weeks or months. If it falls through, it may be pretty late to be starting at ground zero with another firm. Moreover, one firm may offer a lot better deal than another. A logical player will merely rank the top prospects and start working them as promptly as conditions permit.

Some firms pride themselves on the promptness with which they can get back to a company president with a "no" or a tentative proposition. Others, however, appear to pride themselves on the opposite. They can keep you hanging forever, waiting for a "market study" to be completed or making some other equally transparent excuse. What they may *really* be doing is waiting to see if the big sale you said was pending actually materializes, if you have any alternatives, or how desperate for cash you really are. Or the firms may be procrastinating and doing nothing.

If you suspect that any of these possibilities apply, you have a strong signal that it's time to redouble your efforts to find other capital sources more interested in your deal. Don't deliver any ultimatum or deadline—just put them on the back burner. You may need them yet.

A NOTE ON REFERENCES

When you arrive for your presentation, bring along a carefully prepared list of references together with phone numbers. Doing this ahead of time will help the VC to get the due-diligence process underway quickly and easily. It will also enable you to steer the VC's early education to some degree.

Talk beforehand to each person on your list. Be sure they know they will be called, for what reason, and how in general you hope they will respond. Some of your references will be professional, former associates, bosses, and colleagues. Some will be technologists, some will be experts on the market, and a number may be present or prospective customers. In each case be certain that what the caller hears from your references will be good news, or that there is a well-rehearsed reason why perhaps things went wrong. (Why did you leave your job? Why did the beta test unit fail in the customer's lab?) Be sure that you and the reference both tell the same story.

Finally, tell the people on your list that they may get a lot of calls from different people asking the same questions, so *please* to be patient. There is also a particular risk in using the same customer over and over, although this may be unavoidable. The risk is that the customer may get irritable, or even worse, uneasy at the difficulty he or she may perceive you to be having in financing your company. This could in turn translate into a search for another, more stable, supplier. Make sure you stay in touch with your references, let them know how it's going, and most of all, how much you appreciate their help and patience. Remember: Your whole effort may hinge on what the investor hears from them. Be nice to your references.

WHAT IS IN A LETTER OF INTENT?

If you are fortunate enough to get a preliminary offer from one of your target investment firms, it will include at least some of the following elements:

1. A reasonable amount of equity—that is, money paid for stock. In general, the greater the percentage of equity money, the better for the entrepreneur (although study suggests it may be more profitable for the investor, too).

2. A component of straight or convertible debt, ranging from zero to 100 percent of the financing. As explained earlier, some investment firms (for example, SBICs) rely upon interest to help cover their operating costs; others prefer it because, in case of disaster, a bad debt may be written off against ordinary income, rather than becoming a capital loss. Still others seem to enjoy the illusion of control that the borrowing covenants offer. In any case, you may expect the debt to be convertible to stock at the lender's option, or that you will be asked for options (or warrants) that will permit purchase of your stock in the future at a low price. These may be detachable from the debt instrument and will thus live on after the debt is repaid. The debt money you raise will normally be subordinated to permit banks and trade creditors to provide additional short-term capital.

   There is nothing wrong with subordinated convertible-debt financing *per se*, but a higher dollar amount of it is required (relative to straight equity) to ensure that you will have resources to avoid defaulting on interest payments.

3. An employment agreement for each key member of the team. This will spell out maximum salary, benefits, term, and various noncompetition provisions.

4. Provision for life insurance on key team members, with the company or investor as beneficiary.

5. A fractional investor ownership probably ranging between 20 and 75 percent, depending on how early and how risky the deal is. Most investment firms don't require control, but will expect roughly proportional representation on the board.

6. Some sort of consulting agreement. This is not too common, but it can become part of the initial agreement. It might oblige you to buy a certain amount of consulting time per year from the investor.

7. Miscellaneous other provisions, including right of first refusal on any sale of management stock, right of "piggy back" registration of investor shares in any future stock registration, right to veto any new financing, preemptive stock purchase rights to maintain their fraction of ownership, antidilution provisions, and so forth.

You should also not be surprised if the investor comes back with an offer from two, three, or more investors, combined in a "syndication." The purpose of this is either to spread the risk around, to repay favors to other investment firms, or simply to permit investment beyond their statutory percentage ownership or dollars-per-deal limits. One firm will generally be the lead investor, making the earliest commitment and handling relations with your company. This is a fairly good arrangement from the entrepreneur's viewpoint, although it does make for more stockholders to satisfy in negotiating any future offering or financing.

The initial offer will normally be quite informal, probably in the form of a letter or a "term sheet." It will form the basis for negotiation of the specific points, but you can probably improve some aspects of the deal if you are prepared to yield on others. Do not in any case regard the initial offer as the final one; both parties realize that it is merely the opening gambit in a process of negotiation. This negotiation gives the investors a further chance to size up your negotiating skills, maturity, and experience. If this experience turns them off, they can find an excuse to withdraw their offer. No deal is ever final until the check has been deposited in your bank.

Assuming that the basic agreement is at last negotiated to your satisfaction (this may take several meetings, strung over many weeks), you then have the problem of selling it to your own stockholders. If you are the only stockholder, your job is simplified. If you have a number of stockholders, including present and past employees, suppliers of seed capital, etc., you may anticipate some problems. Some are going to feel that the resulting dilution of their ownership is too great, that the stock is being sold too cheaply. Others will resent the fact that restrictions will be placed on the transfer of their stock, or that the new investors will have rights and benefits that the early investors did not.

In general, you will have better luck with your stockholders at this point if you have kept them informed over the weeks of fund-raising with a series of memoranda. Let them know how tough it is to raise capital now, what hard deals are being driven, and how many firms you have approached who had no interest at all. When you do come through, the deal will look a lot more attractive if they know what went into getting it. If you do have some holdouts, you should be aware that minority stockholders have well-defined rights under the law. Discuss your alternatives with your attorney before doing anything.

THE DOCUMENT

Once all parties have agreed in principle, the investor will give you a draft of the document, a two-inch-thick monster of legal and financial detail. You will be horrified when you read it, because you thought those people at the VC firm were so *friendly*. Now they give you a document that apparently strips all rights from you, encumbers the company under endless borrowing covenants, operating rules, restrictions, reporting conventions, personal warranties, and all sorts of other unpleasantries that never came up in the meetings. This will all be dismissed as mere "required formality" or "boilerplate" by the investor, but in fact many new issues of substance are often introduced in the document. Go over it with care, since it may be necessary to initiate an entire new round of negotiation to get it acceptable to you, your investor, and your other stockholders. This can take weeks longer, plus endless hours of your attorney's and accountant's expensive time, and greatly dilute your efforts in running the company. It is at this stage where patience grows thin—where seemingly endless haggling over small points and seemingly petty sharp-shooting on the part of your investor may totally undermine what appeared to be a pleasant business association, and cloud the purpose of the financing itself. Many deals fall apart at this late stage.

THE PROBLEM WITH BRIDGE CAPITAL

Assuming you were short of operating cash when you started the negotiation, you may be in even worse shape after weeks of searching, negotiating, traveling, haggling with stockholders, and paying those endless legal, accounting, and Xerox bills. Your investing firm may acknowledge this and offer to lend your company some "bridge capital" to tide you over until the last details are complete and the final money comes in. Very generous, you think. However, unless you are *very* sure the deal is going through, and *completely* sure of the integrity of the investor, avoid the bridge capital if possible. Cut whatever corners are necessary to keep the company going without it. (See Chapter 7.) The reasons are as follows:

1. You probably will have to pledge the founders' stock as security for the loan, since everything else is already pledged. This means legally that *any* default condition however minor (such as late interest payment or inability to meet net-worth tests), and the company is theirs.

2. If the deal falls through, the note is probably due and payable in full, with perhaps a thirty-day grace period. *Then* where is the money going to come from? This puts tremendous pressure on you to concede negotiating points you shouldn't, just to keep the deal from falling apart. At that point, in fact, there ceases to be a negotiation; it is fundamentally a dictation of terms by the investor.

Perhaps if you are an exceptionally strong negotiator, or are dealing with an unusually cooperative investor, such provisions will not be attached to the bridge capital note. Otherwise, look out.

THE NEGOTIATION PROCESS

Your negotiation with your prospective investors will probably leave you with a heightened sense of humility. It may be the first time that you were ever confronted with the fact that

---

negotiating itself is both a science and an art—one at which the investor has an immeasurable advantage, because he or she is negotiating deals constantly.

You, on the other hand, may negotiate only two or three major financings in your company's existence. What can you do to protect yourself? Here are some possibilities (more on negotiating tactics and strategy in Chapter 24):

1. Get a lawyer who is a good negotiator. This is hard to know unless you have already been through a negotiation together, but it is a key selection criterion. Have the lawyer with you, if possible, at any significant negotiating meeting. He or she will be able to give a dozen legal and tax reasons why some point you don't wish to concede *can't* be conceded.

Conversely, a lawyer can attack the legal arguments of the other side stating why they can't do what you want. Your legal counsel will be able to help shape the deal in a tax-minimizing form, and provide the foresight and necessary safeguards against problems you could never imagine. This person will give you an excuse to caucus when the going gets heavy, yet can often maintain the semblance of a friendly rapport with the other side. In general, the adversary process is second nature to lawyers, while it probably isn't to you.

2. Learn as much as possible about the person you're facing. What is his or her background, education, and reputation? What kinds of deals has this businessperson been signing? What are his or her real goals and needs, as opposed to the manifest one of driving the toughest possible bargain for the company?

3. Try to list all the issues that will surface in the negotiation. Try to guess which are negotiable and which nonnegotiable for the other side. How far are you prepared to move on your negotiable issues? Remember, a point that may be very important to the other side to win may be a concession of little significance to you—and *vice versa*. If you've thought this through in advance, the process of making these tradeoffs at the bargaining table will be much less agonizing.

4. Try to maintain an atmosphere of openness and geniality during the sessions. A little levity can help to relieve the tension and make it easier for both sides to concede points that should be conceded. When the going gets really heavy and you know you're being clobbered, just call a recess for some hours or days. Tell them you have to talk that one over with your auditors, your directors, your stockholders, your priest, etc. If this isn't possible, at least suggest sending out for some sandwiches— anything to break the momentum of the meeting.

5. Remember, the true objective of negotiation is not to kill the other side. It is to strike a deal that is better for everybody than the initial conditions. Each side should concede points of lesser value to it for points of greater value. Naturally, your adversary may not take this Olympian view of matters, but you should enter the process with this attitude, nonetheless.

Sometimes, for no apparent reason, a negotiation will bog down. The investor just seems to lose interest in the deal, is always out of town, or in some other way permits the momentum to die. At this point you must ask yourself if the loss of interest is real, or merely a negotiating tactic to make you more "reasonable." If this happens well along in the process, it is clearly serious.

You should take the initiative and try to find out what the trouble is. At the same time, it may be timely to introduce yourself to some additional prospective investors, to help reduce the psychological pressure on yourself to close this deal. Since you will now have a long process of education behind you, as well as calibration on the value of your deal, the next negotiation with the new investor may go much more smoothly and swiftly than the first.

CONVENTIONAL WISDOM: Don't shop the deal.

REALITY: You *have* to shop the deal.

REFERENCES

1. Levin, Edward. *Levin's Laws: Tactics for Winning Without Intimidation.* New York: M. Evans & Co., 1980.
2. Nierenberg, Gerard I. *The Art of Negotiating.* New York: Hawthorne Books, 1968.
     The original negotiation book. Spells out Nierenberg's needs theory.
3. Nierenberg, Gerard I. and Calero, Henry A. *Meta-talk—Guide to Hidden Meanings in Conversations.* New York: Trident Press, 1973.
     Guidelines for interpreting behavior in negotiation settings.
4. Karrass, Chester Louis. *The Negotiating Game.* New York: World Publishing Co., 1970.

13

Accounting— Inside and Out

President-and-treasurer disease is corporate cancer. The president's job is to take the assets of the corporation and drive them forward as fast as he can. And it is the treasurer's job to say, 'Yes, but. . . .' These two qualities do not rest easily in the minds of one man.   . . Arthur Snyder, Investor

It is hard for entrepreneurs to appreciate fully accounting and what it can do for them. Most tend to view the accountant as a bean-counter, a sort of scorekeeper sitting on the sidelines, rather than as a player on the field with the first team. This is a great mistake.

Every business organization has need for orderly collection and deployment of quantitative information. This information has two broad uses: *inside uses*, to give the manager the plans and data required to run the company; and *outside uses*, to permit reporting the results of the operation to the outside world, including stockholders, directors, the IRS, regulatory bodies, and research organizations. These two functions, while proceeding from the same data base, are really quite different. The former looks ahead, tries to show the manager where the company's going, how to control future costs, what problems to anticipate. The second is largely historical, generated by the book, for the record. While you will have some latitude for experimentation and innovation in the first area, you must conform to rather orthodox forms in the second. In both, you need competent help.

ACCOUNTING AS A LANGUAGE

Accounting is much more than a function; it is a language, a means of communication among all segments of the business community. It assumes a reference base called the "accounting model of the enterprise." While other models of the enterprise are, of course, possible, the accounting model is the accepted form, and is likely to be for some time. To the extent that the entrepreneur does not speak the language of accounting nor feels intuitively comfortable with the accounting model, he or she is at a severe disadvantage in the business world. The entrepreneur must be, literally, as facile in accounting concepts as the physicist is with mathematical ideas. Accounting is a fundamental tool of the trade.

For the entrepreneur to rely solely on common sense and hired hands is unnecessarily risky. To understand what you're asking your accountant to do, let alone evaluate his or her work, *you* must have some basic accounting knowledge. This knowledge may come from reading (see references) or, better, from some formal training in accounting. Nearly every town and city has some sort of college, university extension, adult education, or commercial school where the basics of accounting are taught. The entrepreneur who has had no accounting should seriously consider enrolling in such a program. You don't have to pass the CPA exam, but you do need the basics. In addition to basic courses, you may be able to find a somewhat more advanced course offering of an appropriate character in cost accounting and control. Consider taking it, as well.

ACCOUNTING HELP: HOW MUCH AND WHAT KIND?

In the fetal stages of your venture, you probably found it necessary to obtain some part-time accounting help to set up your books, pay bills, do posting, reconcile the bank statement, and, perhaps, prepare monthly financial reports. Now, with some capital in the venture and shipping dates approaching, the problems change in kind as well as in size. You may find that your brother-in-law's accountant working on Saturdays simply can't keep up with the volume any longer. What you need is an accountant, possibly a part-time one, but certainly one with the experience and energy to do what needs doing. There are bills to verify and to post, checks to write, invoices to be issued, collections to be pushed, suppliers to be cajoled, deposits to be made, checkbooks to be balanced, operating statements to be prepared, tax returns to be filed, and a myriad of other tasks, large and small, which are custodial in nature but which must be pursued with diligence. In addition, there is a creative side to the job, for which your accountant must have some time and energy. You must have this employee's assistance in developing cash flow projections, budgets, standard costs, and cost accounting systems. These are all tasks for which text book models are inadequate. Your systems must be designed to fit the context of your company and to accommodate the needs of the people who will use them.

You do not need Albert Einstein to do all this. What you do need is a solid accounting person who has actually set up systems in the past—not merely posted the books and turned the crank on an inherited accounting mechanism. You need somebody who is fundamentally methodical, orderly, and neat. If your workload will permit part-time personnel (say, afternoons only), you may very well be filling this role with someone who has put a full-time career on hold to raise children, or, perhaps, with a retired person. In hiring, don't worry about keeping a person for ten years; if he or she can help you get through the next two years, that's what you need now. To locate such a person, some newspaper ads or a few inquiries through your auditing firm should net you some acceptable candidates.

As the company grows, the duties of the accountant become both more numerous and more demanding. The need for cost accounting and budgets becomes more pressing, and there are additional interfaces with suppliers, bankers, and customers to be managed professionally. At this point, your accountant will probably come to you expressing a need for some more help—more billing clerks, a cost accounting clerk, another secretary, etc. This, however, is a very critical moment, and you should not act immediately on the advice of your accountant. This is very likely the juncture at which you should instead hire a controller to reorganize your accounting and control function for the next stage of growth, oversee your accounting staff, and raise the entire professional level of the activity. There will, of course, be the possibility of promoting the accountant to controller; however, this is only rarely a good idea. The person you were able to hire eighteen months ago to do all the detail work would, had he or she the qualifications to be a controller, never have taken your job offer. Do not mistake ambition for talent in this area. Enlist your auditing firm in recruiting for this job; it is an extremely critical role. A good controller can make a company to the extent that probably few other employees can. For a poor one, the reverse applies with a vengeance.

AUDITORS

Entrepreneurs often misunderstand what, actually, the auditing firm does. It is not the FBI. It does come into your firm and go over every last transaction with a fine-tooth comb. Your auditors probably cannot tell you if you have a thief in the stockroom or an embezzler in the accounts receivable office. Their function is to examine your accounting and control *procedures* and determine whether they are adequate and whether they are being followed. In the process of so doing, some sampling of accounts payable and receivable is necessary, as well as a detailed check on very large accounts with customers and suppliers. In addition, the auditors will in the course of an audit require that a physical inventory be taken under their observation, during the course of which they will investigate both the condition and the value of this asset. The auditors will want to see any contracts of a major nature, stockholder lists, certificates of indebtedness, and other documents with significant bearing on the company's worth.

Needless to say, this is a rather long and sometimes arduous process for the entrepreneur and the accountant. Normally it is done only once per year, although additional partial-year audits may be necessary in connection with financing efforts. The result of this effort is the "certified statement," in which the auditing firm certifies that they have examined the accounts and accounting methods of the firm and found them in accordance with "generally accepted accounting practice." However, you will eventually discover that these practices are far from being universal, and that there is broad latitude and flexibility in their application. Some businesses are believed to exploit this flexibility, with the acquiescence of their auditors, so as to mislead the readers of their financial statements.

SIGNIFICANCE OF CERTIFIED STATEMENTS

There are, roughly speaking, three levels of "quality" in year-end statements:

1. *Unaudited.* These statements, even though they may be prepared by your auditor, have little weight with outside persons, because they are merely prepared from the books of account without benefit of auditing.
2. *Audited, uncertified.* These statements are the result of a partial audit, in which most but not all of the steps may have been taken. For example, it may be that the auditor was unable to witness the taking of inventory, although the other tests have been performed.

3. *Certified.* This is the most believable, because it means that all steps have been taken, and the auditing firm has stuck its neck out as far as possible.

Young firms sometimes fail to obtain certification of statements in the early years; they either wish to avoid auditing fees or don't appreciate its significance. However, if in later years you decide to take the public financing route, you must be able to supply certified statements for the last five years to the SEC. This can be rather clumsy, because it is very difficult for the auditor to certify the activities of five years ago—or even five days ago—if he or she happens not to have witnessed your inventory-taking. For this reason, and simply because more people will believe them, be sure *all* your year-end statements are certified.

SELECTION OF AN AUDITING FIRM

This is rather easy, as there are only six firms in the country that you should consider, provided you are a firm with national growth aspirations. These are the "big six" public accounting firms. They are Arthur Andersen & Co., Coopers & Lybrand, Deloitte & Touche, Ernst & Young, Peat Marwick Main & Co., and Price, Waterhouse Co.

There are several persuasive arguments for the use of smaller, highly competent local accounting firms. Their advocates will argue that you get more personalized service; that you are more likely to get a senior auditor on your account; that you can later switch to a "big six" firm if necessary; that the rates are lower; that you will have the same person year after year on your audit.

Countering this, however, is the central fact that out-of-town people simply will not *believe* the statements prepared by an obscure accounting firm of whose reputation they know nothing. Investment bankers in particular have what amounts to a horror of small local firms. If you enlist one of the big six on Day One, the issue will simply never arise.

It is possible that the big six firm will charge somewhat more than the local firm. However, it is also possible that it may have more to offer in terms of backup services over and above auditing. Most have small business sections designed to help entrepreneurs in setting up systems and in other types of business problems. All have management consulting sections, which may be capable of in-depth work on some specific problem you may have. It is also true that if you object to the person assigned to your firm, the large firm will have the depth to send in someone more suitable.

The big six are all similar in that they are large and internationally recognized. However, there are significant differences among them in terms in size, operating policies, and clout. One may be much better in your geographical area, while another may have the stronger office in a different location. Ask your attorney, banker, VC, and any other businessperson whom they like in the area; then go call on the top two or three prospects and see which one you prefer. As with other such choices, the views of other entrepreneurs may be quite helpful here.

THE AUDIT

The auditing firm you select is your big friend—until the day of your first audit. From that point forward your auditors may seem to become your adversary. They will criticize your lousy cash control system. They will wish to create reserves for bad debts in excess of anything you can imagine, and also to reserve for specific accounts which may be a bit slow in collecting. They will raise cain with your inventory, insisting that at least half of it is obsolete and should be written off at once. They will find your cost accounting inadequate to determine the actual labor and materials content of your work-in-process. They will insist you write off your capitalized development costs. They will discover that a couple of your accounts receivable claim never to have seen an invoice from your firm. In short, they will appear to be doing everything possible to reduce your bottom-line profit, for which you have labored so long and hard.

This experience, repeated annually, tends to produce a mild paranoia among company presidents. However, you should remember that auditors are, ultimately, only your hired hands. If you disagree with their stand on important issues, take them to task; special circumstances may justify your view in their minds. If not, you can still do as you please anyway, and let them note their objection in a footnote to the certified statement. If difficulties persist, you may be justified in changing auditors. The great umbrella of "generally accepted accounting practice" may, in the hands of a different firm, cover you, too.

OTHER BIG SIX FUNCTIONS

In certain areas, such as tax law, you may wonder whether to start with your accounting firm or your lawyer. The answer almost always is to start with your accounting firm. Often it has specialized staff, including lawyers, who can fill your need professionally at a cost far lower than that of your law firm.

There are many other resources at your disposal as well. These may include locating investors, searching for acquisition or merger partners, general management consulting, strategic partner identification, corporate tax advice, personal tax planning, and help in disputes with tax authorities. Some firms will actually set up your bookkeeping and accounting system and sell you the needed software. Be sure that you explore these resources at the time you select a firm, and make it a point to have lunch with your "principal" once a year, just to stay abreast of what's available.

BUDGETS AND CONTROL

The budget is a rather key tool in your effort to operate your company.

It is, in essence, the connecting linkage between your business plan and your organization; the piston rod connecting your power source with your drive wheels.

Formal budgets serve a lot of useful purposes, and only a very foolish president would try to function for long without them. The budget is

1. *A tool for implementing plans.* In this role, the budget states in detail how much money and calendar time is to be allocated for each purpose in the pursuit of the business plan. It states who will spend the monies, what his or her authorization will be, and for what materials and services it will be spent. To this extent, the company's budgets are more or less an elaboration of the financial projections of the business plan.

2. *A tool for communication.* The budget and the process that produces it constitutes one of the principal means of communicating the exact plan of operation throughout the organization. As finally published, the budget will tell everyone precisely what the spending limits will be for accomplishing each task. It is your *only quantitative statement* of corporate priorities. To the extent that your managers submit budgetary proposals for consideration, they are communicating in a most quantitative form their plans and priorities for carrying out their functions.

3. *A tool for cost control.* By considering in advance the necessary amounts for each class of expenditure and by getting each manager committed to

that statement of expenditures, you have the rudiments for achieving financial control. By reporting actual expenditures against budget, you have a monthly historical record of (a) how good your budget was, (b) how good a job your people have done in controlling costs, and (c) where immediate corrective action is needed. In areas where tighter control is indicated, you will want to take steps toward the *prevention* (as opposed to reporting) of over-budget expenditures. You may wish to have your accountant maintain *daily* tallies of expenditure requests, purchase orders cut, and so forth, and notify the appropriate parties when the budget for a particular item is *about* to be exceeded. It is only at this level that you actually have control of costs. The monthly budget-versus-actual profit and loss statement will only highlight major areas of overrun or underrun for future management action, but the money is already gone. *Caution:* Budgets can also hide a good deal of information. For example, a department that is consistently within its overall budget may be using savings in one area to hide gross inefficiency or other problems in another. Be sure your budget has enough detail to pinpoint the reality of the situation.

4. *A tool for assessment of employee performance.* Sad to say, the ability to meet goals on budget is among the few quantitative measures of employee performance available to presidents. For this reason it is probably overstressed, but unsatisfactory performance in the spending area usually connotes problems. Each manager must assume responsibility for the controllable (i.e., non-overhead or distributed) costs of his or her area of the business. To the extent that managers help to set their own goals and budgets, they must be responsible for meeting them—not merely for mounting a forensic attack on the "unrealistic" budget. Unless every manager accepts this fundamental responsibility, your business plan, your cash projections, and your profit plan will all be meaningless.

For all of these reasons, it is imperative that even startup ventures establish some form of formal budgeting as early as feasible. When resources are limited, there will be hard tradeoffs to be made, and everyone on the team should have a voice in how these are made and implemented. Probably once per quarter is adequate for a full budget update. Procedurally, one starts with an updated sales forecast and works down through the P&L line items entering costs as they *will be* (as opposed to *have been*) during the next four quarters. Avoid the temptation merely to insert last quarter's estimates; challenge each line item, and be sure that it deserves all that is being spent on it. Where could cuts be made if necessary? Improvements postponed, capital equipment deferred? For which jobs are we overspecifying skills? These are the sorts of questions that should be asked, every quarter at least, of each operating manager. This is the meaning of "zero-base budgeting."

Your first few budgets will probably be terrible; they will evoke a hue and cry from their victims, and the results may be rather discouraging to you. Don't quit trying, however; keep refining, improving categories, pushing for compliance, and creating an attitude of recognition for the people who achieve their targets. This is the only way that your costs will come under your control and stay there.

Final note: Don't overdo it. Too much detail and too much frequency can drown a budget system in its own paperwork. Be sure the system is your servant—not your master.

CONVENTIONAL WISDOM: The accountant should sit on the sidelines and keep score.

REALITY: A good accountant will be right out there on the field with you.

REFERENCES

1. Lasser, J. K. *Handbook of Accounting Methods.* 3rd ed. New York: Van Nostrand Co., Inc., 1964.

    This book gives suggested forms and methods on an industry-by-industry basis. Also has good sections on electronic data processing in accounting, stock registration, and other practical issues. Good reference book.
2. Heckert, J. B., Willson, J. D. *Business Budgeting and Control.* 3rd ed. New York: The Roland Press, 1967.

    This is an excellent work, showing in some detail how to develop business plans into budgets, then controlling the firm through the budgets. Takes up where accounting texts leave off.

14

Care and Feeding of Bankers

A banker is a fellow who offers to lend you his umbrella when it isn't raining.   .. Anonymous

It is common currency among entrepreneurs that bankers are parsimonious, hidebound, unimaginative, and timid to the point of irrationality. However, it is time the truth were bared: *some are not.* It is incumbent on the entrepreneur bent on survival to find a bank in that small category and cultivate a relationship as one would cultivate a garden of beautiful flowers.

DIFFERENCES AMONG BANKS

To the outsider looking in, most banks look alike. They all offer about the same services, pay about the same interest on deposits, charge about the same on comparable loans. However, there are differences among banks. Some of the more obvious gross differences are in asset size (general clout), net worth (stability), region served, number of specialized departments, and general prestige. However, most of these don't make too much difference to the entrepreneur. The differences that *do* matter include the following:

1. Source of income. If you are dealing with a bank that depends mainly on mortgages for income, your loan requirements aren't going to get much priority.

2. Capacity for working with small firms. Banks vary radically in this regard. Some regard a startup company as just one more bad risk; others see it as an opportunity. Some have departments or SBIC connections for dealing with the smaller enterprise. Have they made unsecured loans to small firms lately?

3. Reputation for staying in when the going gets rough. Did they call their small business demand notes (or fail to renew) in the last recession when even their old, established customers were crying for cash, or did they hang in there? You can get some interesting insight into bank behavior by talking to entrepreneurs who have been in business for a decade or more.

4. General creativity of approach. Do they just look at your balance sheet and faint, or do they try to suggest constructive financial alternatives— for example, rotating receivables financing, factoring, leasing, negotiating contract advances? Some banks are more adept at this than others. Also, within a given bank, individual officers tend to vary widely in level of creativity.

SELECTING A BANK

Bank selection, though not so irreversible as many other business decisions, is a very important step for the entrepreneur. You begin investing in a good relationship, starting Day One. If your choice is a poor one and you have to switch after two years, that's two years of effort and investment in credibility down the drain. Select the right bank early, and begin grooming it against the day you really need it; when your cash crunch finally comes, it will be too late to start.

Following are some guidelines for bank selection:

1. Develop a list of criteria, then refine them into questions you will put to the various bank officers you interview.

2. Ask other entrepreneurs to describe their experiences with their banks. After you've talked with a few people, a general pattern may begin to

emerge. Be sure to find out who their lending officer is at each candidate bank.

3. Ask your accounting firm, your lawyer, your investors, and your close advisor for suggestions on banking connections.
4. Talk to a few different banks, even if you're convinced you know where you ought to be banking. Try to calibrate the differences for yourself.
5. In interviewing the officer, be sure to ask for some small-business customer references.

In the selection process, keep in mind that institutions are only agglomerations of people and that, as their personal makeup changes, so do their policies and attitudes. For example, a bank with a long historical record of working with smaller firms may have lost one or two sparkplug officers who emphasized and championed that part of the business—and not be, therefore, too interested in more new-venture business. Or, some banks just may have attracted so much small firm business that they are not seeking more. Or, money may be so tight at the moment that they are not seeking any but the very highest quality lending opportunities. Thus, what you must search out is a bank and officer that you can work with *now* and *over the next several years*. What it did in the past is important, but not in itself decisive.

GROOMING THE RELATIONSHIP

To the extent that your side of the banking relationship is active rather than passive, you will be maximizing your chances of long term cooperation. Some of the steps you can take without investing much energy include the following.

1. Keep your banker informed. This applies *whether or not* you have a loan outstanding. Place this person on your PR mailing list, your key customer newsletter list, and the like. Be sure your banker gets a set of operating statements monthly and the audited annual statements while they're still fresh.
2. See your banker in person. These people are big believers in pressing the flesh. Once per quarter might be about right. Have him or her to your office to review the operating results and the projections. Have a look at the plant, review R&D in progress. Fill your banker in on key customers and prospects, and get his or her subconscious working on possible other business sources for you. Have lunch, and establish some human contact. Get this person *interested* in what the company and you

are doing. Remember, if you do a good job now, you'll want to take your banker with you in your *next* company. Likewise, if your officer changes banks, it may be beneficial to move your account with him or her. Banking is, at the root, a business of people, and of mutual confidence and assumed integrity.

3. Start borrowing. Even if the company has $1 million cash from fund-raising, now is the time to begin establishing a record for businesslike borrowing and punctual repayment. It is also time to let the bank start making a few dollars on your account, which they will be only too happy to do—if you have a bundle of cash. If you don't, then you probably need a bank loan, and it's high time to start learning to use bank credit constructively.

4. Meet your targets. Everything said in Chapter 23 about meeting targets applies in spades to the banking relationship. If you acquire a reputation for sloppy cash management, poor planning, or feeble follow-through on your plans, your bank will be luke warm on your account—*even if you're growing and profitable.* A few minor targets met *on-time,* and *on-budget* early in the game will let the banker stop worrying so much about you. Be sure the banker (and everyone else) knows about it when targets are hit.

MISCELLANEOUS SERVICES OF BANKS

There are a number of formal and informal services your bank can render once you're rolling together. These can be worth a lot of money and should be used:

1. Credit checks. You probably won't be able to justify the annual fees for credit agencies such as Dun & Bradstreet at first, and maybe you'll never need to. Your bank has access to all of them. This can also be a useful route for sizing up prospective customers and competition.

2. Equity financing. Banks with SBICs can work directly with you; others can often put you in touch with investors or investment bankers who would not otherwise be accessible to you.

3. Product leasing. If you sell capital equipment, the bank may be willing to help you develop a leasing plan to offer to your customers.

4. Equipment financing. When you need capital equipment, your banker may be able to show you how to evaluate the purchasing and leasing options.

5. Export-related services. Banks with strong international departments can advise you on letters of credit, export credit insurance, foreign bank drafts, and other arcana of international finance.

6. Payroll and other accounting. Banks increasingly offer data processing services to their customers; their rates are of necessity competitive with outside data processing services.

7. Tax advice and services. Certain banks are set up to do a substantial amount of tax-related work for company clients.

8. General business advice. Your officer may prove to be a valuable sounding board and source of advice on business problems. You may get suggestions as to possible sources of business, ways to deal with particular delinquent accounts, methods for setting up payroll and other labor-intensive accounts. Besides sources for additional capital, your banker may know firms that might be interested in acquiring or being acquired.

DAY-TO-DAY BANKING

It may be desirable to maintain a small account with a local bank with offices very nearby. This will not be for the purpose of borrowing but for the convenience of your employees. They need a place to cash their paychecks and do personal banking. Your accountant will occasionally need a certified or cashier's check on short notice and a safe deposit box for certain documents. Your petty cash box will need refreshing periodically. These are all functions for which you want a nearby bank. In addition to this bank, you may wish at some point to establish a discreet account with a *third* bank, in which to keep a portion of the company assets to protect them against being frozen by a creditor's committee or a court action. Such an action, brought to make you do something you don't want to do, can be extremely awkward if you have not anticipated it.

PARTING SHOT: Remember, your banker is the one who's going to rent you working capital that you'd otherwise have to buy with undervalued stock. This person's going to do a lot, therefore, toward making you rich. Treat your relationship accordingly.

CONVENTIONAL WISDOM: All banks are pretty much alike.

REALITY: All banks are pretty much alike—until you ask for a loan.

REFERENCES

1. Ronstadt, Robert C. *Entrepreneurship—Text Cases and Notes.* Dover, Mass.: Lord Publishing Co., 1984.

    See entire section on debt financing, which includes concise, useful information on banking for new ventures.

2. Wayne, William. *How to Succeed in Business When the Chips are Down,* New York: McGraw-Hill, 1972.

    This book, written by someone who has obviously been through the mill, is full of advice on dealing under duress with bankers.

15

That Next Round of Financing

"Take the money and run." —*Woody Allen*

FINANCING FUTURE GROWTH

Raising money for a small, growing firm is seldom easy. However, difficulty comes in all sizes and, in the present context, raising money to continue the growth of sales and profits is a snap, compared to raising money to finance past losses.

The company that has met its targets and has the firm support of its stockholders, bankers, and employees has a variety of choices it can make. It may seek additional funding from its old stockholders, it may seek out funding from venture capital firms, it may arrange a private placement of stock through an investment banker, or it may elect to go public. Possibly it will be attractive enough at this point to elicit acquisition interest from another company. Its optimum strategy at this point is to maximize the net worth of the existing stockholders, given the total scenario of events that each choice implies.

The course of action with the highest present value (future revenues discounted back to the present) would, normally, be the one selected. This may or may not be the same course of action that yields the highest immediate return. For example, you may receive an offer to buy the entire company for $1 million ($1.00/share, assuming one million shares exist).

The founders and the original investors walk away with a pocket full of cash and a handsome capital gain. You may also have the alternative, however, of selling one third of the company for $250,000 in working capital. Not too attractive, you say. Not only is the value per share lower, but neither you nor the other stockholders get any cash. Plus the old investors grumble that they payed as much, but took all the risk. However, based on present growth, you think that the $200,000 would carry the firm another ten months, by which time a small Regulation D public offering could be arranged. In such an offering, the company could raise perhaps $1 million for 20 percent of the stock: thereafter a secondary issue might later be arranged to generate some working capital and stockholder liquidity, perhaps in twelve more months. Let us then compare two possible cases, with some illustrative numbers.

Case 1: Sell Out for $1 Million

	Number of Shares Owned	Cost Basis	Sale Price	Net Gain
Founders @ $.01	750,000	$7,500	$750,000	$742,500
Original Investors @ $.50	250,000	125,000	250,000	125,000

In this case, the founders will probably be required to stay and operate the company for two to five years, depending on the buyer.

Case 2: Sell one third of Company for $250,000, then go public for $1 million = 20%*

Founders @ $.01	750,000	$7,500.	$3,000,000	$2,992,500
Original Investors @ $.50	250,000	125,000	1,000,000	875,000
New Investors @ $.50	500,000	250,000	2,000,000	1,750,000
Public @ $2.67	375,000	1,000,000	1,500,000	500,000

*Assumes that a secondary offering at $4.00 is possible. However, this value will be only a paper gain for a substantial period of time for the founders.

It is to be acknowledged that the foregoing example contains some heroic assumptions; to wit, that the management and original stockholders had perfect knowledge of some unknowables:

1. The price and time when the company could go public.
2. The price and time when a secondary offering and registration of letter stock would be feasible.
3. The ability of the management and initial investors to sell all their stock in the secondary offering. However, this is not necessary if we simply take the market price of $4.00 as a reasonable basis for computing "gain."

The principal point is that decisions based on the relative "dilution" of capital value, loss of "control" or immediacy of cashout can be very poor decisions. The public offering remains the major avenue for realization of the full rewards of entrepreneurship. If you relinquish the possibility too early or too cheaply, you will have lost the ball game in the final inning. In the illustration, our founders quadrupled their gains over the sellout case; moreover, had they sold out they probably would have relinquished their opportunity to engage in entrepreneurship again for the next several years, due to their employment agreements. Thus the opportunity cost of the sellout is probably even in excess of the loss in sale price. A little simulation along these lines, geared at various assumptions about the future, can help a great deal in clearing up your own thinking.

An on-target company seeking Round Two capital has a rather broader range of choices available than it had for Round One. Many venture capital and other institutions invest *only* in Round Two situations; most venture capitalists are more comfortable with this situation. You may also be able to entice in low-cost funds from insurance companies, college endowments, or other quasi-fiduciary institutions once you have a winning track record.

WHO NEEDS THOSE GUYS?

A peculiar phenomenon occurs in Round Two financing with sufficient frequency to warrant some comment. It is the "who-needs-those-guys" effect—"those guys" being the old investors. It often happens that after struggling with the entrepreneur through the pains and risks of startup and the agonizing initial couple of years of operations, the original investors cannot or will not put up the Round Two money. They may be fully invested by then in other ventures; they may have specific preference for startup or Round One investments or, they may simply have reached what they consider a prudent limit for investment in one deal.

At this stage then, the entrepreneur starts looking for new sources of money. Enter Mr. Round Two Deal Man. He looks at the company and likes it—*except* for one thing: those old stockholders hold "too much" of the company. *Who needs those guys?* this investor asks you. After all, *they* aren't going to contribute any further to the company's progress. *They* will simply be sitting on a pile of cheap stock that rightfully ought to be in the hands of management and new investors. *They* are just going to be a pain in the neck, a source of trouble and a possible veto on later financial dealings. Let's get them out.

Herein lie the seeds of a great error. When Mr. Round Two says, "Let's you and them fight," he is setting forces in motion which could tear your fragile new company apart, literally. If he makes an offer contingent on forcing out the old stockholders (by offering an unreasonably low price and insisting everyone participate, for example), he will be pitting you against them, with nothing to lose himself. If the deal falls through, he walks away to another one. Meanwhile, he has convinced you that the old backers are a bunch of mendacious parasites, while they are now convinced that you are a thief and a bounder trying to deny them a reasonable reward for taking the front-end risk and hanging in with you. The damage that is thereby inflicted on the company may be irreparable. You will no longer be partners and the emphasis will shift from a joint seeking of corporate goals to one of maneuvering, one-upmanship, and defense of personal interest. It is now impossible, because of the suspicions created, to approach *any* new investor with a unified front, and no investor wants to buy into a fratricidal family struggle. Moreover, your manifest willingness to dump your old investors over the side will permit the prospective Mr. Round Two to project himself vividly into their position a couple years hence.

This is not to say that there is never cause to take out some old investors in seeking new capital. Some may want out; others may be willing to get out, if they feel that it is in the company's best interest. However, if they feel you attempted to cheat them or to force them out on unfair terms, they will always resent it, and it will come back to haunt you. You personally have nothing to lose by pressing Mr. Round Two for a fairer deal for your old investors. He may not agree, but he should at least respect your commitment to treating investors fairly.

FINANCING PAST LOSSES

Any reasonably intelligent entrepreneur can probably find ample capital for Rounds Two, Three, and Four, if his or her company is growing, profitable, and reasonably near target. The real test of entrepreneurial skill, however, comes when you are in some combination of the following circumstances:

1. You are out of cash.
2. You are losing money.
3. You are far behind plan.
4. Capital intended for market development and production buildup ha? been eaten up by development delays and operating losses.

If this is your situation, you have your work cut out for you.

The first thing to do is to take a hard look at the next few months' cash flow and determine whether you can keep the doors open. There is nothing so certain to sabotage any negotiation for capital than the joint recognition that the company is in utterly desperate straits. It is, in fact, no longer a negotiation, but a unilateral dictation of terms.

If you see that the company is headed full speed for a cash cliff, take immediate steps to alleviate it. Drastic measures are warranted, even though they may be somewhat embarrassing to your "growth company" image. It is vitally important to get the cash flow positive and be negotiating from a sustainable position. It will also vastly enhance your position to be able to show that the company is currently in the black (if only temporarily) in addition to having positive cash.

The measures you will take will be the obvious ones: cut personnel expenses by discharging some people, furloughing the more valuable people, and asking the key people to accept some deferral and temporary cut in salary. Try a four-day week (thirty-two hours) in the shop for a while; if people sense that it is only temporary you may not lose anybody. Cut all other discretionary expenses, and consider various forms of postponement of buying on such items as operating supplies, expendable tools, and materials. Stretch out your vendors and arrange financing on any unpledged assets. Try selling off under-utilized equipment and inventory. Try subleasing some plant space. In addition, you must consider lending the company some money yourself and obtaining short-term loans from whatever quarter possible.

When your business plan has been fully updated for selling purposes, you should take to the road. Put your stockholders to work as well, exercising their contacts and making pitches to possible investors.

Your selling posture would include the following:

1. The company is about to take off and realize its multi-million dollar potential.
2. The heavy risks and expenses are all behind now, and the bill was footed by someone else.

3. The commitment and determination of the management team have been amply tested by the tough times you've been through.

4. The adverse market conditions (if any) have been as tough on the competition as on you. In fact, they may be about to throw in the towel.

5. The prolonged development cycle, with its attendant expense, has resulted in a far better product than originally conceived.

6. There's still time for an astute investor to get in on the ground floor (indeed, you haven't even left it yet).

ACQUIRING AN ACQUIRER

You may discover after some exposure to the investment community that the money you need at this stage simply is not available on any kind of acceptable terms. If so, it's time to start looking for a company with some logical reason for wanting to acquire you. There are, of course, many non–investment reasons why a going concern would be interested in buying you, despite your past record and current distress:

1. Quick entry into a new (your) market.

2. Expansion of their present market by annexing your customers.

3. A cheaper, faster way into a new technology or product than designing it from scratch.

4. A source of supply for some needed products or capability (vertical integration).

5. Captive customers for some of *their* products.

6. A means of absorbing existing overheads (factory space, machine time, sales force, dealer base).

7. A quick way to establish a regional or U.S. presence.

8. A source of some pizzazz to get their stock moving.

Armed with this list of possible motives, start your search for possible corporate partners, first on a local basis, then widening the circle. This may not be the point at which you would normally have wanted to be bought out but acquisition may be the right answer. The acquiring company may be able to add a lot of things besides money to make your venture go, and the personal risks to you may be diminished a full order of magnitude.

Enlist your accounting firm, your law firm, local business associations, business lobbying groups, consultants, trade associations, as well as your shareholders and directors in this process. Selling a company is like selling any other piece of capital goods. It may take fifty sales calls to find three real prospects, of which only one can be closed. Make sure your search is extensive enough from the outset, and

---

don't slide into the physiological trap of pinning a lot of hope on the success of any single prospect. Find lots of prospects.

Keep in mind too that a medium-sized firm may be a much better partner for you than a Fortune 1000 firm. It is especially desirable that the firm still be run by its founder, who hasn't forgotten how to make a decision. An acquisition decision by a large company can take a year or more to make and implement, and the one thing you don't have is time.

Other routes may be open to you at this point. One is Chapter 11 reorganization, discussed in another chapter of this book. Another is government lending agencies designed more or less specifically for the firm in temporary or reversible straits. The SBA offers direct loans (often unavailable due to lack of funds) as well as bank loan guarantees for firms unable to meet normal bank lending standards. State or regional agencies (such as Massachusetts Business Development Corporation) make loans to struggling firms. Your chances with these people are best if you're a substantial employer, but let them judge that. Go see anybody whom you even suspect is in the economic development business. Your state legislator may be a good contact to steer you to the right doors and help you to kick them open. If a federal program appears to have some glimmer of salvation, you should also keep your Congressperson or Senator aware of your activities. Don't forget that they have a big stake in the economic welfare of their constituents.

For you, the entrepreneur, the toughest part of this whole business may be in keeping your own faith alive. With faith, anything is possible (if improbable); without it, you won't be able to convince anybody. You may at times have to indulge in a little autohypnosis to keep on going, but a confident, enthusiastic, and optimistic attitude is essential—and contagious. You must evince the belief that the hurdle you confront is the last major one between the company and the Big Hit.

CONVENTIONAL WISDOM: Each round of financing is easier than the last.

REALITY: Each round of financing is easier than the last, if you're on-target.

REFERENCES

1. Hutchinson, G. S. *Why, When, and How to Go Public.* New York: Presidents Publishing House, 1970.

   Offers prudent, if somewhat orthodox, advice and procedures for going public. Best book I've found on the subject.

2. Mancuso, Joseph R. *How to Start, Finance, and Manage Your Own Small Business.* Englewood Cliffs, N.J.: Prentice Hall, 1978.

   See Chapter 6 on raising new money.

III
PEOPLE

16

People in Small Firms— General Considerations

Youth gets together his materials to build a bridge to the moon, or perchance a palace or temple on earth and, at length, the middle-aged man concludes to build a woodshed with them. . . Henry David Thoreau

The most important resource of any company is its people. As an entrepreneur, one of your most important jobs for the next several years will be the recruiting, training, motivating, and, where necessary, thinning out of your staff. Much of your energy will be consumed with such issues as training a new sales force, creating compensation and incentive packages, struggling with rivalries and conflicts within your team, trying to maintain a creative climate, and getting rid of people who don't work out. To the extent of your efficiency and success in these tasks, you will probably be efficient and successful in building your company.

THE FALLACY OF HIRING FOR FUTURE NEEDS

In Chapter 4 we addressed the issue of over-specification of partners in the zero and startup phases of the enterprise. The same general point can be made for any employee. You are doing a disservice to both the person and the company to hire somebody who is overqualified for the job at hand.

The practice of overhiring is sometimes justified by the argument that, while the candidate's talents aren't needed now, in a year or two he or she will be fully utilized. Using this justification, many firms have exploited recessionary conditions in hiring $50,000-per-year people to do junior engineering for $30,000, with very disappointing results for all concerned. Hiring an overqualified person can result in several problems:

1. In hiring the top candidate for the job, you will normally be overpaying relative to what it would otherwise cost to get the job done.

2. If you take advantage of unusual market conditions to hire a person for less than normal worth, you will invest money and effort in training, only to lose this employee as soon as a normal job market returns.

3. In the very early stages, before the company has significant substance, you will have to pay more in terms of salary, options, stock, and other nonsalary incentives to attract a top employee than you will later.

4. If the person is from a larger company (which may, in all likelihood, be the case), he or she will be accustomed to staff, clerical help, substantial budgets, and other trappings of office. Such an employee may function poorly in the Spartan environment you offer, or worse, persuade you to add the overheads long before you should.

5. If bored by the detail and do-it-yourself drudgery inherent in a new-company job, this employee may quit long before his or her talents are actually needed by the company.

As an entrepreneur, your responsibility is to survive the first couple of years, not to "build for the future" with people who won't be needed until year three.

Therefore, match your hiring to the actual job, as it will be for the next one and a half to two years. The future can take care of itself.

THE OUTGROWN EMPLOYEE

In one version of *The Peter Principle*,[1] an employee gets successive promotions until reaching his or her "level of incompetence," after which this person advances no further and prevents the further progress of the organiza-

---

[1] Apologies to Lawrence J. Peter.

tion in his or her area. In the new enterprise context, however, *The Peter Principle* works somewhat differently. Instead of the individual being promoted up the pyramid, the pyramid grows under the individual. The resulting situation, however, is the same. In the new enterprise it is more serious, though, in that the employee who does not grow with a job can effectively block the progress of the entire company. You don't *have* the option of working around the employee—you must usually get rid of this person, or subordinate him or her to a new manager from outside. Either can present some unpleasantness.

For example, assume you have hired a manufacturing manager who is hard-working, loyal, and extremely competent—as long as he only has about twenty-five employees whom he can oversee directly. He enjoys first-line contact and trains and motivates workers beautifully. But now your organization has grown. You now have one hundred workers, and three foremen. Your old manufacturing manager, however, is not thriving on your success. He dislikes supervising foremen, he misses the direct contact with the workers, and feels that the foremen are doing a poor job of training and supervising them. Production is falling more or less permanently behind schedule, quality is slipping a bit, and fire drills and confrontations have begun to replace planning as a management method. What do you do now?

The simplest answer might be to get rid of the guy. However, he is a good man, a friend by now, and has been with the company virtually from startup. He will walk out with some stock that can no longer motivate the performance of another employee. Moreover, he's well-liked by the team and his ejection could have a devastating effect on morale.

A second answer is to bring in a higher-power manufacturing manager and make the old one a foreman under him. This might work, but the old manager is likely to feel humiliated by his demotion and to resent the fact that he no longer reports directly to the president. These factors may undermine his efficiency greatly.

A third course is to create a sinecure (such as Vice President for Manufacturing Coordination), but this is costly and will arouse the resentment of everyone.

There is no single correct answer to such a situation. Your best bet overall is likely to be to get rid of the guy, even though it's painful. At least, once it's over it will eventually be forgotten. If you keep him on, you may just be buying yourself a future of trouble and lost opportunity. Change the scenario a bit, and substitute Chief Engineer, Controller, or Sales Manager for Manufacturing Manager, and you have a drama that occurs in just about every small company sooner or later.

TALENT VERSUS EXPERIENCE

A different consequence of the overhiring dilemma arises from the entrepreneur's own tendency toward insecurity in a new marketplace. It always seems like a better bet to hire somebody who has been in the industry a while, who has a reasonable track record, and so forth. This applies with particular emphasis to hiring sales personnel. An alternative, of course, is simply to hire a very good junior salesperson who you hope will grow into the position quickly enough to compensate for lack of experience. If, of course, it were possible to hire someone with both talent and experience, the dilemma would never arise. However, you will usually be obliged to settle for one or the other.

If it comes to a showdown between talent and experience, you will usually be better off to err on the side of talent. The older, more experienced hand may be ideal for some jobs. However, it is more often the case that in the new enterprise such experience becomes a liability rather than an asset. This candidate's previous success may have been a function of the market dominance of his or her former employer, or of an early product advantage, or of some market condition that no longer applies. To be effective, this person may require a full product line, an applications engineering staff, a big ad budget, and a big-company reputation to back up product credibility. You will be unable to support such an employee fully in any of these areas. The junior person, on the other hand, will be out to make his or her mark and will be willing to pour in the energy and time needed to develop *your* product, *your* market, *your* company. The newcomer will be more challenged to innovate and to work around the resource limitations inherent in the situation. Finally, even though there may be significant age difference between the two of you, there is likely to be a much better relation between employee and president. Both will be in a learning mode. Both will be innovating and improvising. Both should be capable of taking a fresh look at what the competition is doing well and poorly and at what the market really needs. To avoid creating a case of the blind leading the blind, both should be looking outside the company for some experienced guidance. This can come from directors, the company godparent, professional associations, or elsewhere. Via this route, hiring a bright junior person can sometimes be much less risky for the company than taking on someone with "many years of experience."

CREATING CREATIVE ENVIRONMENTS

Endless books, articles, and dissertations have been written on the problem of establishing and maintaining a climate of creativity in the business enterprise. A few of the better examples are to be found among the references to this chapter. However, most begin with the assumption that where creativity is concerned, the more the better. A few irreverent words on this subject may therefore be in order.

Creativity is to the organization what food is to an organism. With too little, it will anguish and die of malnutrition. With too much, it will become bloated, arteriosclerotic, immobile, and will die. As with nourishment in organisms, there is a range of creativity that is optimum for a given organization. Business enterprises vary drastically in their capacity to utilize creativity. An aerospace firm developing space-flight hardware, for example, inherently requires and consumes more ideas than a firm making plumbing supplies. In the former, the ratio of scientists and engineers to direct workers may be one to one. In the latter it may be one to one thousand.

In the earliest stages of your venture you will not be troubled with the need to strike this balance. Everyone on the team will be innovating, setting up their areas of functional responsibility, and trying to relate them to the needs of the company. Everyone is excited, working hard, and highly motivated. It is precisely this atmosphere of heady involvement, in fact, which permits you to attract still more first-class people. The excitement, involvement, and creativity substitute for the security of the larger employer.

However, as the orders begin to come in, as delivery pressure mounts, and as day-to-day operating problems begin to replace the yeasty excitement of a year ago, you will begin to confront the first real challenge: to maintain an atmosphere of creativity without overdoing it. Your methods for accomplishing this will of necessity change as the company expands in size and changes in character. In general, the larger you get, the harder the task will become.

In a creative environment, ideas are sincerely elicited, evaluated impartially, and implemented as warranted, in order to be proven. There is an openness of communication, a minimum of perceptible hierarchy, and a willingness to suspend judgment of the ideas of others until they are fully explained and understood. There is a sharing of power among staff and a willingness to become involved in problem-solving that, strictly speaking, falls outside one's range of immediate responsibility. There is recognition and perhaps tangible reward for the inventor (who thought up the idea) and the innovator (who implemented it).

At the opposite end of the spectrum, the noncreative environment is often characterized by authoritarian innovation from the top down, by an attitude among subordinates that says "I don't get paid to think about that," by defensive tactics, by not-invented-here attitudes, and by contests to see who can shoot down a co-worker's idea first (perhaps in retaliation for the shooting down of one's own pet idea). There is little effort to elicit ideas and little recognition for even those whose ideas are implemented. Efforts to elicit ideas on a single problem in this environment are likely to be regarded as being manipulative. Surprisingly, this kind of politicized atmosphere can set in quite early in certain young firms, particularly those with strong, autocratic founders.

We will not provide here a long check list of all the things you can do to maintain a climate of creativity in your firm. The context and personalities dictate almost entirely what will work in a given organization. For hourly people, you may wish to try a suggestion system with cash awards. For professional personnel, try leaving your door open to everybody. Try brain-storming sessions for specific problems (such as new product definition). When someone's idea is implemented, make sure everybody knows about it. Spread some praise around. Keep criticism for lost sales, missed delivery dates, etc., to a low level—attack your problems, not your people. Try to keep creativity focused on real problems and on solutions that are affordable and can realistically be implemented.

The overcreative environment is occasionally found in technology companies—especially those trying to make a transition from consulting or R&D to products. There is positive competition to see who can be the most "creative"; and an emphasis upon generation of myriads of clever ideas, rather than evaluation and practical implementation, makes it impossible for anyone to focus on any common objective. The resources of the company become dissipated in the pursuit of too many ideas and, as a consequence, none gets carried to complete fruition.

SMALL BUSINESS TYPES WE CAN DO WITHOUT

THE DEAD FOUNDER: This person made quite a contribution a few years ago as co-founder, fund-raiser, and general go-getter. However, a set routine and the security of a steady paycheck seem to have robbed this person of the vitality and push needed in his or her area. This founder now seems more interested in boats or roses than in the company. Subordinates must work around the dead founder to get anything done.

THE EMPIRE BUILDER: Was hired as an expert on some problem area (such as quality control), but tends to see his or her function as the central *raison d'être* for the company. Constantly jockeying for more staff, newer equipment, and enlarged sphere of power. Writes flood of memos depicting the shortcomings of other departments and underscoring preeminence of his or her own.

DRAGON PERSON: Often a legacy from the past, found in some accounting or administrative capacity. His or her efforts to collect receivables and to approve expense accounts and police budgets seldom fail to patronize and offend customers and coworkers alike. Frequently invokes the old startup days when he or she formed a real team with the boss.

THE SALES EAGLE: Came recommended as the top sales executive in the industry. Commands highest salary and incentive package in the firm (including yours). Never fails to speculate on how far he or she would be now with Colossus Computers, if only he or she had stayed there. No shortage of complaints about lack of staff, budget, company's high prices, cheap-looking literature, etc., all of which are used to explain why the sales forecast is consistently missed.

THE TECHNICAL WUNDERKIND: Conceptual genius hired to beef up the original engineering department. Misses no opportunity to show up the incompetence of whoever designed the original product. Frequently throws up hands in despair, refuses to go on with the old design, insisting that a clean new design is the only answer. New design materializes, generally one year late, over budget, and with the most meager of documentation. Old design still selling well and carrying the company. Old engineers now work for competition.

THE GOOD HARDNOSED BUSINESSPERSON: When things aren't going well, the normal instinct of investors and directors is to sideline the founder and send in the "good hardnosed businessperson," someone of "mature judgment" and "sound principles" (and generally someone who knows absolutely nothing about your business). You will be appointed Vice Chairman. The newcomer will join up and within about three days will have cut out the dead wood (i.e., your best young people from engineering and the sales staff). This person will then impose daily budget review meetings to get costs under control, raise all prices 20 percent to the delight of your competition, and double the service contract fee, to the dismay of your customers. The product will be cheapened up, sales commissions will be reduced, and the ad budget eliminated. If the company survives, it may be due only to the hardnosed business person's predictably early departure.

CONVENTIONAL WISDOM: The new firm needs all the creativity it can get. The more the better.

REALITY: As with any resource, there is an appropriate level of creativity for every firm.

REFERENCES

1. Carlin, G. S. *How to Motivate and Persuade People.* West Nyack, N.Y.: Parker Publishing Co., 1964.

   Practical, usable ideas on the entrepreneur's number one problem: motivating and persuading employees, customers, suppliers, and financial backers.

2. Bartlett, Joseph W. *Venture Capital Law, Business Strategies and Investment Planning.* New York: John Wiley & Sons, 1988.

   See Section 11,"Key Employee Compensation."

3. Taylor, Jack W. *How to Select and Develop Leaders.* New York: McGraw-Hill Co., 1962.

   A fairly good, pragmatic guide to identifying and developing leadership and other talents among your associates and employees.

4. Exton, William, Jr. *Motivational Leverage—A New Approach to Managing People.* West Nyack, N.Y.: Parker Publishing Co., 1975.

   Lots of things besides money motivate your people. Find out what.

17

Acquiring and Divesting People

"Hell is—other people!" ... *Jean Paul Sartre*

A considerable amount of your personal energies during the first several quarters of operation will be consumed by the establishment and implementation of policies and practices for dealing with personnel. Acquiring and divesting people can be considered among the most highly entrepreneurial of your tasks. To the extent that it is done reasonably well, every other task in the new enterprise will be just that much easier to do. This chapter focuses on some practical considerations to help you do the job well.

COMPENSATION PACKAGES

Beyond the privilege of working in your exciting, creative environment, your prospective employee will be looking for a few other things, including salary, vacation, holidays, sick leave, insurance, stock purchase plans, profit sharing, commissions, bonuses, and perhaps education payment. A few words may be in order on each.

Salary

In offering a salary, do not attempt to induce employees to accept a salary lower than their market worth by relying on the glamour of the new enter-prise or stressing the vague future stock benefits. Pay them their full market worth, then use the other intangibles, like stock, to get twice the effort from them for the money. It's O.K. for the founding group to operate on partial salaries for a while to conserve cash or enhance operating profits, but it's totally unrealistic to expect first-rate people to come on board as employees for less than their worth. Various state human resource surveys, as well as personnel managers of other firms, can give you guidance in setting salaries, if you're in doubt. A search firm, if you use one, can also provide some guidance.

Vacation, sick leave, holidays

Your vacation policy will probably be dictated for you by the practices of the region you're in. At the outset, forget about plans that increase the vacation time as tenure reaches ten, then twenty years. Your principal decision in this regard will be whether to have a two-week plant shutdown each year or whether to permit staggered or partial vacations for your people. Holidays and sick leave policies will also be dictated to a large degree by the practices of the area in which you're located.

Insurance

The immediate need is for some form of group medical coverage, just as soon as you qualify. It is much better to start at least a modest plan with high deductibles and minimal benefits than risk having anybody wiped out finan-cially by medical costs. Start out with the company paying only a fraction of the cost, then build up this fraction (with suitable fanfare) as the company grows. Many medical packages can be supplemented with a small amount of life insurance (say, one year's salary). Such term life insurance is rather inex-pensive and should be considered, since many of your nonprofessional people will have no other personal life insurance.

It may be that your group is too small to qualify for attractive rates of group insurance plans. If this is the case, you may be able to find trade associations, professional societies, local business associations, or even pooled-insurance groups who, by offering coverage to all their members, can themselves qualify for group rates from the insurer. However obtained, this coverage is the most fundamental obligation of the employer, and should be implemented as promptly as circumstances permit.

Stock Plans

Where small companies are concerned, everybody wants a piece of the action. Since the subject is going to come up virtually every time you interview somebody for a professional job, it is desirable to have the policy for non-founder stock purchase worked out and committed to writing in advance of recruiting. Stock purchase and stock option plans abound, but they have only one purpose: to motivate *those within the company*. They act as an incentive to those who are working to earn them; they act as a double incentive to those who already have them. Your attorney will be able to review for you the several types of stock option plans, together with their business benefits and tax characteristics.

Try to design a plan sufficiently flexible so that you will not have to abandon it in the first exceptional situation. Make sure that each new employee "earns" his or her way in—include stock as part of an initial offer, but be sure this stock "vests" over three to five years.

In negotiating a job offer, be concrete on the subject of stock. Don't make vague promises that you would be unwilling to put in writing, and be certain that stock purchase privileges are related to performance in an agreed-upon way.

Profit Sharing Plan

Forget it. It will be a long time before there are any profits to share. It will be longer yet before there is excess cash to pay out on a plan. Therefore, its existence will only create disappointed employees. One exception is the "401-K" plan, still available at the time of this writing. Such plans permit tax-deferred saving by employees, optionally matched by employer.

Bonuses and Commissions

Bonuses may be among the best managerial tools available to the small-company president. The bonus may be cash or merchandise (which should, nonetheless, be declared as income by its recipient). It should be offered to motivate accomplishment of a specific task outside the employee's normal job expectations: for example, getting twenty new dealers recruited by June 1, solving the electrical interface problem in the system, reducing accounts receivable from eighty to forty days. Avoid getting trapped by paying a Christmas or year-end bonus to all employees. Today's privilege has a way of becoming tomorrow's birthright. Concentrate on task-specific achievements.

The awarding of a bonus should be accompanied by recognition and fanfare as an example to all.

Commissions are the classical way to motivate performance among salespeople and of keeping your costs variable. The smaller company should have high commission rates with the lowest tolerable salary structure.

Finally, a suggestion system, together with cash bonuses related to the savings from the suggestion, can be an excellent way to maintain morale in the operating departments, while taking advantage of peoples' inherent creativity. Even the sweeper probably has some idea that could save you plenty.

Education Payments

In a new company, especially a technology venture, some of your employees will be disposed toward continuing their education in work-related fields. Even small companies find that the cost of partial or complete tuition reimbursement is often justified as a recruiting incentive and as a way of upgrading the abilities of people on the job. In some geographic areas it may, in fact, be a virtual competitive necessity. Most firms insist that courses be job-related and some tie the amount of reimbursement to grade received.

Other Benefits

You may find that certain other employee benefits may be very popular without adding much actual cost. These include vested savings plans, credit unions, sports, parties, luncheon facilities, etc. It is very easy to go overboard in this department—especially when you, the boss, are expected to show up for the bowling tournament. However, don't underestimate the importance of these things to your people, especially among the non-professionals of the company. In this area, it is often best for everyone if the initiatives come from the employees themselves.

One area in which you can compete with large local firms very favorably is in the area of work hours. Increasingly, people want to control their work schedules, and you may be able to accommodate this desire at little or no cost. You should consider the following:

1. *Four-Day Week.* Typically, this involves a ten-hour workday, with half the firm getting off Fridays and half Mondays. And, if some employees prefer the 5-day week, you can readily accommodate them, too. Some firms use this in the summer only.

2. *Flextime.* Flextime was pioneered in Europe. It permits employees to set their own starting and quitting times, provided they are present during a five-hour "core period." This is especially popular among those with long commutes.

3. *Parents' Hours.* Consider a short day, say five hours, permitting employees to leave home after the children have left for school and to arrive home before they do. This is also a help for one-car families, as it permits one spouse to drive the other to and from work.

4. *Employ Retired People.* One of the best sources of talent and experience in any community is retired people. A retired inspector, draftsman, toolmaker, bookkeeper, or other skilled person can work a few hours per week and contribute a great deal to the growing firm and at very modest cost.

RECRUITING

Now you have it all together: a hot company, a creative working environment, and a well-thought-out compensation package. Now, how do you find a prospective employee?

Your tactics in finding good prospects will, of course, depend upon the job to be filled. However, try to exercise the lowest-cost sources first, as recruitment can be very expensive. The following are places you can advertise for employees, in order of ascending cost:

1. *School placement bureaus.* Colleges, technical institutes, secretarial schools, and vocational high schools all maintain offices both for the placement of new graduates and for alumni changing jobs. If you're looking for technicians, don't overlook community or government-sponsored training and retraining programs.

2. *Signs.* A conspicuous sign on your plant for nonprofessional help may net you some candidates, and it is an indication of company growth to outsiders.

3. *Professional Societies.* A low-cost notice in the society journal, newslet
ter, or bulletin board at the Annual Convention can net you many prom
ising resumes.

4. *Government employment agencies.* State governments offer placemen
services for both professional and nonprofessional people, at no cost t
users.

5. *Firms known to be laying off.* The placement directors of such firms wil
be glad to hear from you although, of course, you must realize that the
best employees are not the first to be let go. This nonetheless can be
good source of leads.

6. *Newspaper advertising.* This is not inexpensive, especially when pur
sued in national publications such as the *Wall Street Journal* and *Electronic News.* However, it can be quite effective since the newspaper i
the first place a person looking around will inquire—it costs nothing i
effort or commitment to look at the paper. Even if the reader is stil
employed, your ad may just spark the desire to make a change. You need
not be splashy with your ad, but it should be large enough to convey
reasonable amount of information and the impression of substance.

7. *Personnel agencies.* Private agencies vary in quality from lousy to excel
lent. They also vary in the types of personnel they are effective i
recruiting. One way in which they are alike, however, is expense. None
is cheap. For a secretary, the fee might be two weeks' salary; for a
engineer or a manager, it could be one to two months' salary. As soon a
you run an advertisement in the papers, you may be beseiged by agen
cies who have "just the one for the job." Your best strategy is to keep
them at bay until you're sure the other sources are not going to come
through for you. Then, do some inquiring and visit the agencies. Some
will engage in limited search on your behalf—others will just fire off
resumes of everybody in their files. Instead of a mechanical engineer,
you may end up reading the resume of a locomotive engineer!

8. *Personnel search agencies.* Now you're talking about real money. The
professional headhunters usually don't operate on a results basis—they
generally want a retainer fee, drawn against a commission of 25 to 30
percent of one year's salary. They are normally employed by larger
companies for filling the higher management posts. The headhunter
tries to find the top three or four professionals in the field, then ap
proaches them discreetly in behalf of his unnamed client. This probably
is not a recruitment channel available or appropriate to most new ven
tures, except for the most senior jobs.

INTERVIEWING

Once you've lavished money, energy, and calendar time in trying to find suitable candidates, it's a pity to blow it all in the interview. Yet this is precisely what happens in an unnecessarily large number of cases. The prospect gets rejected for the wrong reasons, hired for the wrong reasons, or gets an offer that is not accepted.

Employment interviewing is a subject about which a good deal is known. A couple of better references on the subject are listed at the end of this chapter. It is probably well worth your while as a company president to spend a long evening reading some of this material and developing a more or less formal interview strategy. By so doing, you'll learn a lot more about the candidate, you'll avoid missing any critical areas, and you'll do a much better job of selling your company to the person you want.

THE NEW EMPLOYEE

In addition to the normal procedural details of signing up for health plans, withholding, and so forth, your new employee should be asked to sign an Invention Disclosure Agreement. If this is not among the first things he or she signs coming on board, you will have great difficulty in getting the employee to sign it later especially if this person has been in your firm's R&D function and has made some valuable discovery! One of the first actions of the startup company president should be to work with the attorney and develop a suitable agreement of this type for all appropriate employees. To delay it is to invite downstream problems.

Although few new companies have a formal training program of any sort, there should be a single individual responsible for the training of each new recruit, and you should commit to writing the exact steps to be taken in integrating the new employee into the organization. For a production person, this might include familiarization with company rules, policy, production methods, workmanship standards, and related information. For a new controller, it would perhaps include exposure to the operating business plan, familiarization with the existing accounting system and financial history of the company, and orientation with regard to major customers and vendors.

In small companies, it is often difficult to write satisfactory job descriptions, because people tend, after a while in the firm, to structure the job to suit themselves. One of the strengths of the small business environment is, in

fact, the ability to accommodate itself to the skills and interests of the individ
ual employees to a degree not often possible in the large firm. Nonetheless, i
is very necessary that the president be sure that a job description is in fac
written for *every* position to be filled. This description, in addition to describ
ing the job to be done immediately, should describe the directions of growth,
and responsibilities and functions that might be added to the job. It shoulc
specify the minimum, desired, and optimal qualifications that a successfu
candidate would have. Although it may need modification in the future, sucl
a description is absolutely necessary for several reasons. It helps managemen
decide if an employee is needed at all (a question that sometimes doesn't ever
get asked!), how to budget for the job, how to advertise the position, and how
to communicate the job to the candidate. It also helps to establish the performance criteria for the new employee.

DIVESTING PEOPLE

One of the least pleasant duties of the entrepreneur is getting rid of people
who (a) haven't performed as expected, or (b) must be jettisoned in a company
cutback. Most entrepreneurs encounter the first case fairly often and the
second at least once in the first two to four years of operation. These two cases
are sufficiently different to warrant some individual comment.

The Low Performer

Most entrepreneurs seem to put off the inevitable long past the point where it
is obvious that a particular employee is not going to hack it. There may be
pressure to give the person "just one more chance." There may be extenuat-
ing circumstances that could "explain" his or her lack of performance. There
may be some areas in which this employee is doing a good job and, with some
more help, may improve. Forget it. You're only kidding yourself. You are
telling yourself that you're being humane, being fair. However, in reality, you
know this person isn't going to make it. So you're only sparing yourself the
discomfort of acting.

    When you do act, it should be decisive and clean. Repeated warnings,
probationary periods, and so forth probably just prolong the agony. If a visibly
low performer stays around, you damage the morale of the entire team, and
worse, handicap the functional area for which this employee is responsible.
Give the person notice (usually two weeks), but tell him or her to use the two
weeks to look for another job. (You do not want a person who's been fired
around the plant or office for two weeks).

In your termination interview, try to be fair. Tell the employee why he or she is being terminated. Spare the soft soap (e.g., "You're just overqualified for our job."). Help this person to understand where things went wrong, so he or she can find a more appropriate opening or operational method in the future. The terminated employee won't be grateful, but at least won't spend the rest of his or her life wondering why this happened. To help ease the transition, you should make sure that medical insurance is extended to cover his or her interval of unemployment. You should steer this person toward state agencies for personnel placement, unemployment insurance, and other benefits to which he or she may be entitled. You may be able to suggest companies that you know are hiring, or job training programs that can improve his or her areas of weakness. In short, by helping to make the best of this exemployee's opportunities, you are doing the person a much bigger favor than you would by keeping him or her on for a few more months.

The Cutback

This situation is much worse than the low performer. The company has hit some rough sailing—maybe a business recession. Now you are obliged to terminate not only some marginal people, but also some people who have been doing a good job. And you may be putting them on the street at the very time that other firms are also laying off, as, for example, during a recession. This is the sort of thing ulcers are made of.

Just deciding who's going to be thrown out of the boat to lighten the load is a difficult process. You should probably not even discuss it with your partners in the office, since rumors have a way of starting (particularly when business conditions have everyone apprehensive anyway) and then undermine morale and performance, thereby worsening a bad situation. Your main job is to make the cuts without demolishing the morale of the remaining troops. This is a challenge, to say the least.

While emerging business conditions may make this impossible, you should strive to make your total cut at once, as opposed to a few every Friday. The effect will be stunning, but will challenge those remaining to close ranks and try to get the job done without the people who have gone. In the other case, everyone will be wondering all week who's going to be the next to go. Your less effective people will start digging in and mounting defensive tactics. Your better people will start looking around, and some of them may find other jobs and leave. The net result is that the initiative is taken away from you, the morale of the team is undermined, and the best people leave or wish they could. Make your bloodletting as clean, brief, and complete as possible.

You can take the same steps to assist the victims as you did for the low performer. In addition, you may wish to call up the personnel directors of other employers in the area and let them know who is available. If the cutbacks are largely regional, you may be able to make contact with firms in other areas, too. If the cutback is the result of a severe recession, there may be special agencies established for counseling job seekers, to which you can refer the terminated employees.

In all, this is not a happy experience for entrepreneurs. The fact that almost everybody has to face it sooner or later may be some consolation.

A NOTE ON THE PERSONNEL FUNCTION

In the small company the function of personnel management tends to be an orphan for quite a while. Just the management of employee records, withholding statements, pre-employment medical exams, coordination of health insurance claims, etc., can be a substantial burden. If you're very lucky, you may find a secretary or accounting clerk whose inclinations tend in this direction. If so, give him or her the job, and fill in with other work. The person who handles time sheets and payroll may be a good choice for the responsibility. This will prevent wide dispersion of salary or other personal data. Just be sure somebody is responsible for the whole job.

Fairly early in your growth, you should develop a personnel manual dealing with every phase of employment, including rules, policies, benefits, patent policy, etc. The easiest way to do a good job on this is to get somebody else's and edit it to suit your needs.

Before long, however, it is likely that the growth of your firm will dictate the hiring of a personnel manager (or "human resources manager"). The workload and the need for professionalization of this function will dictate that a quality person be brought in. Soon, too, your board should form a compensation committee, which includes the CEO. This committee reviews overall compensation policy, usually approves specific salaries and benefits for all officers (president and vice presidents), and all stock or option awards. Having such a committee takes a lot of pressure off you. Also, the establishment and administration of bonus plans is generally left to the committee.

CONVENTIONAL WISDOM: Small companies have limited resources, so people expect to earn a little less.

REALITY: Small companies have limited resources (and benefits) so people expect to earn a little more.

REFERENCES

1. Black, J. M. *How to Get Results from Interviewing*. New York: McGraw-Hill Co., 1970.

    A very practical guide to planning interview strategy. Covers specific cases such as hiring, promotion, discipline, and exit.

2. Hariton, Theodore. *Interview! The Executive's Guide to Selecting the Right Personnel*. New York: Hastings House Publishing Co., 1970.

    An excellent guide to hiring interviews. Very practical, incorporating suggested forms and interview formats. Must reading.

3. O'Neal, F. H. *Expulsion or Oppression of Business Associates—"Squeeze-outs" in Small Enterprises*. Durham, N.C.: Duke University, 1961.

    One of the few books on a delicate topic: how to be a successful squeezer or avoid being a squeezee.

IV
MARKETING

18

Selling

"Nothing happens until you get a purchase order."
—Anonymous

Selling is the central activity of the business enterprise. If you have this ability, you will always be able to find a useful product to sell; if you have only the ability to engineer or produce products, you may be a bankruptcy looking for some place to happen. The value of selling is often driven home to manufacturers in a dismaying but forceful way: the firm selling its output through an independent sales organization (for example, Sears, Roebuck or Radio Shack) usually at some point realizes that the selling organization is making much higher gross margins and net profits than the manufacturer. Is this unfair, or merely the marketplace placing a proper valuation on the function of selling?

MARKETING VERSUS SELLING

Many people use the word *marketing* when in fact what they mean is *selling*. Selling is in fact a subset of marketing. The other functions of the marketing department include all of those activities that make it possible to get a sale.

These include market research, product specification, product management, pricing policy, literature preparation, advertising, publicity, packaging, product roll-out, product services and support, user training, training of customer service personnel, establishment of OEM sales arrangements, analysis of competition, and selection of sales channels. All of this is necessary and usually must be in place before the sales department can go out to ask for the order.

IMAGE VERSUS REALITY

In the very earliest phases of company growth, there will be a great divergence between the image you wish to project to the market and the actual substance to back it up. It is doubly important at this phase that your actions, statements, literature, and advertising do not bespeak an amateur, unprofessional, or fly-by-night operation. We have addressed this issue in Chapter 5 with regard to the preparation of initial literature. However, it applies to other phases of your selling efforts as well.

Most of your customers and prospective customers will never see more of your company than your salesforce, advertisements, documentation, and products. Most will not see your plant, your beautiful lobby and conference room, your spiffy shop, etc. This is fortunate. Remember, although the plant may be a source of great pride to you, it still looks pretty small-time to a visitor from IBM considering your product. Be sure that the things that customers *do* see are not small-time. You want them to have the impression of a solid, growing company that is going to be around to back up its products, to supply their future needs, to be a source of pride, if your product is included in his. Remember that the buyers feel their necks are out a mile if they are purchasing from you, rather than from your much larger competitor. Poor literature, clumsy presentation, improvised product documentation, etc., only add to their inherent sense of unease. Do these things *right* even if it costs a few dollars. They are as much a part of your product as the hardware itself.

LITERATURE: Be sure that it looks at least as good as your best competitors'. List a variety of models, options, and accessories, even if they aren't exactly ready for delivery yet.

Find a designer to work with you, by looking at other firms' good literature and finding out who does it.

Stress user benefits, not specifications. Stress only the specifications that matter, that set you apart from the competition. Use only first-rate photogra-

phy and be sure your diagrams and art say "professional." Use cutaway drawings to show unique function and consider cartoons to illustrate user benefits.
Remember, color sells. Design your brochure with an integral, tear-off return
card. Don't forget your phone number and leave room for dealers or reps to
add their sticker. Finally, an "800" phone number is often a help in eliciting
responses and can be obtained very inexpensively via answering services.

In addition to product literature, one of the things a small firm can do
better than anyone is to write the bible for the industry. This can be anywhere
from four to one hundred pages long, and could describe the technology, the
applications, the economics, the benefits, the alternative ways of using the
product, the accessories, and the whole unabridged story. The Digital Equipment Corporation Logic Handbook was for many years the chief exemplar of
this type of sales aid. Once it exists, the bible can be the subject of press
releases, free giveaway offers, trade-show handouts, and training aid for
schools and seminars. Consider, where would Christianity be without *its*
main "sales tool"—the Bible?

PRICING AND PRICE LISTS: Try to stay within the conventions of
the industry, at least initially. You should use the same methods of discount-
ing, commercial terms, and so forth, that your customer is accustomed to.
Don't try to innovate initially.

ADVERTISING: If you can't justify the cost of competing at a respect-
able level with your competitors, consider dropping magazine advertising
altogether. Or use the occasional big ad with less frequency, hitting the
annual buyer's guide issues and other big yearly publications. Try some innovation instead. Use some direct mailings, telemarketing, recorded cassette
pitches, demonstration van, etc. Think of ways to make yourself appear more
innovative than your competitor.

PROMOTION: This is the area in which you can shine at reasonable cost.
Create monthly press releases on new products, new developments, new
building, new contracts, new overseas agents, etc. Write articles for the trade
press and the popular press. Present papers at the society meetings. Hold
application seminars at strategic locations around the country and invite the
press as well as customers. You can come off looking much better than a less
ambitious competitor.

PRODUCT DOCUMENTATION: Be sure that your operation manu-
als, instruction sheets, maintenance manuals, etc., are up to the standards of
the industry. Nothing makes an expensive, engineered product look sillier

than sending a blueprint of a circuit diagram instead of a professional-looking manual. This documentation is part of your product. Treat it accordingly.

ADVERTISING AGENCIES

It is probable that at the outset at least you do not need a regular ad agency. What you *do* need is, ideally, a part-time artist and layout person who has worked for an agency. You need good advice and good art in designing letterheads, logo, literature, and perhaps occasional ads. The artist can also be helpful in the design of trade show exhibits, visual aids for speeches, and so on. Find the right person for this role and you will save yourself thousands of dollars and untold aggravation.

As your company progresses and an advertising agency appears justified, do some shopping. Some will want to take over your whole marketing effort. Others will want to push for big, commissionable magazine ad budgets. Some will want to give you a whole funky new image. But you don't want any of this. What you want is a small, hard-working, cost-conscious, and practical agency that will do what you want at a price you can afford. And even then, you will want to keep some of the work with your part-time person—especially for the literature, which requires some continuity of appearance.

Your agency may also wish to handle your public relations and publicity. This is seldom a good idea, because of the fact that editors and reporters like to talk to the president. Moreover, product releases and stories written by you will be much easier to generate, cheaper, and better in quality. Just be sure it gets done.

PUBLIC RELATIONS AGENCIES

PR agencies, like ad agencies, are often ill-equipped to deal with the needs and the budget limitations of startup firms. Often your best bet is to find someone who has worked for a PR agency, but who now wishes to free-lance. Such a person can make a very valuable contribution, especially if personally acquainted with the key editors in your relevant trade presses. The freelancer can write and place your press releases, your product releases, and your business press stories. And, over time, this process can lay a groundwork of investor name recognition for the day when your firm goes public. The best arrangement is probably to pay the person on a per-task basis, guaranteeing at least one day per month.

RICING

The pricing of your product offers opportunity for many commonly-committed errors. Here are some of them:

1. Basing price on cost of manufacture, rather than on value to customer. Engineers are particularly prone to price new products on "cost-plus-overhead-plus-profit" formulas, neglecting the fact that the product may be worth far more to the user.
2. Basing price on present low overheads, rather than projecting into the future to see how the overheads will grow.
3. Failing to include allowance for warranty costs, future servicemen, design amortization, application engineering, cost of capital, dealer discounts, rep commissions, etc.
4. Assuming that, because you are the newest firm in the field, you must of necessity have the lowest prices to get established. Your product strategy might, on the contrary, be to build the Cadillac of the industry, leaving the larger volume sales to other competitors.
5. Failure even to estimate the demand elasticity for the product. How much *would* sales volume increase if prices were lowered 10 or 20 percent? Is your product unique enough to command a premium over others if you increase the price? Finally, what is your *maximum-profit* price, given the price-volume curve?
6. Failure to employ some version of "market skimming": starting off with a high price until demand is saturated, then lowering the price gradually. This way, in theory at least, each person gets a chance to pay his or her maximum price for the product.

High pricing has its perils for the new company, like any other prescriptive measure. For example, if your prices and profits are outrageously high, you may be inviting early competition that would not otherwise enter your market. Remember, too, that your latecomer competition will have little of the market research, product development, and lost-motion cost that you incurred, and will therefore be in a position to undercut your prices substantially.

This factor not withstanding, the burden of proof is definitely on the low, rather than the high, price in a new business venture. It's a lot easier to lower them if you err on the high side, than the other way around.

It is often possible for a young company to engage in some discreet price experimentation, without screwing up the whole sales effort. You can try different prices in different regions, for example. You can create some intermediate "models" to test price sensitivity and competitor reaction. You can offer short term discounts and other "shadow reductions," again with the goal of seeing what your price-volume curve really looks like.

CONTINUOUS MARKET RESEARCH

In Chapter 4, "Measuring the Need," we treated the development of a first-cut market research project which would have a specific result for fund-raising purposes. However, market research does not end there; it is a continuous process in which the president is subliminally engaged all the time. Observing the needs the company can fill and scanning the literature for new developments, pricing trends, competitor actions, availability of customer funding, analysis of customers or competitors are all ways in which the company president must be attuned to signals from the marketplace. In addition, the company may be engaged in a series of more or less continuous formal market analyses of products you are contemplating introducing. Scanning *all* the relevant periodicals, traveling to visit customers and work with salespersons, attending trade shows, professional meetings, seminars, etc., are the principal means of staying open to market intelligence. Do not permit your new sales manager to isolate you from contact with customers, salespersons, or reps. These are your communication lines with reality. Guard them jealously.

BUILDING A REP ORGANIZATION

Independent sales representatives are the marketing backbone of many industries. For present purposes, let us also include in this category agents, discount dealers, jobbers, distributors, value-added resellers, and others who sell your products without actually being on your payroll.

Unless reps are completely unsuitable or unavailable for your product, you will wish to consider using reps as your initial sales organization. The advantages and disadvantages of reps, as opposed to direct salespersons, are as follows:

ADVANTAGES:

1. Reps require no fixed cost. Reps get paid only when they make a sale. Dealers who stock your product pay in advance as a rule. Both effects greatly enhance the cash flow and minimize the capital requirements of the small company.
2. Reps have knowledge of territory and prospective customers.

3. Reps may have several reasons to visit a prospect (i.e., several product lines of interest). Thus their frequency of contact per customer may be higher than that of your own salesforce.

4. Reps may have special capabilities to offer you or your customer, such as installation and repair services, application engineering, stocking against special needs, etc.

5. They may be conducting their own advertising and promotion efforts and be willing to share in the costs of advertising your product in their territories.

6. Reps may offer supplies, services, and hardware that are complementary to yours.

7. You can build a rep organization fast. Direct sales organizations can take years and millions to get up to speed.

DISADVANTAGES:

1. Most reps have many lines but devote most of their energies to selling one or two established, bread-and-butter lines.

2. Reps may not push even a successful line too hard, for fear that the company may decide to replace them with a direct salesforce at lower total cost.

3. Many reps can function effectively only as finders, and require a great deal of factory personnel support actually to close a sale.

4. Reps are difficult to monitor, train, and motivate. The successful reps may lack the time, the unsuccessful ones the inclination, to work intensively with you in building up your market.

Despite the disadvantages, however, reps give the young company a running start on the market. They represent the only way that many small firms can even consider establishing national marketing in the first year of operation, so rejoice that they exist and make it your challenge to learn to use them well.

IDENTIFYING AND RECRUITING REPS

There are several more or less orthodox ways to identify possible reps. The first is through searching in trade directories. Although these are often out of date, due to frequent changes of line (and identity) among reps, directories can tell you what reps are in a given area, what types of lines they handle, what types of customers they service. You may be able to find the reps of your competitor or of a maker of complementary products. Identification can also proceed through associations of reps and dealers. These may be national (e.g., the Electronic Representatives Association) or local rep organizations. Chambers of commerce, at both city and state levels, often maintain lists of reps and agents as well. Also, if you can identify a friendly manufacturer of complementary products, you can simply call the manufacturer's sales manager and inquire whether he or she has a good rep in Dayton. This person may welcome the chance to pool data with you.

Recruitment normally begins with a phone call or a letter outlining your product, your company, and your prospects in the rep's territory. If the rep is not interested, he or she can often tell you who else to talk to. If the rep is, your next step is to pay an office visit. Ideally, this visit should include scheduling two or three actual sales calls to prospective customers in the territory. This gives you some opportunity to assess the rep's contacts and selling approach, while at the same time allowing the rep to calibrate the customers' interest in your product. Since you've gone to the trouble and expense of visiting this person, don't leave without making the direct sales calls. If he or she seems reluctant, this may tell you something too.

Before signing on a rep, you should both have some understanding as to the range of sales volume that you might realistically expect from the territory for the ensuing several quarters. The rep may be a much better judge of this than you are. You will also want a signed contract. These are normally quite informal; reps and other sales managers are a good source of samples. Finally, you should check this person out with his or her other principals as well as with some local customers.

SUCCEEDING WITH REPS

Recruiting a rep organization is one thing; making it a success is another. The initial blush of enthusiasm wanes quickly on both sides as the hard digging of actually building sales begins in earnest. You both are destined for a number of disappointments. You may think the rep personally flubbed the biggest contract you've gone after yet. He or she may seem to be always and forever requesting some nonstandard product modification, or unrealistic price concession. The *rep* may think *you're* an idiot because you wouldn't promise to deliver fast enough to get the order. He or she will probably consider your company unresponsive to market needs. In short, there are many more opportunities for the relationship to run awry than to run smoothly. The smart president will anticipate this and work hard to make the relationship work. Here are some things you can do:

1. Contact every rep once a week, by phone or in person, even if there's no pressing reason to do so. Ask what's going on and how you can help. Make the rep feel he or she is part of the company.

2. Supply plenty of qualified sales leads for the rep to follow. Don't oblige this person to go sit in the lobby and talk cold to purchasing managers (most reps won't anyway). This is one important function of your advertising/promotion program.

3. Offer all reps a decent sales manual. Don't force them to rely only on your data sheets and price lists. Include applications notes, competitive comparisons, glossy product photos, including "inside the box" shots. Give them sales arguments. List the possible objections and the counter-arguments. Give the reps a list of happy users for customer reference. Provide reprints of impressive journal articles. Give them transparencies, slides or VCR tapes. Include specimen proposals. Give the reps up-to-date competitive product comparisons and the latest information on the competitor companies. In short, give these people all the ammunition you can think of—they are out there in the trenches for you and they need it.

4. Try gimmicks to keep reps informed and keep their attention. A newsletter, describing new company developments, product of the month, Rep of the Month, territory sales volumes, etc., can be inexpensive and effective. Send them copies of all the press release packages you send out. Try sales contests, prizes, incentives, "this-month-only" discounts, or double commissions on specific products you want to push. Let them know you're alive. Remember, you're competing for their time with all their other principal companies.

5. Get someone out in the field to work with the reps. Be ready to jump on a plane when the call for help comes. Be prepared to close the first few orders yourself. Support the reps when they need support. Take an occasional swing through the boondocks and work with each rep. Get on a first-name basis with each of his or her sales people.

6. Follow up your sales leads. Keep your own lists, find out politely but firmly what's been done on each of them. Let the rep know you appreciate the follow-up, and are interested in the unsuccessful quotations as well as the hot ones.

7. Pay your commissions on time. Nothing throws cold water on a rep relationship faster than unpaid commissions. Some companies, when they get in a cash crunch, include commissions in the deferrable expense category. You could not make a bigger mistake. Loss of a key rep can cripple a company for many quarters. You'd be better off laying off a few plant personnel than risk the dissolution of your sales organization.

8. Have an annual sales meeting. Put on the dog a bit. Let the reps pay their transportation, while you pay hotels and meals. Let them meet all your people and see the plant. Have some sales sessions, some technical sessions, some gripe sessions. Work on specific problems individually. In short, let them become a part of your team—this, basically, is what a good rep *wants* to do.

9. Deliver on your product promises. Nothing gets the rep in hot water with a customer faster than late delivery, improper operation, balky warranty service, or other forms of bungling by the factory. A rep *must believe* that the product he or she sells is going to be the answer to a customer's prayers. If the rep believes anything less, your chances of getting sales are seriously compromised. If, as is often the case in a small company, the rep has a very souring experience with you, you may want to get rid of this person, even though he or she has not resigned and may not even be at fault. Once confidence has been damaged, it may not be possible to restore it.

   Remember, the rep needs the long-term goodwill of those big customers a whole lot more than he or she needs you. When the chips are down, the rep will be forced to side with the customers and find a better source for the product they want.

10. Avoid "house" accounts. Nothing is more demoralizing to reps, even if they initially agreed to it, than to see large shipments going into their territories without commission to them. Even if they understand it, they will never appreciate it—especially if it's a company they have to call on for other principals anyway. On your part, it may be tempting to exclude one fat customer you've already developed on your own, from the first rep that comes along. A reasonable compromise may be to offer the rep the house account as soon as his or her total volume from other customers passes an agreed-upon target, say $200,000. Then he or she has a great incentive, and you are not risking handing over a commission check each month to a do-nothing rep. Or, some would argue, you want ideally to give the rep enough volume at the outset to make your line one of his or her most important—another way to command a major portion of the rep's energies.

BEYOND REPS

It is commonly believed that the direct salesforce is always the best way to sell. Salaried salespeople, it is argued, are easier to control and motivate, have no conflicting loyalties, are able to spend full time on your product, and, when volume passes breakeven, are cheaper. These are persuasive arguments. However, there are many companies with the volume, cash flow, and profits to sustain direct sales forces who stay with reps exclusively, and there are many more who use a mixture of reps and salespeople. So the jury is still out on this question. Or, more accurately, there is a profit-maximizing mix in each case, depending upon the product, rep quality, market characteristics, and other variables. For this reason you should carefully assess the question of whether to replace all reps as soon as possible with a direct salesforce. It is just possible that that nice break-even volume may follow your old rep to your competitor's organization.

A realistic intermediate step is the establishment of regional offices, each a one-person operation initially, charged with coordinating sales and service for a specified territory. The regional managers can then work directly with your reps in the territory, recruit and train their own reps or, perhaps, handle some of the territory on a direct sales basis themselves. Through this route, your move toward national marketing is advanced one large step further without foreclosing any options. Finally, when and if the time comes for additional direct salespeople, you have the framework in existence for their deployment and supervision.

INTERNATIONAL MARKETING

Marketing and selling overseas is no longer optional—it is a virtual necessity for any successful high-growth company in the nineties.

Here are some of the reasons:

1. For most technology products, half the market is outside the U.S. If you don't seize it someone else will—and will next invade your turf.
2. At the time of this writing, the dollar is at an historic low against Japanese and European currencies, creating a tremendous price pull for U.S. products.
3. Trade barriers are definitely falling, although not as fast as many had hoped a decade ago. Barriers between the U.S. and Canada will shortly disappear altogether. One dark cloud: the fear that the new EEC will create a "fortress Europa" against U.S. and Asian imports.
4. The U.S. no longer has preeminence in many technologies. Therefore, the old strategy of selling the obsolete models overseas is dead.

5. The time lags between U.S. and foreign adoption have correspondingly disappeared. Today it is essential to roll out new products in several countries almost simultaneously.

No longer does the small company have the luxury of using cash flow from domestic sales to support the building of international marketing a few years later. The ever-shortening product cycle virtually dooms such a strategy.

Terrific. Now, in addition to getting the product to work, setting up your team, getting some U.S. customers, and finding money, you now have to worry about selling in six or eight additional countries, most of whom don't even speak English! However, before you reach for the black bottle, consider the following:

1. Everyone *wants* you to succeed in selling overseas and wants to help you. The U.S. Department of Commerce, state departments of commerce, the bank, the Exim bank, and innumerable other entities actively promote exports.

2. In many countries, the reps and distributors are far more competent and autonomous than their counterparts here. They are much more likely to be able to service the equipment they sell, write needed software, and provide needed accessories and peripheral devices. They are accustomed to functioning independently of their foreign suppliers. Often they have means of financing customer purchases as well.

3. Foreign reps often expect to pay cash for products up front and usually expect to buy demo equipment or a modest initial inventory.

4. In many countries the rep is well-connected politically and is quite sophisticated about how to get government business (don't even ask!).

5. Commercial attachés in U.S. embassies abroad have no other job than to promote U.S. product sales. They can help you to find and meet foreign dealers, reps, and resellers. They can steer you to major industrial and government buying points. They can provide intelligence on competitors, market size, growth rate, and many other subjects, all at very little cost.

6. Many young U.S. companies are finding that offshore corporations can be very effective partners, providing not only capital but also ready-made channels of distribution, local manufacture, and service and support at a level that no young company could afford. You should begin thinking right away about who the ideal corporate strategic partner in each of your markets would be, and develop a strategy for getting together.

7. If your venture capital group includes a foreign VC, exercise this person's contacts in the home market to get you together with potential strategic partners.

Naturally, all of this is a drain on management energy and money. Moreover, it takes a long time, so the time to start is now.

Chances are you will want to be the international marketing manager for the first year or so. This is the only way you will ever get a feel for the process, and hence understand what needs doing by your international marketing manager when you hire one. When you do hire one, this person should probably report to you—not to your U.S. Vice President of Sales and Marketing.

OUR JOB AS CHEERLEADER

As Napoleon Bonaparte observed, an army marches on its stomach. In precisely the same sense, a sales organization marches on its heart (or transverse colon, or whatever other organ is used to store enthusiasm and morale). *You*—nobody else—are the sparkplug to whom everyone is looking for the zeal, the confidence, and the incentive to get out of bed in the morning and face some hostile customers, traffic jams, a lobby full of competitors, and the various snarlups that enrich the salesperson's day.

You are a permanent cheerleader, morale officer, and chaplain rolled up in one.

You must be accessible to reps, salespeople, and regional managers. You must show them that *sales*—not engineering, not accounting, not manufacturing—comes first in your outfit.

You must be willing to put your hand in the fire occasionally to add conviction to your rhetoric. You're the one who has to whip up enthusiasm for the new product, the new lower prices, and the new demonstrator van. You're the one who has to head off delivery trouble, take over negotiations with problem customers, authorize special concessions to meet competition. Likewise, you are the one who must set the sales goals and enlist the commitment of all concerned with reaching those goals. You're the one responsible for seeing that the successful salesperson or rep receives more than a paycheck or a commission check—that he or she also receives recognition from everyone in your organization. Or, if warranted, a cordial kick in the tailfeathers. Salespeople are supposed to be self-starters, but it is neverthe less incumbent on you to be sure that the ignition key gets turned.

SELLING CAN BE LEARNED

Even the entrepreneur who is not a great natural salesperson can learn a good deal about the art of selling without long costly trial-and-error education Much is known about selling, since people have been doing it for so long Regardless of the market you serve, it is likely that there exists some sale: course, weekend workshop, or seminar related more or less directly to you situation. These may be run by colleges, by the SBA, by the America Marketing Association chapter, the local representatives' association, etc. It i not beneath your dignity to enroll in such a course or even to insist that you salespeople or partners do also. It is almost certain that you will gain some different perspective, insight, and usable ideas from the experience as well a get a chance to meet other salespeople with problems comparable to you own.

You can also learn a good deal by studying the marketing methods o companies that have been successful and by talking to their executives to gain some understanding of why they did what they did. The president of anothe growing firm, perhaps a stage or two ahead of your own, can be a good sounding board for marketing and other ideas.

CONVENTIONAL WISDOM: Sell, sell, sell.

REALITY: *Sell, sell, sell.*

REFERENCES

1. Hanan, Mark. *High-Tech Growth Strategies.* Englewood Cliffs, N.J.: Prentice Hall, 1983.

    Fast-paced and readable. Stresses market segmentation, targeting and prod- uct definition. Excellent implementation advice.
2. Haas, K. B., and Ernest, J. W. *Creative Salesmanship: Understanding Essen- tials.* Beverly Hills, California: The Glencoe Press, 1969.

    A practical, though academically respectable, treatment of the entire topic of selling. It gives a particularly good treatment of buyer psychology and closing techniques.
3. Kotler, Philip. *Marketing Management, Analysis and Control.* Englewood Cliffs, N.J.: Prentice Hall, 1967.

A very good basic marketing text covering each phase clearly and completely. Could be considered a reference work for the new president.

4. Valentine, Charles F. *The Arthur Young International Business Guide*. New York: John Wiley & Sons, 1988.

A clear and practical step-by-step program for small business exports. Good lists of state agencies and overseas contacts.

5. DeVoe, Merril. *How to Tailor Your Sales Organization to Your Markets*. Englewood Cliffs, N.J.: Prentice Hall, 1964.

Very pragmatic, how-to-do-it information on organizing, recruiting, and motivating a sales team. Very good.

6. Steinkamp, W. H. *How to Sell and Market Industrial Products*. Philadelphia: Chilton Book Co., 1970.

Similar in level and competence to #3, but focused on the industrial product.

7. Gissel, P. *Lauching the New Industrial Product*. New York: American Management Association, 1972.

Brief and very practical, although directed more toward the established firm. It will tell you how you should do it if you had the people, money, and established market momentum.

8. Krause, Wm. H. *How to Hire and Motivate Manufacturers' Representatives*. New York: AMACOM, 1976.

Written by a sales rep, this is the best practical resource I have seen on the subject.

19

The Customer

It is naught, it is naught, saith the buyer: but when he is gone his way, then he boasteth.   .. Proverbs 20:14

The customer is, by definition, someone who needs what you can supply. He or she is the only reason for the existence of your business. Your greatest challenge will be to identify this person and to analyze and satisfy his or her needs.

IDENTIFYING CUSTOMERS

Before your business plan was even put to bed, you had a list of prospective customers for your product. These were people whom you had surveyed, people known to be buying similar products, and people surmised to require your product. Now, however, you are in the marketplace, and have rung all those doorbells, and have closed a few sales. What now? To build up a dynamic list of prospective, qualified customers is a big job. To keep it current and keep the deadbeats off it is a bigger job yet. Among your tools will be the following:

1. *Leads from advertising.* Readers' service ("bingo") card replies are of low to average quality and require further qualification via return mail or phone contact with respondents. Direct letter replies and telephone contacts originating from advertising are among your best leads. Returns from direct mail campaigns are likely to be of higher quality, especially if the respondents must supply some data on their needs.

2. *Leads from trade shows.* These may be readily qualified on the spot by the employee who talked to the prospect. The prospect has also had the advantage, in most cases, of having seen the actual product at the show, further qualifying him or herself.

3. *Leads from trade directories.* If your product is bought mainly by hospitals with intensive care units, you can readily find most of your prospects in a directory. If it is bought by people who own sports cars, you probably can't. Between these extremes lie many classes of customers who can often be reached and qualified by mailings generated from lists extracted for trade directories.

4. *Personal knowledge of reps and employees.* This may be among your most valuable source for early prospects, because it has already been prescreened.

5. *Self-identification.* Some examples of this are the Commerce Business Daily, advertisements soliciting proposals, form letters sent to suppliers, and government solicitations from firms on bidders lists.

6. *Leads from data bases.* This is similar to the directory approach, but may permit greater pinpointing starting from a bigger sample. For example, the Dun & Bradstreet tapes might permit you to do a direct mailing to every firm performing ferrous casting operations, hiring over fifty employees, and located in the eastern half of the United States.

As your list of prospects grows, it can become a mailing list for direct mailing pieces, company announcements, newsletters, new literature, and price lists. Try to reach your list on a regular (say monthly) basis, just as you try to contact each rep weekly. Make it a habit to let your prospects hear from you. Be sure that the reps have all the names for their territory so they can follow through. Try to keep the list in two sections: the mass list and the "top hundred." Keep it current. Make its maintenance the special responsibility of one person in the company.

ANALYZING CUSTOMER NEEDS

In some business (such as ball bearings) the customers' requirements are rather straightforward (they need ball bearings). In other cases, however, it isn't so easy. In most capital equipment decisions, for example, there may be several equally feasible definitions of need. If a customer wishes, for example, to improve his or her accounting procedures, this person may "need" a computer, or a time-sharing service, or a bookkeeping service bureau, or an accounting machine, or maybe just a better accountant. If your firm sells computers, it is immediately incumbent upon you to determine whether your computer really *is* the way to solve this customer's problem. If you think it might be, then your problem is to convince the customer that he or she (a) needs a computer, and (b) needs *your* computer. In other words, you have three distinct chances to lose the sale. But note: the customer's need was for a solution. This person may have had some preconception of the way to solve it; however, if you honestly disagree with him or her, it is best to state your belief. If you sell the customer something that is mismatched in cost and capability to actual needs, he or she will not be grateful.

During the course of introducing your product and analyzing customer needs, you may detect a substantial misfit. You may be selling a high-performance unit for $5,000, when in fact the market keeps asking for a minimal unit in the $2,000 range. You may have developed a technically advanced electronic actuator, when most needs could be satisfied by an inexpensive pneumatic unit. Or, perhaps you're marketing a nicely packaged laboratory instrument which, if stripped, could be sold on volume OEM basis to builders of larger laboratory systems. The point is that regardless of how hard you tried to analyze the market before starting your sales effort, your analysis is probably, in the heat of battle, going to prove wrong in some respects. One of the great strengths of small companies is their ability to adapt and change direction quickly. Don't permit yourself to get locked into a losing situation by your business plan. The feedback from customers should be the principal consideration.

In analyzing the specific needs of prospective customers, try to remain sensitive also to their *other* needs as well. In selling chart recorders, for example, you may discover that there is a great need for chart paper that will not curl when humidity rises. This might be a profitable additional business opportunity for your firm if a suitable paper can be found and marketed through your organization. What else does this customer buy, anyway? If he or she buys typewriters, can you also offer adding machines? Desks? Dictating equipment? If the customer buys machine tools can you also sell this person cutters? Measuring machines? Gages? If he or she buys pressure transducers, can you offer a complete system with electronics? Your main cost in business for a long time is going to be that of reaching living, breathing customers. Make it your challenge to see how many of the needs of each one your firm can reasonably attempt to fill. Try not to freeze the definition of your business too early; the longer you can remain opportunistic, the better the chances you may uncover a much better opportunity than the one you set out to pursue.

ERVICING THE RELATIONSHIP

A major customer, even a difficult one, is a priceless asset. However, it is surprising how many entrepreneurs are prone to ignore their existing customers in the thrill of the chase after new ones. Yet, logically, the emphasis should be reversed. The existing customer requires much less effort and cost to sell additional volume; if you do a good job with this person, he or she will become your staunch advocate, enabling you to sell other firms more easily. Such a customer will provide the cash flow upon which your further marketing will be based. Therefore, be sure that you have exhausted every opportunity to satisfy this person, before turning your energies to the chase. This may mean the following:

1. Occasional personal contact, just to make sure everything's O.K. (and to find out what the competition is saying to your customer, what he or she thinks of your salesman and of your product).

2. Rapid field service when required. Follow-up procedures should be instituted to make sure the problem was actually solved. Don't take your technician's word for this.

3. Personal involvement in any negotiations involving substantial purchase quantities or deviation from normal specifications.

4. Occasional surveillance of the accounts receivable to make sure that petty items, such as spare parts or service bill-backs, are not creating irritation with the customer. Be prepared to bend (conspicuously) on these small matters.

5. Little remembrances. While Christmas gifts and the like are normally considered to be in poor taste and are actively discouraged by most major firms, there are exceptional circumstances. If you feel that a particular customer relationship would be enhanced by a gift in good taste and no rules dictate otherwise, it is probably O.K. Occasional entertain-

ment for the customer may be better, however, since it creates an atmosphere of personal rapport without the possible nuances of a gift.

As a final note on the value of customer relationships, try asking yourself these questions:

1. How much have we invested in direct negotiations, work hours, phone bills, travel, and face-to-face contact with this customer?
2. How many prospects did we have to sift before finding this customer? What did that cost us?
3. How much did we spend in advertising, promotion, and prospecting before we even came up with that list of prospects? How many months? How many work-hours?

If most firms performed this calculation honestly, they would be astounded at the amount of actual hard dollars they have invested in each customer relationship. Be sure that each relationship is secure and fully exploited before rushing forth to invest in further ones.

HANDLING PROBLEMS

No matter how hard you try, sooner or later you're going to foul up. When it comes, it may be a real beauty. Picture this: You are two months late in delivering a machine to your customer. You've heard three times this week from this company's attorneys, but at last the machine has gone out the door. Next, the truck gets re-routed to Los Angeles instead of Minneapolis. Two weeks and several pints of blood later, the unit is delivered. Then you get a call at midnight from their president, informing you that the unit delivered was metric, and they ordered English.

What do you do now? Well, the first thing to do is face the fact that *you*, not your regional manager, your chief engineer, or your sales manager, had better handle this. When everything goes haywire, the customer expects to hear from the president—not from a hired hand. Trying to delegate at this point will make things worse. Depending upon the value of the customer and the possibility of some retaliatory action on this company's part, you may be well advised to propose a meeting at their plant, as opposed to trying to solve the problem over the phone. This has two advantages:

1. Offering to get on a plane the next morning underscores the great concern on the part of your company. It reveals how *extraordinary* this

circumstance is (never mind that it also happened last week to somebody else).

2. The time it takes for the meeting to occur gives everybody a chance to cool down and consider realistic solutions. At this point, your skill as a negotiator will be put to the test. You must be willing to appear ready to make the situation right, even at substantial sacrifice to your firm. This proffered sacrifice may take the form of unbilled overtime to correct the problem; compensation for direct loss suffered by the customer; replacement or substitution of a loaner unit while the other is being corrected; offering other compensatory considerations, such as extended payment terms and discounts.

At this point, in reading the fine print on the back of your quotation form, you may discover some loophole or other that may seem to absolve you of liability for costs resulting from this problem. *Invoke the fine print at your own peril.* If the customer believes to have been slickered, you can forget about ever selling this person's company anything or using it as a reference again. Your safest tactic at this point is to ask the customer what *he or she* thinks is fair. This, in effect, places the burden of fairness upon the customer, and the demands may turn out to be unexpectedly reasonable.

In resolving problems of this sort, it is necessary to take the long view of the short-run concessions you may be considering. What did it cost us in dollars and calendar time to get this customer? What will it cost us to replace the company? What will be the volume and profitability of sales over the next couple of years if we keep it? You may be much better off to relinquish the profit on this particular sale (or to take a loss) than to lose the customer. This negotiation is also a good opportunity to further solidify the loyalty of your customer by your manifest integrity and desire to make the situation right.

THE PROBLEM CUSTOMER

Every company eventually acquires a few problem customers. It is often difficult to balance the benefits of their business against the time, aggravation, and petty costs of doing business with them. These customers may fall into the following classes:

1. The slow payers. Slow payment may be their business policy, and will likely be justified by a succession of "lost" invoices, product "deficiencies," etc. These customers may tell you that prior to the sale, they told your sales rep that they would pay when their customer pays them.

2. The specs changers. These customers either feel that their needs are so unique that they *must* have a special version of your product (at the price of the standard), or feels that, until delivery, they have the right to keep on making changes in the specifications at no cost.

3. The backroom lawyers. These people pride themselves on their night school law degrees, and miss no opportunity to show their skill in out flanking suppliers. They will find loopholes in your contract justifying eternal free service, exclusivity with their firm, product return privileges, and God knows what else.

4. The wheeler-dealers. These are the customers who let you know, none too subtly, that they have found another supplier willing to supply the same product as you for about 60% of your price. They will change suppliers for such marginal advantages that the changeover costs negate them, but they pride themselves on being tough negotiators. Anyway their bosses only hear about the savings they have made, not the costs of obtaining them.

These and other problem customers can absorb a very large portion of your time and energy in maintaining their business and heading off additional problems. When such customers have identified themselves, weigh realistically the benefits and costs of keeping them—then, if you must cut them off, have no compunction. It is simply impossible to work with certain types of firms, and your decision connotes no failure on your part.

It is especially easy for new firms to acquire problem customers for several reasons.

1. The customer may already have been rejected by all the established suppliers in the industry and see you as a new victim.

2. The new firm often has inadequate or nonexistent credit check procedures or other sources of market intelligence.

3. The salesperson for the new firm will feel great pressure or temptation to take on what is perhaps a visibly marginal account just to meet quota.

4. The new venture may seem like a softer touch to the problem customer than the bigger, older suppliers. When the heat is on, this customer will pay them first and let you wait.

The entrepreneur who intends to survive should be aware of these perils and be sure that some mechanism exists for a suitable degree of screening new prospective customers. It's much better for all concerned to request payment in advance "until credit is established," even at the risk of affronting a customer, than to spend the next two years trying to collect.

ENFORCING CONTRACTS

It often develops that a business contract undertaken in good faith by buyer and seller becomes inappropriate to the emerging situation. For example, a company may contract to purchase a thousand of your units, but discover that it can only use two hundred. Completing the contract may be very poor business for the company—in fact, it may put him out of business. Another firm may buy your equipment, only to discover that the job intended cannot be done on it—despite the fact that the specifications of your equipment were clearly stated in your quotation, and regardless of the fact that you do not warrant "fitness for purpose."

You have a contract. The question is, to what extent do you enforce it? This is a business decision, not a legal one. If you succeed in pushing your contractual demands down the customer's throat, you no longer have a customer. In fact, this company may become a very costly adversary in a court room. In selecting a route of action, you must again take the long view: what was the cost to obtain this customer? What is its future value to us? What will be the cost of enforcing our contract? What will be the *net* dollar gain on this contract from so doing? Will our willingness to negotiate simply be interpreted as softness, encouraging future transgressions? These are hard questions, but they should be asked *before* calling in the lawyers. A court action usually benefits nobody; it is, rather, evidence of failure and ineptitude on the part of both parties in solving their mutual probems to their better advantage. Above all, try to avoid involving your ego and emotions in a situation where, objectively speaking, you've been had. So doing merely diminishes the possibility of achieving any sort of rational decision and robs your energies from more creative enterprises.

CONVENTIONAL WISDOM: You can delegate responsibility for customer relations to your marketing department while you attend to more important matters.

REALITY: You isolate yourself from your customers and their problems at your peril. You don't have anything more important to do.

REFERENCES

1. Hanan, Mack. *Hi-Tech Growth Strategies.* Englewood Cliffs, N.J.: Prentice Hall, 1983.
        See especially Chapter 3, "Targeting Growth Customers," and Chapter 10, "Growing Key Customers." Sophisticated, practical ideas.

2. Bender, Paul S. *Design and Operation of Customer Service Systems*. New York: AMACOM, 1976.

This short book explores the entire spectrum of the company's relationship to its customers, covering not just product service but all forms of support, including the setting of internal standards. Excellent.

3. Gannon, Thomas A., ed. *Product Service Management*. New York: AMACOM, 1972.

Seven sections by various authors on organizing, delivering, training, and administering all phases of product services. Short and sweet.

4. Redding, Harold T., and Knight, G.H. III. *The Dun & Bradstreet Handbook of Credits and Collections*. New York: Crowell, 1974.

This highly indexed manual offers you or your controller extensive and useful advice on how and when to extend credit, where to look for credit information on your customer, and how to manage the collection process. The whole ballgame is lost if you can't collect your money, so here's how to do it!

20

Competitors and What to Do about Them

He that wrestles with us strengthens our nerves and sharpens our skill. Our antagonist is our helper.   . . . Edmund Burke

WHO IS A COMPETITOR?

Your very earliest efforts to assess the market for your proposed product included an initial look at the competition. Once you are in business, however, it will become apparent that your initial definition of competitor may have been rather narrow. Most entrepreneurs tend to think of the competitor as the firm which has very nearly the same product for the same markets as their own. However, some reflection will reveal that the term "competition" is in fact much harder to define.

Conceptually, the competition is any other entity which is competing for the same funds that you are competing for. This means that the cinema operator is not just competing with other cinemas in the area; the business is competing with all other entertainment media (such as sporting events and stage shows). The builder of hydraulic motors is not just in competition with other hydraulic motor firms—this builder is in competition with electric and

179

pneumatic motors, too. The vendor of consulting services is in competition not only with other consultants, but also with in-house experts within the client's firm. In determining what sales appeal will be most successful, you must first place yourself in your customer's shoes and imagine what the buyer's real alternatives are. Then, and only then, can you compile a convincing case contrasting your solution to the others.

COMPETITORS AS AN IDEA SOURCE

Enlightened imitation is among the surest roads to business success.

It is beneath the dignity of no businessperson to imitate, adapt, and improve upon the innovations of other companies. The incredible trajectory of the Japanese economy has been, until very recently, the result of intelligent adaptation and improvement of nonoriginal ideas. On the other hand, England, long a pioneer in the inventive technologies, has been far less successful in innovation and adaptation of existing ideas for commercial uses. The enormous advantage that the imitator has over the innovator is that the imitator does not have the development costs, the market testing, the unsuccessful false starts, and the tremendous lead times that plague the true innovator. Remember, the pioneer is the one who gets an arrow in the back.

None of which is to say that your imitation must be blatant or unimaginative. Skillful adaptation implies learning from the mistakes as well as from the successes of the innovator. Very often the second, third, or fourth imitator is the one who really rings the commercial bell after having the benefit of observing the mistakes and weaknesses of several other competitors. After all, IBM did not invent the computer, nor were they the first to market it. McDonald's did not invent the hamburger or the fast-food franchise.

When observing (where possible) some of the failures of your competitors, consider this important question: What products have they introduced with fanfare, but silently deleted from their last catalog? We all have our little Edsel, after all. Just be sure that your fantastic new design is not already somebody else's Edsel.

COMPETITORS AS A BASIS FOR COMPARISON

In addition to such obvious comparisons as price, specifications, and share-of-market, some other comparisons may prove instructive to the extent they can be made. They include these factors:

1. Gross margins
2. Overall profitability
3. Allocation of sales dollars to labor, material, R&D, advertising, etc.
4. Marketing setup, salesforce incentives, dealer policy
5. Areas of product development
6. Current market research in progress
7. Quantity and costs of material purchases
8. Current production and shipping rates
9. Identity of major customers
10. Pricing policies, formulas

Depending upon your situation, there may be a number of other things you ought to know about your competitor. This knowledge is almost essential for intelligent development of offensive strategy and defensive tactics. It is especially critical for the new enterprise for these reasons:

1. New ventures are very often established because of a market gap, an oversight, or a quirk in the competitive structure. If this is about to change without your knowledge, the game may already be over.
2. The established company, including competitors, can afford a few mistakes; one major mistake will probably kill the new venture. The easiest way to make a mistake is by misreading the competition both in terms of its plans and its probable reaction to your own planned actions.

INDING OUT ABOUT COMPETITORS

Short of calling in the CIA, there are ways in which one can learn as much as necessary about competitors. The following list is only suggestive; the imaginative entrepreneur will be able to come up with others as the occasion demands.

1. *Financial sources.* In addition to annual and interim reports, public companies must file various other classes of financial data and other information with government bodies. These include NYSE listing applications, SEC Forms 10-K and 10-Q, include offering circulars for new security issues, and, in some states, annual statements of condition. In addition, you can obtain Dun & Bradstreet or NCO reports. You can check with City Hall to find out whether financing statements have been

filed pledging collateral. You may also be able to unearth a financial analyst who has recently studied the company and can give you some insights without disclosing sensitive information.

2. *Former employees.* One can often learn a good deal about a firm from its former employees—especially disgruntled ones. Even present employees are often a good source of intelligence when, for example, they are interviewed in response to a job opening you have advertised.

3. *Dealers, reps, distributors.* These people are usually anxious to fill a sympathetic ear with their grievances against your competitor, whom they represent. You will learn about late deliveries, quality problems, design deficiencies, late commissions (cash problems), and field service problems to a degree that may astound you. Everybody has problems— even your smooth-looking competitor.

4. *Suppliers.* A classical example occurred a few years ago, wherein a firm making motors had always carefully guarded its volume data. Its competitor, however, discovered the source for one of the key purchased components in the motors, which *in turn* had one key purchased component. The level two vendor unconsciously gave away the monthly shipping volume of a customer's customer without ever having heard of the motor manufacturer. There are several ways to approach your competitor's supplier. The best way is as a potential customer. You'd like to see the shop; you'd like to see what sort of work they are doing for others in the industry; you'd like to get some idea of how much they could ship you when volume is required. In short, give the supplier as many opportunities as you can to tell you what a great job is being done for your competitor.

5. *Professional meetings.* Pay attention to what the competitor's scientists are saying about their work. Their president might be quite chagrined at the amount of competitive information being disclosed in the name of scientific progress. Observe also what they are writing in the professional journals.

6. *Other companies' salespeople.* While competitor A's salespeople will probably be quite close-mouthed about their company's activities, they may be quite effusive (and knowledgeable) about the activities of your mutual competitor B. What-are-those-bastards-up-to-now is a favorite game played in hotel bars across the nation every night. Likewise, the salespeople for their suppliers can be a source of some occasional insight.

7. *Unethical sources.* While there is in reality a continuum of "ethicalness" from pure white to pure black, most of us think we know about where the line is. Methods such as the Watergate plumbing, espionage tech

niques, bribery, employee "plants," etc., are not unknown in business. Clearly, these methods raise a host of ethical questions. Ethical questions aside, however, such questionable methods seldom justify the cost of possible exposure and are likely to backfire. Once your own integrity is called into question, there is no real way to repair the damage. Richard Eells and Peter Nehemkis offer the following guide to where the line falls (please see their book listing under *References* at the end of this chapter):

LEGITIMATE METHODS:

1. Published materials and public documents, e.g., court records and government reports.
2. Disclosure made by employees or obtained without subterfuge
3. Market surveys and consultants' reports
4. Financial reports and securities analysts' research surveys of individual companies, annual company reports, and interviews and speeches by corporate executives
5. Trade fairs, exhibits, and competitors' brochures
6. Analyses of competitors' products (i.e., reverse engineering), comparison shopping, and special consultants' reports
7. Reports by salesmen and purchasing agents

DUBIOUS OR CRIMINAL METHODS:

1. Employment interviews with individuals who worked for a competitor (during which the discussion touches on the competitor's know-how, manufacturing costs, and other proprietary information)
2. Camouflaged questioning and "drawing out" of competitors' employees at technical meetings
3. Direct observation of a device or piece of equipment clandestinely (usually involving surreptitious photography)
4. False job interviews with a competitor's employee (i.e., when there is no real intention to hire)
5. Breach of confidentiality in negotiations for a licensing agreement (in which access to a trade secret is acquired and pirated)
6. Hiring a professional investigator to obtain a trade secret or using prostitutes for the same purpose
7. Hiring an employee away from a competitor to obtain specific know-how or other trade secrets

8. Trespassing on a competitor's property in the course of a clandestin espionage operation

9. Bribing a competitor's supplier or employee to obtain trade secrets

10. Planting an agent on a competitor's payroll for the purpose of securin; trade secrets

11. Eavesdropping on competitors (e.g., by wiretapping or bugging)

12. Theft of drawings, samples, documents, and similar confidential prop erty belonging to a competitor

13. Obtain trade secrets through blackmail of key employees who hav deliberately compromised themselves through a sexual indiscretion

14. Penetrating a competitor's computer system to scrutinize, manipulate o extract secret, proprietary information

COMPETITIVE STRUCTURE

There are, roughly speaking, three distinct types of competitive structures

Type A: The market dominated by one large competitor. IBM is th classic example in the computer industry.

Type B: The market shared by five to twenty fairly comparable firms The semiconductor industry might be cited as an example.

Type C: The fragmented market shared by dozens of small competitors Film processing is an industry of this type.

In picking new markets for your firm, you are probably better off witl either Type A or Type C competition than Type B. In Type A, you will not be a likely to encounter immediate retaliatory action, and your pricing may be pro tected under the large company's pricing umbrella. Granted, you may be ver; weak when at last that company retaliates, but usually you can find some job i isn't doing too well and prosper at filling the gap. Also, the large company risk anti-trust action in moving to limit your competition.

A Type C market permits a vigorous firm to establish market dominanc rather quickly by outselling or buying out the small competitors. If you car become the dominant force in this market, then you will be establishing th pricing, the standards, and the rate-of-change for the industry.

Type B markets, in contrast to the others, are tough to enter becaus competitors have strong incentive to retaliate quickly to additional competi tive pressures, and because market dominance will be difficult if not impossi ble to achieve, and because existing competition among equals probably has eliminated any comfortable price umbrella allowing you no temporary period of extraordinary profits to offset startup costs.

HIRING COMPETITORS' PERSONNEL

The hiring of competitors' personnel is as much a part of the American competitive tradition as the spitball. The rate of success of new ventures, it could be argued, would be greatly diminished were it not for the ready availability of experienced (i.e., competitors') personnel. One of the reasons, in fact, why it is much easier to start a company in America than in many other countries is the lack of any excessive employee loyalty and the general absence of ethical sanctions against job-hoppers. In the U.S., the job is considered to be something you do until something better comes along. In more traditional societies such as Japan and Germany, on the other hand, your employer is a sort of alter-parent to whom you owe loyalty in return for security.

Often, there is simply no alternative to hiring competitors' personnel. If there is a scarcity of skills, you and your local competitor are almost automatically bidding up the price for these skills. However, even in cases where there is a choice, many firms believe they are better off to hire the competitor's employee, rather than recruiting from outside the industry.

The reasons are pretty obvious:

1. Firms help themselves *and* handicap the competitor in a single act.
2. The employee will likely require minimal training and break-in time since he or she already knows the business.
3. Firms may be able to elicit important information from the employee regarding the competitor's operations and customers.

However, the advantages can be short-lived, since two can play the game. Moreover, the job-hopper doesn't become a loyal employee just because he or she comes to work for you; this person may be working for another competitor (or maybe the original one) in another year with *your* business plan in his or her file.

Economists have argued that, on the whole, job-hopping may benefit the economy by promoting competition; information flows so freely between companies that nobody can keep a secret for very long. This is slight comfort to the entrepreneur interested in survival, however. Perfect competition is exactly what this businessperson *doesn't* need. Employee-swapping, like price cutting, is one of those things most businesspeople would like to see go away; however, until human nature changes significantly, it is with us to stay. The pragmatic entrepreneur must be resigned to playing the game, initially at least, by whatever rules the particular industry dictates.

CONVENTIONAL WISDOM: Free competition is what makes America great.

REALITY: Free competition is what makes entrepreneurs grate.

REFERENCES

1. Eells, Richard, & Nehemkis, Peter. *Corporate Intelligence and Espionage: A Blueprint for Executive Decision Making.* Copyright © 1984 by The Trustees of Columbia University in the City of New York. Reprinted with permission of The Free Press, a Division of Macmillan, Inc.

   An excellent work on current U.S. corporate practices, with a strong section on ethics. Also an extensive discussion of Soviet industrial espionage methods.

2. Greene, Richard M., Jr., ed. *Business Intelligence and Espionage.* Homewood, Ill.: Dow Jones Irwin, 1966.

   This book of readings will tell you more than you want to know about this subject. And, if you choose not to employ the methods discussed, at least you'll know how your competitor is finding out about you. Suggests many sources available in any good library.

21

Going International

*"You can count on your fingers the American companies
which are maximizing their full potential in
international markets."*   *. . Mark McCormack*

HY GO OFFSHORE?

As a high-tech firm, you will be a multinational, whether you like it or not.
This is the reality of the 1990s and beyond for almost every technology
entrepreneur. In the old days, "foreign marketing" was something the venture thought about only after the company was fully established in the U.S.A.
Even the term was revealing; foreign marketing was something that was
vaguely alien to the American entrepreneur. The markets, if they existed,
seemed small, far-away, and relatively unimportant.

In the nineties, this mindset is as obsolete as the vacuum tube. Here are
the main reasons:

1. The U.S. no longer enjoys a significant technological lead in most areas.
   Indeed, the Japanese and increasingly the Europeans are pulling ahead
   in many significant areas. No longer can the entrepreneur regard the

offshore market as a sort of dumping-ground to extend the life of older model products; this is simply no longer acceptable to foreign buyers

2. Product lives are becoming steadily shorter. Therefore, to realize a acceptable return on R&D investment, marketing efforts must increas ingly be launched at major markets simultaneously.

3. Communications are improving. Foreign buyers read the same pres and attend the same trade shows and professional meetings. They are fully aware of the state of the art and the state of world pricing.

4. Increasingly, your sources will be offshore. Some U.S. firms (such as Sur Microsystems) are already fully dependent upon the technology of off shore vendors. This can only increase.

5. The offshore market is enormous. For most technology-based products the U.S. now constitutes somewhat less than half the world market. I would be a poor entrepreneur who turned a blind eye on half the poten tial market. Your job will be to find economic ways to reach those markets.

6. The dollar is currently weak. This means that U.S. manufacturers have an historical (if temporary) opportunity to sell in Europe and Japan a very competitive prices.

BENEFITS FLOW BOTH WAYS

Appropriately, most small companies are motivated by the large potential fo additional sales that offshore markets offer. However, this is only the begin ning of the potential benefits. Here are some examples:

1. Other countries may find wholly new applications for your product Different economic and social contexts may reveal totally new market you hadn't thought of. Computer imaging developed for medical applica tions in the West may find its way into oil exploration in the Middle East. Combustion systems developed for energy production in the U.S may find their way into waste disposal facilities in Europe or Japan.

2. Other countries are a potential source of low-cost technology for you Once there, you may discover complementary or even superior technol ogy, often developed with heavy government subsidies, looking for out lets in the U.S. This could save your firm years and millions.

3. Other countries are sources of products. You may discover that Germany has products that could be comarketed with your own. When feasible,

this eliminates the cost, lead-time, and risk of developing your own products to achieve the same revenue result.

4. Other countries can be an attractive source of production for domestic and U.S. markets. In some cases it may be cheaper (as in the Pacific Rim nations). In others, it may be necessary to add some more "local content" to overcome quotas or tariff barriers (which is why Japanese cars are increasingly made in the U.S.).

5. Other countries can be a low-cost site for your R&D. Some countries (such as Israel, Ireland, and Canada) offer attractive government R&D subsidies and legions of well-trained, English-speaking technologists. Others simply offer more attractive wage-rates. For example, India is making a concerted effort to market its software-development capabilities to firms worldwide.

In short, it is time for American entrepreneurs to open their eyes to today's reality, that there may be a lot of ways to further their ventures' goals by working with capable overseas partners.

HOW TO PROCEED?

If you're like most entrepreneurs, your initial goal will be to find ways to increase your sales via export. This begins by identifying and ranking the countries that are the best markets for your product. This, as in any other form of market analysis, requires some research. Fortunately, you can expect a lot of help, because the U.S. Department of Commerce, various state economic development agencies, and even city governments are eager to see you succeed at exporting. They are all sources of advice, assistance, and data, which can quickly help you to home in on the opportunities and obstacles inherent in each national market for your product.

Once your first several target markets have been identified, you will need to explore the appropriate means of accessing each market, and get some sense of the cost of doing it. Avoid monolithic thinking at this stage. For example, you may discover that in Canada a direct sales office is needed, while in your top several European targets regional distributors are needed, while in Japan you should ally yourself with a trading company. It would be most unusual for a single pattern to work best in every relevant market. Here are your major options:

Agents and Distributors

Every country has local entrepreneurs who import, sell, and support foreign
goods, and they often specialize in American-made products. They can often be
identified through the Department of Commerce's agency identification ser
vices, conducted through the U.S. consulate in the target country. This is a low
cost, high quality service. You may also discover that agents will make them
selves known to *you* as a result of your exposure in the trade press and trade
shows. These people can be checked out by talking with the U.S. Department
of Commerce, a well as by discussions with some of their U.S. principals

It is a surprising fact that dealing with foreign agencies is often easie
than dealing with their U.S. counterparts. This is because they are accus
tomed to acting autonomously, with little support from their U.S. principals
Their average level of technical education may be higher; they may have
significant repair facilities. They may have complementary products, which
can ease the sale of yours; they may be willing to perform software system
integration services that are essential to closing a sale; they may be willing to
buy evaluation or demonstration equipment from you, as part of the initia
deal. In short, foreign agencies are likely to do for themselves many of the
things that you would have to do for U.S. representatives. Moreover, they
usually buy equipment at a discount for resale, reducing the credit and
collection headaches that can come with commissioned rep sales. Finally
these agencies are accustomed to bridging the culture gap. They will often
translate the literature into their own language; they are accustomed to deal
ing with the customs, currency exchange, and export license dimensions
which may be new to you. They also will usually handle the local advertising

On the negative side, foreign agencies will demand prices that are
deeply discounted from U.S. list. They will often conceal the prices that they
are quoting customers, so you cannot know if they are too high or too low
They may also try to insulate you from their customers, out of fear that you
may eventually go direct (as indeed you may). And of course, they will want
the same level of marketing support, fresh products, and involvement in your
company that characterize any good rep marketing relationship. They may
also want too much territory. For example, Germany is a very large country
with several concentrated economic centers. It is often wise to have a sepa
rate agent for each of these centers.

Foreign Sales Offices

Direct "regional offices" located in foreign countries are a luxury that you will
likely forego, at least until your sales exceed $25 million. The establishment
staffing, managing, and financing of such offices are simply beyond the capaci

ties of most small companies. One exception may be Canada, but even there you must also evaluate local agencies carefully. The apparent advantages of direct offices, in terms of cost and control, often prove illusory even for much larger companies.

A strategy that works for some small companies, however, is to establish a Europe–wide support office in some convenient location (the U.K. and Holland are popular). From here your sales manager, perhaps a European national, may supervise roving specialists in training and applications. A major benefit of this arrangement is the higher frequency of agent contact that it permits. Moreover, you may find it advantageous to organize the support office as a corporation, to which additional functions (e.g., assembly or R&D) can be appended. And, should you decide eventually to go direct in some territory, this may provide the launch base.

Corporate Marketing Agreements

Often the best bet for a highly technical product is to find another manufacturer with complementary products, and sell through them. This will give you instant credibility and market entree well beyond what even a good agency can offer. Your corporate partner may well offer a significant applications and service capability, systems integration and software skills, a large sales organization, and substantial advertising, sales organization, and trade show exposure. They may also provide built-in financing to their customers. Finally, there may be some noncommercial benefits to your venture. Your partner may become a source of financing, either directly as an equity investor or indirectly through significant stocking of your product. If your partner has a significant and visible company, the relationship may also give your firm added credibility with U.S. investors.

Trading Companies

Your best bet in Japan and possibly other Pacific Rim markets may turn out to be a trading company. Examples are Marubeni, C. Itoh, Mitsui, and Mitsubishi in Japan; a host of smaller, often specialized firms exist there and elsewhere. The four mentioned are huge commercial combines, doing many billions of dollars annually. They buy and sell worldwide, but most of their sales are to or from Japan. They are often affiliated with banks and with groupings of companies, which may themselves be customers for your product. Different trading companies have different strengths and product marketing emphasis, so be sure you're talking to the one best suited to your product.

The trading companies bring size, financial clout, and brand-name recognition, in Japan and perhaps elsewhere, too. Often they will wish to sell your product in a number of Asian countries besides Japan; this should be explored, but not automatically conceded. There may be better alternatives for Korea, Hong Kong, or Taiwan.

Trading companies can usually provide an excellent market analysis for Japan, identifying major customers, suitable agents, and competitive structure. (Do not be surprised if the analysis indicates the need for some modification in your product specification for Japan.) They also have the ability to finance inventories and demo equipment, and to sponsor some engineering R&D if need be. They may, as previously suggested, sell through outside agents, through their own sales offices, or through a mixture. They may also recommend some corporate partnership as the best means of penetration.

The major trading companies are easily identified. All maintain New York offices, and some have regional offices in major centers. All are interested in talking to U.S. high tech firms, and you will have little difficulty in finding someone to talk to. As in all dealings with Japan, plan on several months of discussions and market analysis before any deal is cut. However, after that they will often move very rapidly.

Strategic Alliances

"Strategic alliance" is one of the buzzwords for the nineties, so add it to your vocabulary right away. It means some sort of economic alliance with another (larger) company in the U.S.A. or elsewhere. In the present context, it can include some or any of the following:

1. One-way or reciprocal marketing agreements
2. Manufacturing of your product by partner under contract or license
3. Joint R&D efforts
4. Arm's length "comarketing" agreements
5. Financial investment in your firm
6. True joint venture corporation, set up with the resources of both companies as an independent entity to exploit a particular technology, product, or market

Often an alliance will begin at one level of commitment (a trial marriage) and evolve into a closer tie. In fact, your partners may eventually become the logical buyers for your company, and may be willing to pay more than anyone if it has become integral to their own business.

OREIGN MARKETING IN CONTEXT

All this is wonderful, you say, but how can I, a struggling startup entrepreneur, possibly do any of this and still get done all the things that I'm already doing? Where will the knowledge, the people, the money, and the time be found?

The answer will not be simple nor necessarily cheap. It will tax your entrepreneurial ingenuity to solve this puzzle—yet solve it you must. You will be shortchanging your company, your team, and your investors if you only address half your market. In conceding it, you will in fact be inviting stiff competition both from more alert U.S. competitors and from hungry offshore competitors who, unopposed in their own markets, will soon find it attractive to challenge you in the U.S.A.

Here are some approaches:

1. Include foreign marketing plans and costs in your initial business plan and raise enough money to finance them.
2. Hire an experienced international sales manager early. If your VP Sales and Marketing is experienced overseas, the international manager can report to him or her. If not, this manager should report to you to avoid distracting others from development of the U.S. market.
3. Consider hiring a consultant to assist you in developing your export strategy. Many capable people are available.
4. Budget some of your own time to attend a few foreign trade shows, read the foreign technical press, and talk with some of the government agencies concerned with developing export markets.

Even if your analysis shows that you should wait a year before executing your plan, it is nonetheless essential that the plan exist now. It will provide you with a framework for evaluation of people and opportunities that come over the transom. More important, it will signal potential investors that you are fully aware of today's borderless markets, and that your company is poised to exploit the international opportunities to their fullest extent. All you need is a little extra money!

CONVENTIONAL WISDOM: First develop the U.S. market, then find some foreign customers for the old product.

REALITY: You must plan *now* for penetration of *all* your markets. Today, a U.S.-only strategy is a prescription for disaster.

REFERENCES

1. Valentine, Charles F. *The Arthur Young Internal Business Guide.* New York
John Wiley & Sons, 1988. (Available through Arthur Young offices)
A very practical road map for your company. Excellent guide to state assis
tance programs and U.S. government agencies.

22

Strategic Partnering

Corporate venturing remains popular with corporations as a supplementary approach to existing R&D and corporate development programs . . William J. Golden Consultant, executive, author

WHAT IS A STRATEGIC PARTNERSHIP?

As mentioned in the preceding chapter, the strategic partnership, or strategic alliance, is a buzzword for the nineties. It represents a broader agenda that many large firms are attempting to establish with smaller firms. In the old days the agenda was quite simple. If you found a small company with a product or technology you liked, you marketed the product, licensed the technology, or bought the company. Today, corporate development officials, more reliant than ever on technology developed elsewhere, are pursuing a broader range of models for cooperating with small companies. This trend also connotes a widespread awareness of the historical fact that simple acquisition of small companies by big ones doesn't always work.

Examples of strategic partnerships can run the gamut from licensing to merger, from R&D sponsorship to joint venture corporations, from component contract manufacture to complete product design, assembly, and test. The partnership can be a hybrid of these or a succession of these.

WHAT'S IN IT FOR THE NEW VENTURE?

Briefly stated, you get access to markets, management, and money.

Markets

The enormous cost and lead-time to set up a strong sales and marketing organization virtually guarantees that certain types of startups are completely reliant upon strategic partnerships from Day One. This is nowhere more evident than in the biotechnology area. Without access to the marketing resources of the major drug companies with whom they pair up, few of these companies would stand any chance of survival. Moreover, their support during the long FDA approval cycle is another major factor in the industry's survival.

The ability to form an alliance with a powerful marketing partner can also be critical in markets where the product life is very short; there may simply be no other way to get your product to market before it is obsolete; this is true in both U.S. and foreign markets.

The partnership may also enable the new firm to overcome a major marketing obstacle inherent in startups: the lack of brand recognition.

Most entrepreneurs rely on the price and performance of their product to penetrate the market. However, there are many other reasons why people buy and don't buy. A major reason why they balk is the discomfort most buyers feel at buying high-ticket products from an unknown startup that may be gone tomorrow. Many have had this experience. Thus, the obvious value of a recognized name on the product.

Management

As mentioned above, the management skill and knowledge needed to get through FDA drug or device approval are not insignificant. Likewise, other skills and contacts are very valuable to startups. The ability to sell to government and military agencies is an important example. The skills and contacts to sell into foreign markets is another, discussed at length in Chapter 21. The knowledge of how to adapt products to esoteric applications (e.g., militarization, flight qualification, or TEMPEST qualification) is another example. Advice on bundling or unbundling your product for specific classes of buyers may also prove valuable. In short, big companies know lots of things that little companies don't. If a partnership gives you access to some of this management knowledge, it could be a major plus for your future venture.

Money

The strategic partner is often a source of significant cash flow for the startup. This may take many forms. It could be a direct equity investment loan, an advance against future deliveries or a progress payment, a technology transfer fee or prepaid royalties, the beneficial effect of filling up a large distribution pipeline with a lot of your products, fees for consulting or sponsored R&D. In short, the direct financial consequences of the partnership can be quite significant. The partnership will give you added credibility with the financial community, enhancing the terms upon which outside financing is available to you.

WHAT'S IN IT FOR THE BIG PARTNER?

Technology

Access to new or interesting technologies is by far the most important driver for strategic partnerships with smaller firms. Even firms with huge research budgets and facilities cannot do everything. Moreover, companies sometimes need to get involved with technologies that are divergent from the mainstream of ongoing research. Also, some fast-breaking technologies (such as superconductors) are moving at such a pace that it would be hard ever to catch up from a cold start.

In certain other fields, it may simply be a make-or-buy decision based on cost. Small companies are far more efficient at R&D, and it may be a lot cheaper to cut a deal with a small firm than start an in-house program. Finally, there is the political expedience of doing some risky projects outside the corporation. If the product or the market fails, it's the venture's neck to a large degree.

Market Windows

An alliance with an innovative small firm may provide the large company with a low-cost, low-risk means of exploring a new market. It may be a new type of product that can be sold by existing salespeople to existing customers. It may be an altogether new group of buyers, whose needs the big partner can get to know through the alliance—buyers who may ultimately be customers for this company's other products. In all events, the partnership may represents a low-profile, low-risk toe in the water.

Potential Acquisitions

Most big firms would rather buy something than structure some elaborate partnership agreement. However, outright acquisition of small firms by big ones often doesn't work out, for a large number of reasons. The failure modes include:

1. No logical point at which to attach the new venture.
2. Departure of the acquisition's inside champion.
3. Inability of the big firm to provide meaningful incentives to the founders, resulting in their departure.
4. Incomplete understanding of the business culture of the small venture. Your weird software genius may not go over so well in Toledo!
5. Insufficient management attention available to make the relationship work. Senior management always seems to have bigger problems.
6. Inappropriateness of the accounting, control, or other procedures to handle the small organization; or heavy-handed implementation by staff with no stake in the outcome.
7. Changing goals and priorities of the parties.
8. The not-invented–here (NIH) factor.

For all these reasons and many others, acquisition of basically unknown small companies has not always proven successful. For this reason, the use of succession of strategic partnerships with small companies has the same advantages of dating a lot before getting engaged to be married. It provides a trial period during which to get to know the team, the product, and the market. It may serve to highlight problems or identify risk areas that must be considered before acquisition. It may, incidentally, provide a good window on the small firm's competitors, one of whom may prove to be a better acquisition candidate than the partner. For all of these reasons, the strategic partnership may be an excellent way to reduce the risk of an unhappy marriage.

WHAT ARE THE FORMS OF STRATEGIC PARTNERSHIPS?

The partnership may take on different forms, or even a succession of forms, of varying degrees of commitment. Here are the major models:

1. Big partner (BP) markets little partner's (LP) products, either on a resale or a referral basis.
2. BP licenses some portion of LP's technology.
3. BP undertakes the contract manufacture of LP's product.
4. BP sponsors contract R&D in LP's product.
5. BP becomes a favored user of LP's product.
6. BP becomes an equity investor in LP.
7. BP and LP form a joint venture company for the exploitation of a particular market or technology. This is usually a separate corporation, controlled by BP.
8. BP and LP engage in joint research activities, perhaps jointly bidding on government R&D contracts that neither could get alone.

There are no doubt many other models, as well. Obviously, a relationship could incorporate elements of several of these, and its structure could vary over time.

HOW DO YOU MAKE IT WORK?

As in marriage, there are a lot more ways for things to go wrong than for things to go right. However, there are a number of principles, which, if observed, should go a long way toward assuring that both BP and LP will be happy with the partnership.

1. Be honest with your partner. Don't, for example, dive into a partnership simply because you think this is the way to get BP to make an investment. Be sure the logic is correct and that the partners are being aboveboard, with no hidden agendas.
2. Be sure the benefits are real. Make sure both sides do enough due-diligence to quantify the present and potential market opportunities.
3. Be clear about what the relationship will cost you. For example, a relationship with BP may foreclose any chance you had of selling to this company's competitors or of concluding a better deal later with someone else.
4. Trade only what's of value to BP. This company may not need rights to every application of your patents; it may not be interested in every geographic or applications market; it may not care if the deal term is short. Be sure you don't throw away opportunities without getting corresponding value in return.

5. Put your best efforts into making it a real partnership. Don't permit an "us versus them" psychology to take root on your team. Air grievances early and fairly. Deliver good value.

6. Establish informal relationships with the highest officials in BP's hierarchy you can reach. Make sure they are kept informed and do not entrust the fate of the partnership to the VP of Corporate Development (a job which typically has a two–to–three–year tenure).

7. Do a professional job of training BP's technical, support, and sales people in your product. Don't rely on BP's flunkies to do your job.

8. Have the courage to end it when the benefits no longer justify the costs. Regardless of what the agreement says, when it is no longer good for both parties, it's time to renegotiate.

In summary, the nineties will be the age of strategic partnership. Many new ventures can benefit from them, and some will be unable to survive without them. But, like any marriage, it will take a lot of effort, patience, and forbearance to reap the benefits.

REFERENCES

1. Hanan, Mack. *Growth Partnering: How to Manage Strategic Alliances for Mutual Profit.* New York: American Management Assn., 1986.

   A short, practical book on growth partnerships; how to structure and manage them.

V
RUNNING THE SHOW

23

A Race with the Clock

Even if you're on the right track, you'll get run over if
you just sit there. . . Will Rogers

The day that your Round One financing is complete (the document signed and the cash in the bank) is the day you begin a contest—perhaps the toughest of your life. It is a race with the clock, or, more accurately, with the calendar. You have succeeded in convincing investors of the merit of your deal. They have delivered. Now it's your turn. In your business plan you yourself wrote the rules and time limits in which the game was to be played. Those dates that once seemed like soft targets to you now take on the character of grim deadlines. Your cash-flow projections tell you when you will run out of cash; whether you can get more at that point depends upon how well you've met your objectives. If you go through the money, and the results aren't visible, it doesn't matter whose fault it is—the game is over.

THE IMPORTANCE OF MEETING TARGETS

In the early phases of operations it is very often tempting to move the target around, rather than to make a genuine effort to hit them. It is nearly alway true, for example, that engineers will want a couple more months to polish the product design before it is released for promotion. Or maybe now tha you've got money in the bank, this is the time to find some nicer quarters— instead of putting the money and energy into the marketing setup as planned Nothing is more upsetting to the initial operations of the company than a immediate abandoning of the plan. Needless to add, this makes your inves tors not a little uncomfortable, as well. Get into the habit of holding your ow dates as earnestly as you hold your customer delivery dates. Get into th habit of meeting targets.

ENTREPRENEURS VERSUS CUSTODIANS

Very early in the game of operating a new company, you may come to recog nize that your own activities fall more or less into two categories: the entrepre neurial and the custodial. Roughly defined, the entrepreneurial tasks involv the *setting up, planning,* and *motivational* activities of the firm. They woul include such things as initiating market research, recruiting a banker, a accountant, an ad agency, finding a building, setting budgets, and so on. Th custodial tasks, by contrast, are such things as tracking budgets, developin; financial reports, purchasing materials, supervising production, refereein; disputes between production and marketing. As a rule, entrepreneurial task are much less delegable than are custodial tasks.

Also, among managers there is a spectrum ranging from pure entrepre neur to pure custodian, along which everyone falls. Although you will b obliged for some period to handle both the entrepreneurial and custodia tasks of your company, it is well to decide, based on your perception o yourself in the spectrum, which tasks you should get rid of by delegation an which you should keep to yourself. You might be successful at delegatin; certain entrepreneurial tasks (such as advertising responsibility) while hang ing on to certain custodial tasks in which you feel a strong interest (such a customer service). Yet, in general, the more of the custodial tasks you can ge rid of without losing control, the better job you're probably going to do as a entrepreneur. However, as the company matures and its operations requir skilled custodians, you may find that you must move aside or move out. It i generally recognized that entrepreneurs often make lousy managers.

HE PRINCIPLE OF ENLIGHTENED MEDIOCRITY

The author is indebted to Nick De Wolf, founder of Teradyne Corporation, for this pungent phrase, which captures so beautifully the essence of what every successful entrepreneur learns sooner or later. Basically, it is this: there is very little hope for a perfectionist trying to run a growing new enterprise. There are *so* many things to be done, *so* many problems to solve that weren't in the business plan, and *so* little time to do it in, that a first-rate job is not only impossible for each—it may be undesirable. It has been asserted, with some truth, that we accomplish about 80 percent of any given project with the first 20 percent of the effort. Which says, mathematically at least, that one should be able to do about five 80 percent quality jobs with the time and energy required to do a *single* 100 percent A+ job on any of them. The entrepreneur who shoots for 80 percent quality will not go far wrong. There are, nevertheless, some areas that you will wish to single out for 100 percent quality treatment. It may be product quality control, customer service, or some one or two other key areas that drastically affect the company's position in the marketplace. In these areas, you must ruthlessly demand perfection; in the others, you should learn to settle for less without getting ulcers. To illustrate a bit further, a certain sort of manager may spend a month working out the details of a computerized production control system for the shop, when in fact, about the same result might be obtained with a couple of wall charts in the production supervisor's office. In fact, the result may be better if the supervisor invented it himself or herself. In learning to settle for 80 percent in most areas, you at least have a fighting chance in your race with the clock.

ASH BALANCE

Among the hardest things for the starting entrepreneur to get onto is the function of cash in the enterprise. It seems incredible to many that a company with growing sales and good profits could go bankrupt, but it happens. It happens because the very condition of growth can create overextension of existing working capital and cash. When and if the company's bank debt is called and cannot be renewed (as in the cash crunch of 1980), good companies as well as bad go down the tube. A major customer's failure, a serious collection problem, or a supplier problem can have the same effect.

The existence of a good-sized lump of cash in the bank following financing tends to defocus the crucial significance of the cash balance as the company's blood supply. Then, one cold morning, it is gone. It has been devoured by the business operations: equipment, materials, salaries, working-process development. At this point it dawns on many managers for the first time wha that cash-flow projection really is: a survival weapon.

A manager who cannot predict a cash shortage in the business is not runnin; the company—the company is running him or her.

An unexpected cash crisis can cause much embarrassment and, in some cases permanent damage (such as bankruptcy) to the company. It may make i impossible to meet such "no-fail" commitments as loan interest, the payrol] or (God forbid) withholding tax payment. To say that this event reduces th confidence of the bank, the staff, or the government is to somewhat under state the case. It is damned serious. Other forms of awkwardness can includ missed shipping dates due to materials withheld by suppliers; panic calls t your investors from suppliers; emergency calls to one's investors to help mee the Friday payroll; major price concessions to customers to obtain early pay ment. Not so nice.

The best and only way to avoid this is to *plan* your cash flow and guard i jealously. Work out a format appropriate to *your* needs with your accountant Schedule your accounts receivable into it *by major customer* so that you ca pinpoint collection problems one by one. Schedule major cash payments b *major supplier* so that aggregation does not hide reality. Try to plan about si: months ahead; review and update weekly. If you see a cash shortage develop ing two months out, now is the time to do something about it. Go see you banker, go over your cash-flow statement with this person, show him or he when and why the shortage will develop, plus when and how the desired loa: will be liquidated. The banker will be far more disposed to cooperate nov than sixty days hence when your checks unexpectedly start bouncing. So eve: if there is no cash shortage now, start operating as though there were. Soone or later there will be. You may be growing faster than expected, another cas] crunch may cause your customers to start delaying payment, or somethin; may go wrong with a major shipment, causing delayed payment. Get contro of your cash today. Your race with the clock can be equated with a race t reverse the direction of the flow from negative to positive before crossin; zero—not unlike pulling an aircraft out of a dive.

MAINTAINING INVESTOR RAPPORT

You can make no greater mistake than shutting your investors off from th progress of the company, or worse, permitting an attitude of suspicion o hostility to develop between you. One of the functions of directors' meeting is, theoretically, to keep the investors informed. Unless the investors insist on them, however, most entrepreneurs can find better things to do with their time than holding a directors' meeting. This, however, in no way absolves you of the need to keep your investors informed. A monthly memorandum to the investors detailing large pending orders, current problems, various nonfinancial milestones attained, significant research results, developments in the marketplace, etc., will be very valuable. Attach recent press clippings, literature, and so forth. Its functions include:

1. Offsetting the impact of the (bad) news in the monthly financial statements.
2. Giving them some interesting information on their deal.
3. Letting them know you care what they think, thereby creating vicarious participation.
4. Establishing a fund of goodwill upon which you can draw when the company is in a cash crisis or when you are raising additional capital and require their votes for approval.

Stockholders who are ignored until there is a problem, or until their votes are needed for some deal that has sprung on the scene, are going to be understandably difficult to deal with. Make the effort to keep them on your side as partners in the venture.

THE ENTREPRENEUR'S CREDIBILITY

As noted earlier, the importance of hitting your early targets can't be overemphasized. This is the honeymoon with the investors, with suppliers, with the bank, with the customers. Your performance will never again be under such intense scrutiny, because they are all still nervous about you, your integrity, your ability to perform.

If all goes along nicely and according to schedule, you have nothing to worry about. Just be sure they all know what a lot of effort it took to do it. If, however, things do not go exactly right, your credibility can still be salvaged. When serious problems arise, you will be very foolish indeed to try to hide them to make yourself look good. Most business problems get worse with time (e.g., quality problems, collections problems, employee dishonesty) and by the time you *have* to acknowledge them, the situation can be very bad indeed. You can have problems *and* investor support if you acknowledge the problem and, if meaningful, ask for help.

Naturally, the same principle applies to your customers and suppliers as well. If you discover that a shipping deadline is going to be blown, it is far better that the customer learn about it immediately from the president rather than from your shipper on the scheduled delivery day. If you're going to be late in paying a large invoice, have the courage to call your supplier personally and explain; give the supplier a chance to plan *his or her* cash requirements around your problem. Tell this person when you will pay and make it happen. These may all seem to be rather obvious, common-sense actions, but when things get rough you're going to need these people. If they doubt your integrity, they won't be there.

PLANNING YOUR TIME

Most entrepreneurs do a much better job at planning the years' activities for the entire company than they do planning their own day. Consequently, they end up taking fourteen hours to accomplish in a day what should be done in ten (hence, including Saturdays, the legendary 84-hour work week). However, despite a certain heroic aura borne by the 84-hour week, it is really dysfunctional and can almost always be shown to be due to poor planning, rather than heroic devotion. It is dysfunctional for the company because:

1. After about ten hours of work, anybody's efficiency tapers off enormously; you will accomplish little more during the next four hours than you would in one hour fresh.

2. It creates an atmosphere of tacit disapproval toward other employees who can't or won't work your hours. This can strain the relations between you and key people.

3. The long hours are naturally necessary when the big push is on. As a steady diet, however, they merely exhaust you and rob you of the vitality necessary to get customers excited about your product or to inspire your own employees.

The better answer is to try planning your day better. A few tips:

1. Identify your own "creativity cycle" during the day and be sure that those hours are reserved for your really creative work.

2. Try scheduling your entire day—not just appointments—scheduling yourself as though you were an expensive production machine (you are). Have specific attainable goals or milestones to be accomplished in each interval of time.

3. Ignore the telephone. Save one hour during the less creative part of your day to return all calls. Do not become the slave of this instrument. Use your secretary to filter off (politely) all but the most vital callers.

4. Work outside the office. If you have a major report, business plan, technical paper, or speech to prepare, go work someplace else (not at home). A library is often the best place to get things done.

5. Try batching, rather than real-time operation. Set up a few regular weekly, bi-weekly, or monthly meetings to keep abreast of progress in specific areas, rather than constantly interrupting your employees' work or letting them interrupt yours.

6. Batch your travel. This is often less costly in out-of-pocket terms, as well as being efficient. If you plan to be gone two solid weeks next March, everyone knows you'll be away and can plan around you.

7. Batch your correspondence. Get used to using a dictating machine instead of dictating to your secretary or handdrafting, so you don't keep interrupting this employee's work. Batching your correspondence permits you to get all files, orders, etc., in order and get it all done quickly.

8. Use the telex or fax instead of committing yourself to long telephone conversations. It is cheaper, just as fast, avoids time-zone problems, and gives a written record. Try using it also instead of writing letters. People will forgive you if you're terse, and remember, the average business letter costs over $12.00 to dictate, type, and send.

9. Set aside some time for thinking—even if it's only a half-hour in the shower each morning. Nothing is more inimical to good management than a constant rat-race with every minute jammed full.

10. Don't overdo priorities. Some things are important—others are merely urgent in a time sense. Some require large blocks of uninterrupted concentration, while others are short and can be fitted into the time interstices between more important or nonschedulable events. Don't get yourself tied up in a system that tackles everything in order of "importance" or "priority."

11. Get some regular exercise. There is no better defense against the physical and emotional wear and tear on the entrepreneur than some daily energetic exercise. It helps you wake up, metabolize your food better, and maintain a higher general level of animal vitality.

12. Get out of the office. Whether to work on a major project, have lunch with your banker, or make some sales calls with the local rep, make it a point to get out of the office and frequently expose yourself to new people and fresh ideas. This helps to revitalize both you and your staff.

13. Employ the principle of enlightened procrastination. It is truly amazing the number of problems which, if ignored, simply disappear. Someone else solves them, or a deadline passes, or the need for their performance disappears, or somebody discovers it really wasn't that important after all. In sorting out your "in" box, you will discover that about 70 percent of its contents can be put in the circular file, 20 percent in a bushel box marked "pending," and the 10 percent remainder earmarked for action sometime this week.

HELPING OTHERS PLAN THEIR TIME

No matter how efficiently you use your time, the ability of the company to meet deadlines depends on your employees' ability to plan theirs. As president, it is up to you to instill a sense of day-to-day urgency to show people why it is essential to get their tasks done on time and to enlist their commitment and pride in making sure it happens.

Task-driven behavior is not natural to many people, especially if they have come from staff jobs in much larger organizations. You must make it clear that here in your small company environment, people are judged on output (tasks completed on time), not input (eight hours put in today). They are expected to finish on schedule, even if it means an occasional evening or weekend invested. Here are some tips to help your people meet their goals:

1. Each professional should have a written schedule, showing when jobs are to be started and completed. The classical Gantt chart, or bar graph, is a good visual format. Progress should be reviewed weekly by supervisor.

2. Flex time should be employed. When deadlines impend, let people work at home or in the office at hours of their own choice.

3. If a critical deadline (such as a major proposal) is due Monday, work the weekend and give the people two other days off.

4. Encourage people to take work along on trips. The long hours in airports and hotels afford excellent uninterrupted intervals for creative work.

5. Try scheduling staff meetings, sales meetings, planning sessions, and other team gatherings outside regular working hours, perhaps at a pleasant place off-site. There are so few prime customer-contact hours in a normal week, that these should be jealously guarded. Plan working breakfasts, Saturday or weekend-long planning retreats, working lunches, etc. Make it pleasant. Provide some food, and if needed, a pleasant hotel or resort for the planning meeting. Save those prime hours.

6. Pay bonuses for specific, extraordinary tasks accomplished. Consider prizes that will be used by the spouse if you want double mileage. After all the spouse is the one who suffers most when the company demands that leisure be rescheduled or foregone.

CONVENTIONAL WISDOM: The entrepreneurs' shortest commodity is time.

REALITY: The shortest commodity is not time, but energy and organization in its use.

REFERENCES

1. Oncken, William Jr. *Managing Management Time—Who's Got the Monkey?* Englewood Cliffs, N.J.: Prentice Hall, Inc., 1984.

     A usable practical book on what happens to our time, written by a consultant who's seen it all.

2. Webber, Ross A. *Time and Management,* New York: Van Nostrand Reinhold Co., 1972.

     A 160-page essay on time and how it gets lost. Offers concrete measures for its management as a corporate resource. This book, although intended for the manager of the established firm, has many important insights for the entrepreneur.

3. Naumes, William. *The Entrepreneurial Manager in the Small Business.* Reading, Mass.: Addison Wesley, 1978.

     Readings and original text on what managers really do.

24

More on Negotiation

Let us never negotiate out of fear, but let us never fear to negotiate.   .. John F. Kennedy

Many successful business executives would, if pressed, acknowledge that nego tiating skill, more than specific business knowledge, administrative technique or other management skills, has influenced their ability to achieve. Negotiatio is the common central element in *all* of business—whether between two came traders in the bazaar, or between a giant corporation and a tough labor union Skill in negotiation appears to be one constant factor in every successful enter prise. It is extraordinary, therefore, that it is seldom if ever treated explicitly i business schools or other management development programs.

Negotiation impinges on nearly every activity in business life, regardles of the size of the enterprise. It is especially crucial, however, in the earl operations of a new company. An established firm has the substance, th ongoing sales, the reputation for delivery and payment, and a huge veste interest to protect. It has much to offer as well as to gain from its opposin negotiators. Contrast this, then, to the situation of the new company: it has n record, no significant substance or proven ability to deliver on its promises

Worse yet, the opposing negotiator may have had some unfavorable experience with small companies. Nonetheless, the only way that substance, track record, and reputation *can* be built by the new firm is through negotiation.

You will at the outset be negotiating lines of credit with suppliers and banks, compensation packages with employees and prospective employees, and complex, multi-dimensional contracts with customers. You may find yourself also negotiating with people who are supposed to be your paid helpers. For example, you may become engaged in a negotiation with your auditor over proper treatment of inventories. You will be negotiating schedules and budgets with each department head. You will be negotiating vacation schedules with your spouse. You will be negotiating with *everyone*.

OUR OPPOSER IS USUALLY AT A GROSS DVANTAGE

In Chapter 11, we observed that the financier with whom you are negotiating for capital is invariably at a great advantage over you, the entrepreneur. This is also true to some significant degree of nearly every other outside entity with whom you may be negotiating in the early stages of growth. Your opposer is negotiating similar deals with other companies every day of the year. This person has heard all your arguments before and knows how to counter them, has seen three better deals than yours already this week, and, moreover, probably understands the strengths and weaknesses of your position better than you do yourself. Finally, your opposer probably needs your patronage a great deal less than you need his or hers—and this person knows it.

In short, the entrepreneur is attempting to negotiate a place in the world for a company at the very time when personal inexperience, coupled with the firm's lack of substance, least qualify him or her for success. Therefore, the entrepreneur should take whatever steps are possible toward improving the probable outcome by:

1. Improving negotiating skills, and
2. Enlisting the skills of experienced negotiators.

HE NEGOTIATING PROCESS

Inexperienced negotiators are often handicapped by their very concept of what a negotiation is supposed to be. They tend to view the process as a form of combat in which there will be a winner and a loser; tactics and strategies will be used, if at all, to drive the other negotiator to the wall. To back this up logically, they would tend to believe that the threat of force (play it my way o else) will elicit the desired concessions from one's opposer.

A little reflection will reveal how invalid this view of negotiation actuall is. First, there would be no negotiation at all if both parties did not perceiv some potential benefit from it. In fact, the purpose of negotiation is precisel to establish how the joint benefits of a new situation can be made to excee the benefits of the old situation.

To put it in economists' terms, you both should be striving toward . *higher* tradeoff curve—not merely forcing one another up and down the sam curve you both started from. Second, it is an experience of everyday life tha "agreements" struck under duress tend only to last until the weaker part *feels* it has the strength to tear them up. If your opposing party feels driven t the wall (whether or not it really *is* a bad deal for him or her) this person' prime energies from this point forward will be directed toward evening th score with you. The fact that your opposer may be violating a contract t accomplish this merely ensures that your lawyer will be able to meet yach payments for another couple of years.

A second handicap with which inexperienced people enter a negotiatin session, is that of a prematurely frozen position (here's our deal, take it o leave it). There is almost no way you could better guarantee that you will no get *anything* you want from a negotiation than by presenting an ultimatum demanding everything. Even if you feel that what you desire is reasonable attainable, and beneficial to some degree to the opposing party, *you* must stil let your opposer reach this conclusion independently. He or she individuall must take the intervening steps. Along the way it is possible that your op poser will come up with alternative formulations that you haven't even consid ered that may be more beneficial for both parties (such as a method o structuring the purchase of a company to minimize the taxes for both sides)

WHY TECHNOLOGISTS ARE OFTEN POOR NEGOTIATORS

The technologist's rational mindset, so valuable in most contexts, can prove ; liability in a negotiating setting. Accustomed to analyzing a problem anc finding the single best solution, this person may be quite unprepared for the irrationality, the posing, the gamesmanship, and the human element tha usually drives negotiations. The need to demand more than you expect to get to work through the entire process, making sure the other side must work fo each point it gets; the interruptions, restarts, and seemingly needless redun dancy of the process—all of these things may build a sense of aggravation, impatience, and finally, a desire just to get the process over with. It is precisely at this point where the newcomer to negotiation might start making concessions that should not get made; where tradeoffs cease to be thought through; where value is left on the table. These are the reasons why a negotiating team, with at least one skilled and experienced player, perhaps a lawyer, is essential.

NOWING YOUR OPPOSER

The better the understanding you have of the individual you will be facing in a major negotiation, the better will be your chances of working successfully together. Some basic facts on this person's education, business background, tax status, and general personality can be truly invaluable. What personal needs is the opposer going to satisfy by entering this negotiation? Sometimes it is difficult to find out much in advance along these lines, especially if the organization with which you are negotiating elects to put in a new person to run the negotiation. However, rather than going at it cold, you may be able to use some tactic, such as a "fact–finding meeting" or other occasion to meet with the individual prior to the actual negotiation. You may also be able to identify someone who has recently dealt with the person in a similar context.

It is also desirable to know a good deal about the organization the negotiator represents. What are its unannounced motives? What are its legal constraints? How far has it gone with firms similar to yours? What is general practice in its industry? What special circumstances might cause it to bend its policies slightly in your case?

For a concrete example let us assume you are applying for a line of credit from a local bank. Its motivation for dealing with you may be a good deal more complex than simply a lender finding another borrower. It may be motivated to deal with you for these reasons:

1. Your firm is local, only a few blocks from its office.
2. Your account, though small, has the possibility of growing very large.
3. Your firm's presence will attract the private accounts of your employees to this bank.
4. It may need to create an image of public servant, friend of small business, or supporter of the prevailing minority in the community.

However, on some investigation you may find that the bank has definite *limits* imposed by regulatory agencies and charters, such as

1. Requiring signature of the principal on unsecured notes
2. Balance sheet tests (such as debt-equity ratio)
3. Avoiding long-term debt, as opposed to seasonal or self-liquidating loan
4. Charging higher rates for riskier loans
5. Lending only on real estate

In addition, it may have operating *policies* which, in times of tight cash funnel money to older customers, instead of shaky new accounts. They may or may not prefer the pledging of assets (e.g., receivables). All of these are facts which, if known in advance, would greatly simplify the entrepreneur' negotiating process. It might, in fact, convince the credit-seeker that no negotiation was even warranted. The point is, the more you can learn in advance about your opposer and the organization, the better.

STRATEGIES AND TACTICS[1]

Negotiation is an art upon which substantial study has been expended, espe cially in the application area of labor relations. It is not the purpose of this book to advance the frontiers of this literature, but merely to catalog a few of the approaches the entrepreneur may find useful and also should anticipate having used against him or her in negotiation. Nierenberg offers the following:

1. *Forbearance.* When the going gets tough, hold off answering, call a recess, suspend discussions, call a "cooling off period." This will some times give the opposition a chance to see the merit of your position, to break the momentum of a negotiation that is going poorly, or just to show that you are under no time pressure to reach agreement.

2. *Surprise.* Often a skilled negotiator may elect to become totally unrea sonable during a negotiation, to take the opposer off balance. Surprise can also take the form of totally altered demands, a whole new set of fact injected, a relaxation of some "non-negotiable" demand, etc.

3. *Fait accompli.* Make your move, then let the other side react as they will. For example, if a final written contract is unsatisfactory, cross out those portions you dislike, initial each correction, and sign the docu ment. Or, if there is disagreement on a price, simply write the check fo

---

[1] The author is much indebted to Gerard I. Nierenberg for several of the key ideas in this section (see References).

the amount you think it should be and let them decide if the difference is worth the cost of collecting it.

4. *Bland withdrawal.* (Who, me?) Sometimes it's better to violate someone's presumed rights temporarily than trying to negotiate initially. For example, you might elect to violate a known patent for a while to get established in a market, calculating that it either won't get enforced or that it will be worth your while to pay whatever the possible penalty would be.

5. *Apparent withdrawal.* This can often be combined with surprise for the desired dramatic effect. Stomping indignantly out of a meeting can be risky but is used effectively by some negotiators. The threat of withdrawal can be equally effective, if the demands of the opposer seem unrealistic.

6. *Reversal.* In one form, this can mean the exacting of symmetric concessions from the opposing side. For example, if the union feels wages should go up because profits went up, oblige them to agree to wage cuts in case profits go down. In another form, reversal could cause you to increase your bargaining demands, rather than lower them in exchange for other concessions. For example, after a recess from financial negotiations in Boston, you could conspicuously "disappear" to New York for a few days, later reopening negotiations with a much higher price-per-share demand. Let your opposer wonder who you saw in New York.

7. *Time limits.* The press of the calendar often provides the best impetus to a speedy conclusion. If your position will be served by time pressure, schedule your meeting a few days before Christmas or before the opposer's plant shutdown. Look how many negotiations are settled in Congress just before recess. Other limitations are useful as well. For example, if you are trying to raise capital and your opposers know your company will be out of cash shortly, they have a very real limit working in their favor.

8. *Feinting.* Yield the concessions you make reluctantly. Make the opposition work for them. Bury the opposers in facts to conceal the weaknesses in your proposition. Make sure they know there is someone else very eager for a piece of your proposition. Let them feel at the end that they should be glad they got as good a deal as they did.

9. *Participation.* Explain *why* the proposed package is unacceptable and ask the opposers' help in showing how your problems with it can be answered. Enlist their ideas in a sincere, nonmanipulative way. This may result in a solution or in their recognition and acknowledgement that their position is unrealistic.

10. *Dissociation.* Make sure the opposers understand why your firm is totally different from those other new ventures in which they lost all that money. Be sure your customer is able to differentiate between your product and all its scurrilous imitators.

11. *Crossroads.* Be prepared to meet any unreasonable new demand with an equally unreasonable counter-demand, until the initial demand is withdrawn. If labor wants a shorter workweek, you agree, provided they give up several paid holidays.

12. *Blanketing.* Inundate the opposers with data, with detailed questions, with prearranged meeting agendas, etc., to take away their initiative.

13. *Randomizing.* This can involve non-negotiating tactics, such as splitting the difference or flipping a coin, aimed at invoking irrational chance to break deadlocks.

14. *Nonrandom sample.* As evidence, you introduce verbatim interview recordings with ten engineers who like your product. Of course, you don't tell them about the other fifty who hate your product.

15. *Salami.* Try for small concessions, a slice at a time. Get them in the habit of saying yes. Tell the customers you only want to give them a sample of your product at an introductory price. Get rid of that manager by first giving him or her a Chevy instead of a Cadillac, then a disagreeable secretary, then no secretary at all, etc. This is especially common as a tactic in large corporations.

16. *Shifting levels.* If your opposers keep pleading that they haven't the authority to grant a concession, then go over their heads. You may then be talking to a higher person with broader understanding, as well as authority. Or, make suppliers justify their prices in terms of their costs instead of benefits to you. Or shift time horizons. Try negotiating for a whole year's supply, rather than simply for the next price-break quantity.

This list of negotiating tactics can be greatly expanded by your own experience as you discover what works well for you.

SOME ADDITIONAL CONSIDERATIONS ON NEGOTIATING

Some advance preparation for any negotiation will serve you well. In addition to scouting the opposer fairly well, you should be sure that you have done your homework in other areas, too. Try to anticipate which way the negotiation will go, and be prepared with countertactics. Try to anticipate objections to your position and have the counterarguments and facts available to back you up. Some people find play-acting simulation a useful preparation. Cite chapter and verse. Be prepared to justify all demands (even your arbitrary ones) in terms of rational considerations or precedents that the other side can not easily reject. For example: "We cannot consider owning less than 51 percent of your stock, because otherwise we cannot file a consolidated earnings statement with the IRS." Or, "I cannot meet your price demand because I would be in violation of the Sherman Anti-trust Act." Let them know you would happily concede the point, if only you had a choice.

Try to maintain control of the place of the meeting, as well as of the agenda. The order, as well as the content, of the agenda can be very important—for example, if there is a time limit, reserve your weakest areas for last, so that they may get cut out altogether. Try to keep the initiative.

Be sure that you get an attorney who is a skilled and experienced negotiator, and that you have this person present as a team member in any significant negotiation. There is no better protection against your own inexperience.

If there are others who must ratify the agreement reached by negotiation (such as key stockholders or partners) try to have them present at the negotiation, or at least keep them fully informed of progress so that they will know not only where you are in terms of your success, but also how you got there. This will make it far easier to enlist their cooperation at the final stage. Try to remember that, to succeed, the final agreement has to be good for everybody. If any principal feels coerced or short-changed, the agreement will probably be in litigation next year.

CONVENTIONAL WISDOM: My gain is your loss.

REALITY: In a professional negotiation, both sides should win.

REFERENCES

1. Nierenberg, G. I. *Creative Business Negotiating*. New York: Hawthorn Books, Inc., 1971.

2. Nierenberg, G. L. *The Art of Negotiating*. New York: Cornerstone Library, 1968.
    References 1 and 2 are about the best books available on the subject of negotiation. Both discuss Nierenberg's "needs theory."

3. Strager, M. *Acquisition and Merger Negotiating Strategy*. New York: Presidents Publishing House, 1971.
    This is a very useful work on negotiating strategy from the viewpoint of the acquiring firm.

25

Lawyers and Their Uses

*It's impossible to tell where what is legal ends and
where justice begins.   . . Anonymous*

Lawyers can do a good deal more for businesspeople than advise them as t
whether or not a proposed course of action is legal. That, in fact, is probabl
the least creative of the many services the right lawyers can render. Beside
being legal advisors, they function as business advisors, negotiators, inter
faces with the financial community, sounding boards for ideas, and, of course
as defenders, should the occasion demand. Top attorneys, rather than bein
mechanics, are artists. They will be able to envision creative solutions t
problems of organization, taxation, and finance that would probably neve
occur to you. They will also be able to look ahead and anticipate problems an
take whatever measures are appropriate to minimize them. They can deploy
wide range of knowledge, experience, and contacts to help you solve you
problems.

AWYERS AS LEGAL ADVISORS

In the mechanical aspects of incorporation, qualifying you to operate in various states, and electing officers, directors, etc., you do not need the top person in the corporate law field. However, if at the outset there are serious questions regarding employment contracts with your previous employer, questions of non-disclosure and noncompetition, or patent agreements, then you'd better have a pretty good lawyer. The earlier in your corporate life you find your permanent attorney, the better the quality of important decisions you'll be making from now on.

Rather early in your venture you will have questions as to the distribution of equity to employees and you will need advice in drafting a stock purchase or stock option plan. There will be employment agreements, or at least invention disclosure agreements for your key people. There will be commercial terms and conditions to be worked out. At the appropriate stage, there will be the need for some legal assistance in the preparation of a business plan for the raising of seed and, later, for the raising of Round One money. These are all activities in which legal and business advice blend to some extent, and you will want the best possible advice in their pursuit.

AWYERS AS BUSINESS ADVISORS

In addition to the business advice needed in drafting company contracts, there are other areas in which it makes sense to enlist the ideas of your attorney. If his or her corporate law practice is an active one, this person has come across many successful and not-so-successful businesspeople and business ideas. This experience is at your disposal. Your attorney can be useful, for example, in suggesting tactics for collection of difficult accounts receivable, in proposing ways to deal with a partner who's gone sour, in dealing with the angry customer, and in structuring transactions to take maximum advantage of tax laws. Your attorney is in a position to have seen every conceivable sort of business problem, and is the best person to help you work around them or work out of them. Finally, though, be sure that you weigh your attorney's business advice, but make your own decisions. Attorneys are much better at identifying alternative courses of action and potential pitfalls than they are at evaluating the business risks and probabilities. That's *your* job.

LAWYERS AS NEGOTIATORS

In a complex negotiation (e.g., a major contract with a customer, a stock underwriting agreement with an investment banker, or a sellout agreement with another firm) an attorney skilled in negotiation will probably save you many times the legal fee (which itself may be quite sizable). The training and experience of attorneys in the adversary process, in the skilled researching of statute and precedent, and in the relativistic defense of the guilty as well as the innocent, all equip the attorney admirably to help you negotiate against other skilled negotiators. He or she can help you to sharpen up the objective of the negotiation, to develop a negotiating strategy, and to help you counter the unexpected turn in discussions. In short, your attorney can be a most formidable ally when you most need one.

LAWYERS AS INVESTOR INTERFACE

When you are raising funds for your venture, your lawyer is a most logical place to ask for suggestions as to possible investors. After all, lawyers usually have a lot of money and a lot of affluent friends. Moreover, yours may have some affluent clients, some of whom might be interested in exactly your kind of deal. Your lawyer will, after having helped you edit your business plan or offering memorandum, have a double incentive to help you pull off the financing—knowing the chances of getting paid will be a whole lot better if you have money. And, after having helped edit or review the document, your lawyer will have a detailed knowledge of your deal which will greatly help him or her in discussing it with other potential investors.

As a result of having handled private placements and public offerings in the past, your attorney should have some acquaintances in the investment banking community who can prove helpful, as well. Finally, your legal advisor may be helpful in identifying and introducing you to your future banker.

LAWYERS AS DEFENDERS

A hoary cliché has it, "When you're playing the game hard, you're going to get called offside once in a while." The penalty may come in the form of a lawsuit by an angry customer or employee; it may be an action brought against you by your stockholders; it may even be a petition for involuntary bankruptcy brought by panicked creditors. In any of the above, you're going to need a lot more from your attorney than legal advice. You're going to need some decisive, intelligent action. This is where experience, skill, and prestige often hold the balance. "When the going gets tough the tough get going." You want a tough partner now.

PICKING A LAWYER

In the selection of an attorney, unlike the selection of an auditor, the person is everything. The attorney may be working in a large, prestigious firm, or in a smaller firm, depending upon personal inclinations. This individual may even work independently. There are those who believe, that other things being equal, you're better off with a good lawyer in a big firm than a good one in a small firm. The arguments are as follows:

1. The large firm has a better-known name, which may in some circumstances be of value. At least it won't handicap you.
2. The larger firm has a range of specialists in such matters as taxation, real estate, securities regulation, etc., who may from time to time be useful to you.
3. The large firm has more people to draw from, since your own lawyer may occasionally not be available.

In behalf of the small firm, you can probably expect more attention from the senior partners, you may find that people are more informal and accessible, and you may discover, too, that as an entrepreneur in his or her own right, your attorney has a generally better gut feel for your situation. It is the author's overall view that the new entrepreneur may be better off with the smaller firm in many cases. However, large versus small firms is not an issue of paramount importance. Selection of the right lawyer is the key issue.

Your best source of leads for good lawyers is other entrepreneurs. Whom are they using? Whom have they dropped? What (if any) difficult situations have they confronted with this attorney and how did it go? What sorts of fees have they experienced? Did the lawyer ask for stock or finders' fees in connection with financing (both considered mildly unethical)? Does this person seem to have plenty of good connections in the business and financial worlds? How has the lawyer been as an informal business advisor? How are his or her negotiating skills? These and other questions should be used to probe for actual information.

Don't settle for an offhand, "Oh, our lawyer's great—you'll really like this person."

Venture capitalists can often be a good source of referrals for lawyers. If your lawyer is known and respected by the venture capital community, chances are your deal will seem more credible and will certainly be easier to negotiate and close. Also, the VCs may have been through some messy situations, and know which lawyers have handled matters well.

Recommendations from bankers, owners of large businesses, and other nonentrepreneurial types are likely to be slightly suspect because the recommenders are suggesting somebody they would wish to have represent them—but their business problems are radically different from your own. As far as the local bar association is concerned, forget it. You might as well be looking in the Yellow Pages.

In interviewing the prospective lawyer, take along your first-cut business plan. Have a list of questions thought out ahead of time. Take up the same issues you raised with the other entrepreneurs. Who are some of this lawyer's other corporate clients? Is there a present or downstream conflict? How much time is this legal advisor going to be able to spend with you? With whom will you work when your lawyer is not available? How about fees? (Anywhere from $50 to $200 per hour may be justifiable). Will this person take some collection cases on a contingency basis? (Probably not if he or she is a top lawyer). How about the candidate's experience in financing, public offerings, and SEC registrations in particular? Your list will grow rather long as you begin to consider all the things you'd like to know about your future lawyer.

In evaluating a lawyer, don't rely on analytical considerations alone: listen to your intuition. Do you like this person? Do you think you could work together creatively as a team in strategy or negotiating sessions? Is this lawyer as tough as you'd like? How is this person going to come across to the types of people you'll be dealing with? Do you get the feeling that this candidate takes a genuine interest in your company? Are you hiring a white-gloved patrician or a street fighter?

Try to interview the top three or four candidates, even though you may be perfectly happy with the very first one. This approach is desirable, if only to see some of the range of types available. Additional acquaintances will never hurt you, either.

PATENT LAWYERS

Patent law is such a specialized field that even large firms do not ordinarily presume to practice it. When the time comes for a patent lawyer (or if you've come to doubt the abilities of your old one), your attorney can probably supply some valuable leads. Now you will be dealing with an area in which analytical considerations count for much, subjective impressions very little. Here, as in selecting your corporate attorney, however, anything but the best may prove very costly in the long run.

You will be particularly lucky if you can find a top patent lawyer who is already working in or familiar with your particular field. This can save some substantial startup time and cost. One way of finding such a person is by examining the key patents in your field and contacting the attorneys who wrote them. An out-of-town patent attorney is probably OK, since the two of you will not have extensive day-to-day dealings, and the dealings you do have can be largely conducted by mail.

As you interview your patent attorney prospect, keep in mind that this person may have to help you defend your patent someday. How effective will the lawyer be in court? What's his or her track record? Who are some clients who have been through the fire with this lawyer?

PECIAL COUNSEL

Just as you choose a specialized lawyer for your patent work, there will be occasions when you will want to employ specialists for other reasons as well. This is customary, and you must not expect your own law firm to be tops or even competent in every aspect of the law. Bankruptcy, for example, is a specialty; in such dire circumstances you don't want to be advised by a generalist. Also securities law, as it may apply to an IPO, may well require special counsel. It may also happen that in some situations (such as a dispute with a customer also represented by your law firm), your firm will disqualify itself and you will need to seek special counsel.

In general, just keep this in mind: There's absolutely nothing so expensive as a second-rate lawyer.

CONVENTIONAL WISDOM: The lawyer's the one you call when you're in trouble.

REALITY: The lawyer's the one you call *before* you're in trouble.

REFERENCES

1. Ronstadt, Robert C. *Entrepreneurship—Text, Cases and Notes.* Dover, Mass. Lord Publishing Co., 1984.

    See especially, "Legal Issues: About Lawyers, Their Selection and Their Use." (p. 565)

2. Vorhees, Theodore. "Selecting a Lawyer for Your Business." *Management Aids for Small Manfacturers*, Annual No. 8 (1962) pp. 66–73.

    Published by the Small Business Administration in Washington, D.C., this publication gives practical advice and checklists for any startup firm.

26

Custodial Operations and How to Avoid Them

"We trained hard ... but it seemed that every time we were beginning to form up into teams we would be reorganized. I was to learn later in life that we tend to meet any new situation by reorganizing; and a wonderful method it can be for creating the illusion of progress while producing confusion, inefficiency, and demoralization." *... Petronius Arbiter, 210 B.C.*

In applying the principle of "enlightened mediocrity" to the day-to-day operations of the company, you must be prepared to strike a reasonable balance between custodial and entrepreneurial duties; then let loose of the rest of the custodial chores. This can be a lot harder than it sounds.

At the outset, you were president, operations manager, plant manager, personnel director, and sales manager and a lot of other things all rolled up together. The distinction between these duties was probably not clear, because you alone were doing them all at once. As the company evolves, you *must* get rid of many, if not most, of these duties, even if you're convinced the people to whom you must delegate them can only do a 70 percent job.

Your primary energies must be focused on the *growing edge* of the company—not on the day-to-day struggles.

You must be free to press market development and to search for new markets and new products. You must have energy and time for working with new customer prospects, with your financial sources, with government agencies, with possible overseas business contacts. You will need to be looking for possible candidates for acquisition and for key staff members. You must, more than anyone else in your firm, assert to the world your firm's leadership. This involves speaking before technical and business groups, membership on industry and government panels, giving interviews to key publications in your industry, and arranging press conferences for new product introduction. You, in short, must be the key, visible interface between your company and the outside world.

The fact that your time is largely allocated to these presidential duties does not mean that you are any less responsible for the ongoing operation of the firm. It simply means that you must establish the means for *delegation, communication of objectives*, and *feedback on performance*—all very elementary Management 101 stuff, you say. However, Management 101 does not tell you how to accomplish this in a tiny company with rapidly-changing problems. Moreover, you may have to redefine the jobs, juggle workforce, and rethink your system about every six months for the first couple of years. Things just don't stay neatly in place in the dynamic, sometimes chaotic, atmosphere of the new enterprise.

Your delegation (organization) plan should be such that only three or four managers report directly to you. Who they are depends on what business you're in. In general, however, they ought to be:

1. Financial Manager (chief accountant, controller, treasurer)
2. Operations Manager (or plant manager, office manager, general manager, etc.)
3. Marketing Manager (or sales manager)
4. Chief Engineer (or VP, Engineering, or Technical Director, etc.)

If you have more than about four line managers reporting to you, you are going to get too involved in custodial management. Some presidents like to have reporting direct such people as Materials Manager (purchasing, inventory control, incoming inspection, etc.), Quality Assurance Manager (Q.C., inspection, final test, standards, etc.), Personnel Manager, and so on. Important though these functions are, to the extent that you become enmeshed in them you will be unable to do your own job.

Following are some general comments on delegating jobs, communicating orders, and eliciting feedback.

Financial Manager

Do not permit this individual to report to anyone but you. The finances of the company are its lifeblood, and you must keep your finger on the pulse. Your financial manager will have a great deal to do, much of which will not require your direct surveillance once the systems are set up to your satisfaction. This manager will probably function very well with one clerk initially, perhaps adding one more for each additional million dollars' volume. The key areas in which you will wish to involve yourself will be:

1. Weekly review of cash flow projections and accounts receivable. A regular one-hour meeting every week will be sufficient except in times of crisis. This regular schedule will permit your accountant to get data together and be prepared.
2. Preparation of budgets. This will occur at least every six months under the general supervision of your financial manager. You will be spending substantial energy at budget time, working out all the compromises between programs desired by the operating groups and those permitted by resources available, and wrestling with the inevitable conflicts.
3. Monthly review of operations, comparing budgeted to actual P&L. This would typically involve your entire team, including key third-level members with budgetary responsibility. These meetings should occur just as soon after monthly closing as humanly possible—ideally not more than ten days into the next month. Otherwise, in the general march of events, people tend to forget what went on, and the conditions causing those overruns will still be uncorrected.

Even if you lack an accounting background, make it a point to look over the general ledger, the cash journal, and accounts payable from time to time—unannounced. This will give you an opportunity to spot certain classes of problems, such as late or incorrect posting, jam-ups in certain accounting areas, impending payable and receivable problems, incorrectly computed rep commissions, improper product price entries, etc. More important, it will help to keep your financial manager on his toes. Ask plenty of questions, even though some may be naive.

Operations Manager

You should meet at least weekly with this person, for a couple of hours. The operations manager will be responsible for many of the major classes of expenditure in the organization, including plant operation, personnel, purchasing, and maybe substantial subcontracting. The manager will also b responsible for the development and holding of shipping schedules and th production schedules to back them up. He or she may also be responsible fo the efficient operation of the office, which can be a hard problem in th growing company. In short, this person may have more different things t worry about than anybody else in the company.

Your operations manager should be given rather great latitude in ap proaching the job. This manager should be the one to originate requests fo labor-saving equipment, design changes to simplify production or procure ment, and various cost-reduction plans. At the same time, the heat is con stantly on this person for on-time delivery, acceptable quality, and on-targe production costs. The manager will also bear the brunt of many personne problems and will spend substantial time hiring and training people.

To understand what's happening in this bailiwick, you should try t attend some weekly operations staff meetings (these may be called productio status meetings or schedule reviews). This is where the real clashes occur where tough decisions get made, where incipient ulcers get their start. Thi meeting is where you find out *why* certain jobs are in trouble, *why* there is bottleneck in Test. You should not intervene in this sort of meeting bu neither should you allow yourself to be excluded from it.

In addition to your weekly meeting with the operations manager, it woul be well to spot check, on a nonscheduled basis, the large-dollar areas under hi or her purview. In many manufacturing companies, for example, purchase account for 50 to 70 percent of all expenditures. It is therefore one of the area you should probe. Is the buyer doing his or her whole job, or just struggling t prevent unanticipated parts shortages? Is the buyer getting multiple quota tions? Maintaining decent vendor records of cost, quality, and delivery? Ac tively seeking functional equivalents for high-cost items? Are your engineer getting suggestions and questions from the buyer? Is this employee the first t raise make-or-buy questions? Is he or she approaching makers of major pur chased items to negotiate annual buys? Is this person, in short, initiating actio or just reacting to the press of events? Inventory and stock control are bot critical areas in some kinds of operations. Be sure that you look at the invento ries and test the methods used to control them from time to time.

Have a look at the phone bills and the copying invoices occasionally You're not being nosey—just interested. Success is the sum of a thousan details performed well.

Sales and Marketing Manager

You'll have plenty of day-to-day contact with this person, in pursuit of majo orders. However, he or she should meet with you monthly and review las month's bookings and the updated forecast for the next quarter. Who are th customers, what are they going to buy, and when? When can we plan to ship? Do this by territory, to give yourself some fix on the effectiveness of each rep or salesperson. Who is making their quotas? How did last month's bookings shape up against forecast? Review the problem areas: contracts lost, customer disputes, salesperson problems. What changes in the product are needed? What additional literature? Advertising? Promotion?

The sales and marketing manager must learn sooner or later to accept responsibility for the fact that sales forecasts are the basis for all planning for the company. If this manager is consistently unable to meet the reasonable forecasts he or she developed, you may have the wrong person in the job. You must not under any circumstances allow this manager to isolate you from contact with the customers or the salesforce. You should make it a point to spend at least a quarter of your time with customers and salespeople. If you lose the feel of your market, you've lost touch with the whole business.

Chief Engineer

If yours is a technology company, the chief engineer should report directly to you. If the emphasis is more on manufacturing and marketing it may be OK for this person to report to the operations manager. In either case, it is incumbent upon you to stay abreast of what's going on in the engineering department. You will want not only a roster of its projects and progress, but also some reading on the department's productivity. Engineers are fond of saying "You can't schedule invention." However true this may be, it is also true that most of what goes on in engineering departments is not invention. It is straightforward application of well-known principles to modify or redesign existing products. You can schedule and budget this work, and the chief engineer has the same sort of managerial responsibility as anybody else on the team for meeting schedule and budget.

On the more creative side of this job, is the chief engineer originating ideas for new products and significant improvements in old ones? Is this person keeping the company abreast of the state of the art or merely implementing modifications as demanded by the marketing department? Does the chief engineer provide any ideas for the production and test people? What little R&D projects are being "bootlegged" because the chief engineer personally believes in them? Does this person make it a point to go out and talk to customers once in a while?

Unless your company is heavily involved in innovation, you may not need a scheduled weekly meeting with the chief engineer. However, you should be a presence in the department from time to time, to nose around and get a feel for what is (or what is not) happening. And once a month, your chief engineer must be accountable for milestones and budgets, along with everyone else.

TOO MUCH INFORMATION

A basic principle of operation that requires some time for most new presidents to grasp is this: *You should try to learn what the minimum level of information is for you to run the company satisfactorily.* It may be a great deal less than you think. It is literally possible to run certain kinds of companies knowing only the daily cash balance or the day's shipments. The less operational information you personally must process and act on, the better.

There may be certain cases in which you will wish to immerse yourself temporarily to solve a problem, which will require a good deal more information than normal. However, resist the temptation of making the person responsible generate a new report on the problem every month from now on. You won't read it. Handle short term problems on an *ad hoc* basis, in sufficient depth so that you can actually assist in the solution. Then let your manager see that the agreed-upon solution is implemented while you move on to a different problem. If you try to monitor everything all the time, you will have time to do no presidential work, and you will not contribute very much to the operations either.

It makes us all feel very important to have lots of staff reports, operating statistics, and computer printouts passing over our desks. However, this stuff all costs money to generate, and you should ask in every case: (a) Does this really need my attention, or could somebody else handle it?, and (b) Was there any reason for this report at all? What would happen if we eliminated it altogether?

Reports and memos are the basic tools of the empire builders in big companies. In the small company, they can quickly be carried to excess simply because everybody has so much to do anyway. The net cost of being underinformed is probably much less than being overinformed.

CONVENTIONAL WISDOM: You can't know too much about your operation.

REALITY: Right.

REFERENCES

1. Kelly, P., Lawyer, K., and Baumback, C. *How to Organize and Operate a Small Business.* 4th ed. Englewood Cliffs, N.J.: Prentice Hall, 1968.

    If you're going to run your company by the book, here's the book to run it by. Covers every phase of small business management, including manufacturing, marketing, accounting, and control.

2. Thurston, D. B. *Manual for the President of a Growing Company.* Englewood Cliffs, N.J.: Prentice Hall, 1962.

    A big book of practical guidance in a nonexhaustive form. Good treatment of many administrative functions.

3. Easton, Allen. *Managing for Negative Growth.* Reston, Virg.: Reston (Prentice Hall), 1976.

    Provides many useful ideas for coping with difficult small-company problems. Deals with cutbacks, illiquidity, and other gut topics. Excellent.

4. Eisenberg, Joseph. *Turnaround Management,* New York: McGraw-Hill Book Co., 1972.

    This is an excellent, hard-nosed treatment of many types of business problems, written from a survival point of view.

27

Millstones and Other Fixed Assets

Beware of all enterprises that require new clothes.
. . Henry David Thoreau

There is something uniquely and tangibly gratifying about having a beautiful plant, modern gleaming equipment, and a fully-integrated operation. It is, in a way, a monument to the entrepreneur—a solid testament that *here* is some one who does things first class.

Regrettably, it is often the case that the monument becomes the tomb stone of the enterprise. In a study of ninety-five small Midwest manufacturing firms, Hoad and Rosko observed that only nine were successes.[1] Of the remainder, fully 45 percent of the entrepreneurs felt that unwise investment in capital equipment had been responsible for their failures. Indeed, it is hard to think of a worse use for venture capital than tying it up in bricks, mortar and machinery. The reasons for this, while obvious, seem to elude a great many entrepreneurs:

[1]Hoad, William M. & Rosko, Peter: *Management Factors Contributing to Success or Failure of New Small Manufacturers.* Ann Arbor, Bureau of Business Research, Graduate School of Business Administration, University of Michigan, 1964.

1. Except in mature firms, the profit arises from sources other than skill in manufacturing. It may be from ingenious product design, proprietary technology, innovative marketing, or just tremendous demand. Very rarely does it arise because you can make things a lot cheaper than anybody else.

2. Tying up capital in machinery means there is that much less for product promotion, inventories, accounts receivable, product development, or the other creative or necessary costs of a growing company.

3. Committing funds to specialized equipment may be greatly increasing the total risk of your company. If the product folds, if a better production process is found, or if it's just plain cheaper to buy it elsewhere, you're stuck. You may, to raise cash, be obliged to dump the machinery at a fraction of its value. If it ties up cash that could otherwise pay creditors, it may be the factor that topples you into bankruptcy.

4. Apparent cost savings due to improved machinery have a way of being very illusory. They are usually computed on a model of full utilization, long runs, minimal downtime, and other factors that are extremely difficult to guarantee in the fluid environment of a new company or a developing market.

5. An elaborate plant usually entails costs that are hidden altogether or are hard to evaluate *ex ante*. These include maintenance, power, materials, production scheduling, and management time and effort.

Therefore, before commiting large amounts of your capital to plant and equipment, weigh carefully the following alternatives:

1. *Buy the product completely made.* Give somebody else the manufacturing headaches and profit, if any. Contrary to intuition, this price may be substantially lower than your true cost to manufacture, simply because the manufacturer is taking on the work to make a contribution to its existing plant overhead. The manufacturer may wish to keep workers employed, to keep machines loaded, or to maintain volume with its vendors. For any number of reasons, it often costs less to have the product made outside. And even if it doesn't, ask yourself if the premium paid isn't less than the aggravation and risk of being in manufacturing.

2. *Buy premade components, and simply assemble.* The same arguments apply as in #1, except that you may be less dependent upon a single source. You will be adding some value; however, it is likely that you will also be adding to working capital requirements, due to additional inventories of parts and work in process.

3. *Rent time in someone else's plant.* If your product requires operations o costly machines (such as large dropforgings, large injection molde parts, and centrifugal castings), you may be able to find a plant with th requisite machinery willing to sell you machine time, possibly at thei marginal cost. Other operations can then be done in your own plant Computers, circuit testers, environmental test equipment, and so fortl can also fit this pattern.

4. *Lease equipment instead of buying it.* This is the final step, short c outright ownership. You may find that the terms of the lease limit you flexibility to a degree, but at least your money is not totally frozen i company–owned plant equipment.

   In the past few years, lessors have become quite sophisticate about leasing equipment to startup companies. In 1980, it was hard t get major lessors interested in a startup with little demonstrated abilit to generate cash to service the lease, and few if any assets to back it up Today however, there are several firms in the "venture leasing" busi ness, who share in the risks and rewards of providing lease capital t young firms. They often take warrants as a condition for writing th lease. Some require no warrants, but require an above-market interes rate. Still others will require a large "down payment," which reduces th amount of money at risk. There are even lease brokers who will find yo a lessor and who may even lend you the down payment, in return fo (you guessed it) warrants.

   Venture leasing is such a dynamic area that it is essential to be up to-date on your options. One good bet for guidance may be to find small company Chief Financial Officer who has just been through it Also, lease brokers may be worth talking to.

5. *Consider used or self-constructed equipment.* Depending upon you industry, if a plant seems inevitable, you may be able to find use equipment that will serve the desired purpose for several years at fraction of new-equipment cost. If you're looking for machine tools presses, and other equipment of this sort, there are national listin services to help you locate the desired piece. If it's electronic productio or test equipment, computers, simulators, environmental chambers laboratory equipment, etc., there are innumerable sources for use equipment of this type. Auctions and bankruptcy sales are among th best places to pick up equipment bargains. If the machine is specia purpose, consider the possibility of making it. You may surprise your self. Give your plant manager a little applause for saving the compan $10,000 cash by a little innovation. Or, pay this person a $1,000 bonus

6. *Use low-cost production space.* If you must manufacture, consider separating your production operation from your front-office functions, such as sales. Then seek out older industrial space, mill buildings, empty school structures, vacant garages, or any other low-cost space that can be cleaned up, painted, and made into efficient, attractive, production space. Consider manufacturing in high-unemployment areas, especially inner-city locations, where substantial grants for plant, equipment, employee-training, and property tax relief may be available, as well as a better pool of labor.

All of these routes should receive consideration before betting the company's future on more plants and equipment.

MAKE-OR-BUY ANALYSIS

The usual industrial engineering approach to make-or-buy analysis, while appropriate to large enterprises, may be quite misleading in the small company context. It focuses, predictably, upon the engineering aspects of unit cost. It does not take explicitly into account the overall corporate questions, concerning additional financial risk, liquidity, alternate use of capital, and risks of dependence on outside sources. These are likely to be much more significant questions then mere unit cost, but they cannot be properly weighed by your purchasing agent alone. They are decisions in which you yourself must participate. Similarly, decisions on optimum purchase quantities of materials are often made without adequate attention to the risks of obsolescence, illiquidity, and alternate uses of capital. Long term supply commitments of any magnitude should involve top management, not just the purchasing agent. The apparent savings of volume buying may be dearly· bought.

THE PLANT-BUILDING INSTINCT

There are a number of reasons in addition to entrepreneurial ego why companies invest unwisely in plans and equipment. These reasons include the following:

1. Relative to non-balance-sheet investments (e.g., market development and advertising, which are expensed), plant investment seems somehow

"prudent"—after all, it's only changing one asset (money) for another (machinery). The apparent net worth of the company is unaffected.

2. The plant-building instinct is strong. Plant managers tend to measure their own worth by the amount of resources they can divert into an ever bigger-and-better plant. Production engineers are quick to point out the "savings" and profit improvement that a more efficient plant would produce. Workers are quick to take up the cry for better conditions, if it seems to be in the air. Finally, even financial backers may seem to give tacit blessing to a big new plant. After all, it's a lot more tangible than all that expensed R&D.

3. There is often a belief, sometimes justifiable, that customers will be impressed by a classy plant and will therefore be influenced to give you the contract. There is no denying that in some cases this is the decisive factor, especially when you are dealing with a large company or the government.

4. Government programs to promote capital investment and "jobs creation," such as the investment tax credit and accelerated depreciation, as well as painless equipment financing offered by manufacturers, both can create the illusion that enormous savings will somehow accrue, thus presenting further temptations to the instinctive plant-builder.

For all these reasons, you may find yourself besieged with demands that a new plant and equipment be purchased. However, you may be the only person in the company who is in a position to perceive the total effect that this will have on the future of the enterprise as a whole. When you have weighed all benefits, costs, and risks, have the conviction to stick by your decision. A good CEO knows how to say no.

Remember, you will have plenty of other chances to play "You bet your company." Fancy plant equipment certainly is not a high enough pot for that sort of bet.

PARTING SHOT: If you've got $500,000 in the bank, do everything you can to keep it there. The cash you save by deferring plant outlays may just be the cash that keeps the company alive next year.

CONVENTIONAL WISDOM: The prudent entrepreneur seeks to minimize unit product costs, thus maximizing profit.

REALITY: The prudent entrepreneur keeps all costs variable, thus maximizing the amount of cash in the bank.

REFERENCES

1. Buskirk, Richard H.; Vaughn, J. *Managing New Enterprises.* St. Paul, Minn.: West Publishing Co., 1976.

    See especially Chapter 19, "Acquiring Production Capabilities." Focused on results (not efficiency), used equipment, subcontractors, etc.

2. Gross, Harry. *Make or Buy.* Englewood Cliffs, N.J.: Prentice Hall 1966.

    A solid treatment of the industrial-engineering viewpoint on make or buy decisions.

28

Managing the R&D Function

"If it works, it's obsolete"   .. Anonymous

It has been the unintended but irresistible tendency of this book to talk i
terms of technology-based companies engaged in the design, manufacture
and marketing of some new product. Such companies, though far from
major portion of startups in any given year, are most often those marked fo
national markets, for significant growth, for venture capital eligibility, an
ultimately, for public offerings. To the extent then, that technology companie
are dependent on the talents of technologists, let us explore some aspects o
living with them.

ENGINEERS AS A SPECIES

As a group, engineers probably create more value than any other segment o
our economy.

238

It is the engineer, not the scientist, the banker, the businessperson, the salesperson, or the stockbroker, who creates the new products, chemistries, materials, machines, computers, satellites, ICBMs, artificial hearts, and nearly everything else that makes our industrial society run. The engineering profession is demanding in terms of native intelligence, educational duration, personal stamina, and professional standards. And unlike most of us, the engineer's performance is judged by the most stringent of yardsticks: the product has to work! No wonder good ones are so hard to find. Yet find them we must in a technology-based company.

WHAT ENGINEERS DO IN STARTUPS

The image of engineers sitting around all day, creating new designs is just a bit misleading. In fact, in the typical small firm most engineering hours are absorbed by tasks that are anything but creative: poring over catalogs looking for parts and components to purchase, so that they need not be reinvented and retooled; prototyping and testing designs that were created months ago, possibly by others; writing specifications, test procedures, operator's manuals, production standards, and myriads of other documents; supervising or performing the drafting of engineering drawings; attending review meetings, vendor meetings, status meetings, technical conferences, and a dozen others; testing the early production units; and so on, *ad nauseam.* The remarkable thing is that there is any time left to do engineering.

Although most of these functions are not "creative" in the strictest sense, all are essential to the success of your fledgling venture. And, given the usual financial constraints, there's no one to delegate them to, so the engineers do them all. While this may be inescapable for a period of time, the sooner you get out of this mode, the better.

As your venture matures, it should be possible gradually to improve the "creativity" component of each engineer's time, by supporting this person with proper drafting, clerical, technical, and manufacturing support. The engineering function in a startup is generally characterized by one other set of constraints: a very narrow time focus. The initial product must get done at all cost, must work, and must be within budget. There is little time or energy to expand on future products, novel features, new application, or new technologies. This constraint makes it much more difficult for the typical engineer to function in a fasttrack startup. An unusual combination of talent and single-mindedness is demanded.

Again, as growth permits, the time-horizons of the engineering department will expand so that different people can be concerned with different

aspects of the future plan. Thus, a current array of tasks might ultimately loo
like this:

Immediate (0–6 mos.)	Intermediate (6–12 mos.)	Long Range (12–36 mos.)
• Get prototype working • Finish production documentation • Develop test fixtures • Write users' manuals	• New customer applications • Cost reduction program • New options and features • New software • Fix field problems	• New technical approac] • Super performance ve] sion • Ultra cheap version • New market requirements

PRODUCT ENGINEERING: SOME TRENDS

In the 1990s, management will have to cope with several trends that wil
significantly impact the nature of the engineering function and the innovativ
process itself. These trends include the following:

Ever-Shorter Product Life-Cycles

The onrush of technology has created something of a Frankenstein for tech
nologists themselves: products may be obsolescent before they are eve
shipped. this is not merely true of your company's products—it is also true o
the products of your suppliers. Thus, if for example you design in a semicon
ductor component that is in full production today, you are almost assured tha
it will have been replaced by something new in the market by the time *you*
product is in full production. Obviously, then, making the correct guesse
about the speed and direction of your vendors' development progress is a
essential as appraising your competition's.

Greater Demand for Customization

Neither the commercial customer nor the private consumer is disposed t
accept whatever is being offered any longer. If the consumer buys a car, he o
she expects a wide range of options, finishes, and accessories. If this perso
buys a printing press, a computer, a chemical plant, or a jetliner, the attitud
is the same: Give me what *I* want. Engineers will still be designing standar

products, to be sure, but they must design products that can adapt, chameleonlike, to the needs of the individual customer in a routine way, without upsetting the engineering or manufacturing functions. This is a major engineering challenge in the 1990s.

Black Box Integration

What goes on in engineering departments will be greatly affected by this continuing trend. In 1900, an engineer designing a locomotive is also expected to design the boiler, the valves, the drive linkages, the wheels, the suspension, the operator controls, and all other parts of the system. Today, not only would there be a specialist for each part—the specialist would be working for other (vendors') companies. The designer would merely specify the components, assemble them in a prototype "system," and turn them over to the manufacturing department, which would in reality be an assembly and test operation. This, of course, is largely how automobiles are built. The advent of pre-engineered modules, such as single-chip computers, monolithic memories, modular power supplies, complex integrated circuits for communication, interfacing, etc., has drastically altered the role of electrical engineers, transforming them into systems designers or even software engineers. Much the same is occurring in other engineering specialties, drastically affecting the content of engineering work, generally but not always for the better.

Computer-Aided Design

Computers, since their invention, have of course been used to perform engineering calculations. Today, however, we are witnessing a new phenomenon. An electrical engineer can sit before a video terminal and specify a design by its inputs and outputs. The computer will then offer up a circuit design that performs the desired function. The engineer can inspect, modify, and even "test" the design by simulation, without ever touching a soldering iron. Then, almost at the press of a workstation key, the engineer can transform the verified design data into the tooling for a custom large-scale integrated circuit, upon which his or her circuit will appear, perhaps replicated thousands of times. The next thing the engineer sees will in fact be the functional prototype of the integrated circuit, ready for testing. When it works, it's ready for production! Similarly, much of the grunt work of structural, mechanical, and civil engineering can now be performed graphically on computers, shortening the design time, eliminating overdesign, and improving the

creative content of the design function. Finally, CAD is permitting increasin
automation of the tooling function by automatically creating programs fo
generating integrated circuits, printed circuit cards, and machined meta
parts. Many believe that we are on the threshhold of explosive growth in thi
area. We'd better be, because it is our only hope of coping with shortene
product life and customized production!

PATENTS

In our generally accelerated technical environments, patents are assuming
somewhat different role from that of the past. Design patents become increas
ingly meaningless when product lives are shorter than the time-cycle t
obtain the patent. The engineering time and effort it takes to follow throug
and obtain a patent must be carefully weighed against the value it would hav
to the company, *vis à vis* keeping the design as a "trade secret."

Patents, to the extent that you they are pursued at all, should hav
significant economic life and should focus on more fundamental techniques
processes, and innovations than perhaps was the case a few years ago. Natu
rally, a strong patent position makes your venture incrementally more attrac
tive to the investment community, but short-lived design patents will no
impress the financial community and will be of little practical value to th
company. Remember, too, that patents only have value to the extent tha
their owners have the money and the energy to defend them. Startup compa
nies are usually short on both.

INDUSTRIAL DESIGN

Industrial design is a highly specialized field, dealing with issues of produc
appearance, ease of use, ease of servicing, packaging, and overall custome
reaction. It is an area in which even large companies are often deficient. Smal
startup ventures should almost always therefore retain an industrial desig
consultant to look at the product and suggest ways in which to make it visuall
and functionally appealing. In so doing, the consultant may also be able t
show you how to reduce its cost by combining functions, changing material
or finishes, repackaging, or by using different types of vendors. These ser
vices will cost you a few thousand dollars, but the result should be well wort
it. Every major city has industrial design firms. Interview a few, look at thei
work, and see what they can offer. Don't try to do industrial design yourself

ARE AND FEEDING OF ENGINEERS

Since much of your startup venture's money may be spent on and by engineers, it behooves one to think carefully about controlling this cost and being sure the company is getting its money's worth.

Recruiting and Hiring

In this era, engineers are scarce; workforce projections indicate that they will be in short supply throughout the balance of this century. Therefore, to compete for the best, you must be entrepreneurial. In searching for prospects, use the list of sources in Chapter 17. In interviewing, stress the things that your little company can offer that Colossus Industries cannot: opportunity to see design all the way through from inception to production; flexible working hours; informal, collegial environment; future opportunity for equity participation; more responsibility than someone the same age could get in a large firm; maximum scope for initiative and creativity; opportunity to grow with growing firm, etc.

In recruiting for scarce talents, be prepared to make an offer on the spot, if necessary, "subject to routine reference checks." Rest assured that your competition is similarly prepared. Be concise but complete in outlining salary, benefits, bonuses, or stock plans, and be sure to mention that this person must sign an invention assignment form. Give the prospect a deadline; make it known that he or she is only one of several strong condidates being considered. You can also be entrepreneurial in enlisting engineering talent from sources different from those used by the large companies. For example:

1. Hire students. Some of the best talent, especially in areas such as software, is in school. Hire them part-time or on a co-op basis. Hire them as temporaries, if they want to lay out for a term to earn money.

2. Consider aliens. Many large companies cannot, or will not, hire aliens, due to defense contracts or corporate policy. However, talented people arrive in the U.S. daily from technically advanced countries such as Canada, England, Russia, Taiwan, and Japan. Many are educated in the U.S. at our top schools. Where a language problem exists, you may be able to get a highly experienced engineer on a very favorable basis for all concerned.

3. Hire retired engineers. For many specialities, such as mechanical engineering, tool design, production engineering, circuit design, and others, a part-time semi-retired engineer may be the ideal worker for your firm. Especially in the mechanical, hydraulic and electro-mechanical areas, this

person's years of experience may prove priceless in a young, inexperience
design group.

Carrots and Sticks

Your primary management tools, as with each other department in your firm
are budgets and schedules. We have all heard the saying, "You can't schedul
invention," but as we have seen, very little invention is, in fact, going on i
your engineering department. Engineers' tasks are highly amenable to track
ing via milestones, and their expenses are readily controllable since the
consist mainly of salaries. As always, judicious alternation of the carrot an
the stick is indicated.

On-time completion of tasks, ingenious solutions to problems, and out
standing work of every type should be singled out for praise and recognition
People should receive recognition for creativity as well as task completion
however, for this establishes the climate in which engineers love to work

The stick, when employed, must be used privately, one-on-one. Ever
effort should be made to attack the problem, not the person. If repeate
experiences show that the talent or motivation is deficient, don't delay takin
the necessary action to terminate. There's no room to hide your mistakes in
small company.

Supporting the Engineer

At the outset, with limited resources, your engineers may have to double i
brass. However, as your resources increase, you will have some hiring latitude
At this juncture, it is important before hiring more engineers to be sure you ar
properly supporting the ones you already have. Do they have enough draftin
help, technicians, and clerical support? Do they have the right instruments
tools, and computation facilities? Do they have, in short, what's needed to ge
the job done right? If not, adding more engineers will make matters worse, no
better. The new engineers won't want to be technicians, either.

Supplementing the Engineer

Most companies have engineering projects of two sorts: the mainstream prod
uct developments and the secondary. The latter might be special options
accessories software packages, or other improvements to the existing produc

line needed urgently by marketing. In such instances, rather than interrupt the larger projects, it may be optimal to contract out the special project to a consultant on an ad hoc basis. This way, the work gets done quickly, you know your costs in advance, and the overall department is not disrupted. Finding the right specialist can often result in a better job than might be done in-house, as well.

Marketing versus Engineering

In small companies, a dynamic can easily be permitted to spring up that is destructive to all concerned. From marketing's viewpoint, it may look as though engineering is not being responsive to the needs of the marketplace, that the competition's engineering is always a lap ahead of ours, and that the engineers are unwilling to interrupt their work schedule to help the company by working on that "special deal."

To the engineers, the same circumstances may look like this: Marketing expects us to offer every feature that every competitor can ever think up; they don't have enough initiative to sell our standard products, so they expect us constantly to custom-engineer specials; and worse, they continually interrupt our work on the new generation product to add some marginal feature to the old product.

This dynamic, left unchecked, can undermine productivity and morale on all sides. To avoid it you may be able to (a) include marketing in engineering reviews, (b) include engineering in all marketing strategy/product line planning efforts, (c) provide an applications engineering function exclusively for marketing's use, or (d) make sure that key engineers periodically make customer calls to stay in touch with the marketplace.

Evaluating your Engineering Function

The engineering function is a costly one and must be subjected to the same investment criteria as any other, despite the fact that the "investment" in product design does not appear on the balance sheet. The engineering investment must be capitalized for planning purposes just like tooling, inventories, and other product costs. A project that pays out with say, three work-years of engineering investment might never pay out if the effort were eventually to require five. Slippages, overruns, re-engineering, fixing units in the field, and late or incomplete production documentation are not generally problems of themselves but are rather symptoms that your engineering investment is being spent poorly. It may be that no corrective measure, short of replacing from the top, will correct the problem—assuming there is still time an money enough to correct it at all.

IN CONCLUSION

You may, from time to time, conclude that your top engineers are a bunch c prima donnas with all that the term implies. Well, you're probably right. Th opera may, in fact, be the appropriate metaphor for a high-technology startup You may be the greatest impressario on earth, have a super orchestra, a fin stage manager, a good director, and talented extras—but without those prim donnas, your show is going nowhere. The sooner you learn to live with them the better.

CONVENTIONAL WISDOM: You can't schedule invention.

REALITY: You can certainly schedule whatever it is your engineering depart ment is doing.

REFERENCES

1. Glasser, Allen. *Research & Development Management.* Englewood Cliffs, N.J. Prentice Hall, 1982.

     A compact and practical guide for managing the entire process. Good sec tions on proposal writing and presentation skills.

2. Parker, R. C. *Management of Innovation.* New York: John Wiley & Sons., 1982

     Excellent for guidelines for product innovation, including eight detailed case histories drawn from different industries.

3. Peiz, Donald C.; Andrews, Frank M. *Scientists in Organizations.* New York: John Wiley & Sons, 1966.

     Explores the dilemma of organizations versus freedom, in a study of 130(scientists doing both research and development. Came up with measures o performance and related it to many variables. Determinants of motivation, dedi cation, and creativity are all discussed.

4. Shames, William A. *Venture Management.* New York: The Free Press (Mac millan), 1974.

     Contains extensive treatment of the business of inventing.

29

Life after Death: Our Beneficent Bankruptcy Laws

Some days nothing *seems to go right.* . . *corollary of* **Murphy's Law**

To most of us, the term "bankruptcy" holds chilling connotations comparable to terminal cancer, execution, or just walking off the edge. The bankrupt businessperson as social leper is a recurrent American theme. Dark though the connotations may be, however, our liberal laws provide a surprising degree of relief for the bankrupt businessperson; indeed, they may be considered as just one more tool of entrepreneurial survival.

HAT IS BANKRUPTCY?

As generally construed, bankruptcy is the chronic inability to pay one's debts.[1] In the academic sense, it would be defined as having a negative net worth (technical insolvency). However, many firms operate with negative net

[1]Bankruptcy should also be differentiated from *failure.* Dun & Bradstreet defines *five* failure modes: failed companies cease operation (a) following a bankruptcy or assignment of

worth and are never declared bankrupt by a court. In a practical sense, the bankrupt firm is usually characterized by negative working capital (current assets minus current liabilities), hence the inability to meet current obligations. Indeed, for many entrepreneurs the only thing that differentiates between current conditions and bankruptcy, then, is a state of mind.

The usual causes of bankruptcy are generally a combination of under capitalization, inept management, and over-expansion. However, there is often a major precipitating factor, such as the failure of a large account receivable, a factory fire, a major lawsuit, or the unwillingness of a lender to renew a note. It is uniquely tragic when a company that is growing, even profitably but absorbing all its cash, is hit by one of these precipitating events. If cash management is poor, assets are illiquid (e.g., tied up in plant equipment or excessive inventory), or lending relationships in poor repair, the result can well be bankruptcy.

WHAT THE LAW SAYS

In ancient Rome, the legal code provided that the bankrupt debtor had to surrender his *person* to the creditor for disposition, without any judicial proceeding at all. The creditor could, presumably, put you to work as a slave or sell you off for that purpose, or possibly donate you for lion-fodder, as wholesome example to other debtors.

By the Middle Ages, things had softened a bit, however. Kings could among other things, grant the bankrupt debtor a delay of payment without consent of creditors. Colonial America was settled, of course, in a significant area, by debtors released from overcrowded English prisons. However, by 1978, when our present Bankruptcy Act was enacted, society had generally come to recognize that not only is it difficult to obtain further payments from a dead or imprisoned debtor, it is also very hard to obtain payment from a liquidated or care-taker-managed company. Clearly, the debtor has made great progress in the last 2,000 years or so.

The Bankruptcy Reform Act of 1978 represented the first Congressional action in forty years to streamline and clarify the intent and operation of our bankruptcy laws. The Act covers all types of bankruptcies and liquidations. However, we will focus only on one portion: the new Chapter XI, which repre

---

assets, (b) following an execution, foreclosure, or attachment with loss to creditors, (c) after involvement in court actions, (d) involving receivership, reorganization, or arrangement, and (e) voluntary compromise with creditors. Note that the company operating under Chapter 11 is *not* a failure in the D&B definition.

sents a merging of the old Chapter 10 (involuntary) and Chapter 11 (voluntary) provisions into a single set of procedures that should be more equitable to both the creditors and the entrepreneur. Chapter 11 works like this:

Voluntary

The entrepreneur (debtor) may, when confronted with the inability to pay debts in a timely way, petition for the protection of the court (the U.S. District Court). The Court may extend protection or dismiss the petition altogether, whichever it deems to be in the creditor's interest. If the petition is accepted, the petitioner then may continue to operate his or her business under a set of legal ground rules designed to protect the creditors. The petitioner then has 120 days in which to submit to the court a Plan of Reorganization which, if accepted, becomes the operating plan for the duration of the case. The court also has the right to appoint a trustee in cases of voluntary bankruptcy, who takes possession of all assets of the company and oversees operations for as long as the court deems necessary. If the debtor has not submitted a plan within 120 days, or if the court has not found the plan acceptable within 180 days, the trustee may submit a plan of his or her own, as may the creditors. The acceptance of a Plan of Reorganization requires at least one of the following:

1. Acceptance by creditor representing two-thirds of the total dollar claims and 51 percent of the individual claims.
2. Acceptance by any other class of interests (such as shareholders) representing two-thirds of the dollar interests of that class.

The court can impose a plan on any dissenting class, so long as it deems it to be "fair and equitable" to that class. Also, if there is more than one qualified plan in front of the court, the court may decide which, if any, to approve. Once a plan is accepted by the court, it becomes the new operating charter for the entrepreneur. The plan may give the entrepreneur quite a lot of latitude. He or she may raise new funds by selling shares, by borrowing money, by leasing or selling assets of the firm, and by continuing operations in the most profitable manner.

Involuntary

Under the Act, the creditors still have the right to petition the court to order a company's reorganization. A petition may be submitted by a group of creditors whose claims total only $5,000. However, if an involuntary petition is submitted, the debtor has the right to contest it; if successful in having i thrown out, the debtor is entitled to court costs, legal fees, and damages. I unsuccessful, the debtor has, as before, 120 days to submit a Plan of Reorga nization. The procedures then are essentially the same as in the voluntar case.

These provisions of the new law are generally quite favorable to th entrepreneur; they give relief from harassment by creditors, stockholders and others as soon as the court accepts the petition. They allow an opportu nity to develop a workable plan to turn the company around, rather than jus assigning a receiver or liquidator. They provide a chance to raise new monie by subordinating the claims of the old creditors; and they give the right t fight off any attempt to place the entrepreneur in involuntary bankruptcy. I short, they give this person far more than the benefit of the doubt, and a fai chance of recovering from his or her straits.

WHAT'S IN A PLAN OF REORGANIZATION?

The Plan of Reorganization for a Chapter 11 reorganization is a little like you financial business plan, in that it must convince some very skeptical people o your ability to make the company profitable. This includes, predictably, finan cial projections, market data, product information, etc. It also includes on other very important item: your plan for treatment of creditors. These in clude, usually, a *reduction* in claim (called "composition of debt"), *extension* o payment date, and often a *substitution* of other securities for debt. Thus, typical Plan of Reorganization could offer the following:

1. Pay off all creditors with claims under $100.
2. Reduce all other claims to $100 and pay them.
3. Distribute one share of common stock for each dollar of claims unpaid

Or you could just resort to the good old $.10 on the dollar method, or schedule of payment in full, over a long period. Many permutations ar possible.

DIVING IN AND DIGGING OUT

Today it looks like the end. The phone never stops ringing, and the creditor aren't just angry—they're starting to panic. You've moved heaven and eartl to collect that enormous account receivable, but to no avail—it looks like you customer is going broke and taking you along. Meanwhile, rumors of creditors' committees have reached your banker, who is getting nervous, too. The stockholders have started to call up to find out what the hell is going on. The brimstone smell of bankruptcy is in the air. What do you do?

The first thing is, don't panic. The second is, get to your attorney fast. If Chapter 11 is the only logical route in your lawyer's judgment, you must not waste time in filing your Petition, before the creditors get organized and file theirs. Once the petition is granted, you have a breathing spell of up to 120 days to file a Plan of Reorganization, and another 60 days while the court and the creditors are considering it. During this time you can, of course, work on the problem that sent you into U.S. District Court in the first place, but chances are you won't get it resolved. So, keep your fingers crossed, and do whatever you can to persuade holdout creditors that their best chance of recovery is your plan.

Once in Chapter 11, you've got your work cut out. You must make the plan work or resign yourself to the liquidation of your company. You must function on less cash than ever before. You'll be obliged to cut staff and overheads to the bone; you'll cut advertising, development, and other discretionary costs. You'll need every tactic in the book to operate under the conditions that will prevail (see Chapter 7, "Operating Without Capital"). You will have to be a veritable Norman Vincent Peale of inspiration and optimism.

There are several groups of people who will require some constant attention and inspiration during this business:

1. *Customers.* Your customers are your only hope of salvation. Their reaction to the announcement of your bankruptcy will be negative, to say the least. Personally call up or write all customers and visit key customers. Explain that the problems are only temporary, that their source of supply is secure, and that your're going to be in business to back up the products they have bought in the past.

   Step up your rate of press announcements of new products, new personnel, new anything, to let the world know you're both alive and kicking.

2. *Creditors.* They are the whole reason for the exercise and have "donated" a major portion of your new working capital. They deserve to be kept informed. Don't avoid them; be open and cooperative, and continue to try to win their confidence—not just their grudging acquiescence.

3. *Stockholders.* Even though they may have no vote, they are still very important to you. They stand to lose more than anybody; moreover, they may be your only hope of getting additional loans or referrals, so you

need them. Send them a monthly memo and let them know how th
Plan of Reorganization is being pursued.

4. *Employees and Reps.* The last thing you want at this stage is defection c
key employees or reps. Keep maximum contact, be a source of inspira
tion, keep everybody focused on the tasks at hand, not on the pas
difficulties. Try sales contests, special incentives, awards for special ac
complishment. If you're feeling a trifle gloomy, don't let anybody kno\
it.

With courage and persistence, you can dig your way out of Chapter 11
Those who have, say it is a uniquely educational experience in hard-nose
management. As a matter of sobering fact, however, it should be noted tha
fewer than one-tenth of the firms that enter Chapter 11 do, in fact, make i
out. Viewed in perspective,

**Chapter 11 is, indeed, a management tool. It permits you to raise workin
capital by the delightfully simple expedient of stealing it (legally) from you
unsecured creditors.**

Then, with the court protecting you from their wrath, you're back on the ol
corner, selling the old goods. Business as usual, except now the stakes hav
been pushed up a notch: This is your last chance to make it. If you repeat th
same mistakes that got you into Chapter 11, you may well expect to end up :
Dun & Bradstreet statistic. But even that's a lot better than rowing a galley o
nourishing a lion.

ALTERNATIVES TO FORMAL BANKRUPTCY

Despite its benefits, Chapter 11 can be costly both to file and work through
A competent bankruptcy lawyer can recommend suitable alternatives tha
have the same effect as Chapter 11, but without court protection. The alterna
tives may be faster and much cheaper. As before, they rely upon the consen
of the creditors, but these people too stand to benefit if a faster cheapei
process will leave more money in the company's treasury. Edmond Freier
muth discusses some of those alternative forms of reorganization (please se
References).

CONVENTIONAL WISDOM: Chapter 11: The end of the line.

REALITY: Chapter 11: One more management tool.

REFERENCES

1. Freiermuth, Edmond P. *Revitalizing Your Business.* Chicago, Ill.: Probus Publishing Co., 1985.

    A little book of invaluable advice, ideas, and step-by-step plans for the entrepreneur whose business is headed down. Explores the informal forms of reorganization, as well as Chapter 11.

2. Freiermuth, Edmond P. *Life After Debt.* Homewood, Ill.: Dow Jones Irwin, 1988.

    This is in some sense the sequel to his 1985 book. Again, it's short, practical, and full of street-smart advice on salvaging your venture.

3. Ma, J. C.; Henney, H. D. "What it Takes to Come Out of Chapter XI." *Credit and Financial Management.* (February, 1962).

    A rather interesting article written by a professor and an entrepreneur who have been through it all.

VI
OVER AND OUT

30

Exit This Way

Getting into a deal is a cinch, compared to getting out.   . . Anonymous

WHY GET OUT?

If you're a typical entrepreneur there will come a time when you will want to get out of your company. This is not necessarily just a matter of cashing out, since (a) it is possible that via a secondary issue you have enough cash, and (b) if you liquidated your entire position you'd have to pay the government, then reinvest it someplace else. However, there are several valid reasons why you might very well wish to get out, among which may be:

1. You have found a better opportunity you wish to pursue, or you want to look for one.
2. You're tired/bored with the old business, even if it's successful. You'd like some new problems, some new people, maybe even a new career.

3. You feel that the major growth phase is over, or possibly you see some serious problems ahead for the company.

4. You feel that the entrepreneurial phase is over and are not sure of your ability/desire to become the skillful custodial manager needed for the next phase of growth.

For these or a number of other reasons you are likely to be looking for a graceful exit somewhere between five and ten years from startup.

LIFE STRATEGY

If you're like most of us, a lot of more planning goes into your business life than into your personal life. If you need some concrete evidence of this, just look at the mess your checkbook is in (unless your spouse does it), and how irrational your cumulative personal investment decisions look. The months and years on the firing line of your company make it appear that the company *is* your life. It isn't. It is merely the dominant component in this phase of your life.

It would be well if, one day each year, you would sit down with your spouse and update your ten-year plan. This might be very useful, even if it merely serves to identify those areas in which there is no agreement, or no possibility of predicting/influencing the outcome. Try setting some goals, just as you do for the business. Remember, a goal differs from a wish. A wish could take the form, "I want to be happy"; a goal would take the form, "By age 45 I wish to retire with a net worth of $750,000." A goal has the characteristics of *concreteness, measurability, time-relations,* and *attainability.* In the absence of any of these four characteristics, you don't have a working goal—you have a wish.

Your goals and schedules might include such items as the following:

1. Your spouse's change in occupation

2. Acquisition of physical assets for personal use (e.g., a new home, country place, boat, airplane)

3. Attainment of a particular investment goal (e.g., assets of $2,000,000 yielding unearned income of $200,000 per year)

4. Your desire to change jobs or career

5. Extensive travel

6. Return to graduate school

7. Ability to assume support of parents
8. Relocating in a desired geographical location.

Your plan must include not only the goals, but the requisite intervening steps for getting there, and the milestones you will establish for measurement of progress toward them. You should also list the risks/obstacles to attainment and the strategies you will employ to overcome them.

To the extent you are able to integrate the progress of your business into your personal ten-year plan, you will be better able to make correct decisions about whether, when, and how to exit from the company. In fact, it will pull many other elements of your personal decision-making focus, as well.

XIT MODES

There are several exit modes from the company. These include, mainly

1. Business failure
2. Getting fired by directors
3. Selling to another firm
4. Selling your stock to private parties, including others in the company
5. Selling your stock in a public secondary offering.

Not all will be available to every entrepreneur, obviously. They differ in rate of personal exit, rate of financial exit, and range of follow-on options.

Business Failure

When the doors are closed involuntarily, it is usually the end of the road for the firm, but not necessarily for the entrepreneur. This person is usually out looking for a new deal the next morning, although the failure of the last one may take some tall explaining. Some ultra-entrepreneurial types have even been known to show up at their firm's liquidation auction, buy up the assets at a nickel on the dollar, and behold: they are back on the old corner Monday morning.

The folding of your company, however, may provide an appropriate juncture to pause and reflect. Was it really bad luck, or are you yourself weak in certain areas that may jeopardize success in future ventures? What lessons can be gleaned from the experience? Try writing yourself an essay on the

experience, complete with prescriptions for dealing with the forces that led t
your last company's downfall.

Getting Fired by Directors

This is, in some respects, more undesirable than business failure, although it i
possible that it leaves you with more assets, therefore more options as to futur
action. Again, some careful analysis of yourself and your company's history is i
order, to establish precisely what went wrong and how to avoid a repeat perfor
mance. Be honest. Was it bad people, bad luck, or bad management?

Selling to Another Firm

This exit route, probably the most common for entrepreneurs, is not necessar
ily an exit at all. In selling your company, it may also be necessary to sel
yourself for a number of years, since without you the value of the enterpris
may be much lower. This is especially true if the selling company is to b
operated as a subsidiary. It is perhaps less true if you are to become a divisio
or a department.

The new role may be bondage or a fantastic opportunity, dependin
upon circumstances and your state of mind. Many companies look to thei
subsidiary acquisitions as a major source of future top executive talent, as wel
as growth and diversification for the parent. Others see the acquisition as
sort of portfolio investment, a part of which is the entrepreneur. This perso
is bought with it and sold with it, as circumstances demand.

The situations of acquired executives vary widely. Some are locked i
only for a given time period; others are locked in by a stock workout arrange
ment, which bases the purchase price on subsequent performance. Some ar
given great latitude—for example, in acquiring other firms. Others are kep
on a very short tether, indeed.

If your firm was originally financed by a large corporation or its ventur
capital subsidiary, you probably have no choice as to whom to sell it to. I
fact, the pricing formula may already exist. If this is not the case, howeve
selecting a corporate partner can require some serious research. If you ar
headed for calamity, you probably haven't much leisure in which to check ou
the fine points. If this is not the case, however, you should review you
prospective bedfellow rather carefully. Before approaching anybody, yo
should develop a list of criteria to aid you, your directors, and perhaps
consultant in the search for appropriate corporate partners. These criteri
could for example include:

1. Size of company
2. Present business
3. Experience in acquisitions. Are they sophisticated, or will they make all their mistakes with you? Will you get a better price from an unsophisticated firm?
4. Familiarity with your industry and market
5. Availability of resources needed by your company (e.g., manufacturing capacity, marketing ability, raw materials, working capital)
6. Geographical location. There are pros and cons to close proximity to one's corporate parent.
7. General progressiveness. While a progressive partner may normally be desirable, sometimes the presence of some new blood is what a company needs to revitalize it, creating a bigger opportunity for the new blood.
8. Ownership status. Is it on the NYSE, OTC, or privately held? What is the history of its stock price?
9. Character and reputation of management

You will be able to think of several dozen more criteria. You should rank or weight them, before putting them to use. Remember, even a bad set of criteria is better than simply selling out on the basis of willingness of the other firm to buy. Your choice should, of course, be heavily influenced by your personal ten-year plan, since you may, in effect, be making a long-term career choice at the same time.

Selling Your Stock to Private Parties

Such a route may be available to you on favorable terms. However, even more than the acquiring corporation, the buyers are likely to need you to run the company for some substantial period of time. To ensure this, they may be willing to offer attractive bonuses, option plans, or other incentives to keep you on board.

A major exception, of course, is the case in which your partners and/or stockholders are buying you out to get rid of you. Your greatest obstacle to rational action at this point may be the involvement of your own ego in the process. If the other members of the team are inalterably opposed to your leadership, it may be best for you, too, if you bow out. You are going to have nothing but trouble from now on if you stay. A fight for the sake of winning may ensure that *everyone* loses out.

The toughest problem at this juncture is in getting a fair price for your stock. If it develops that you can't, consider leaving *with* the stock, and let them figure out how to increase its value. A partial solution of some stock and some cash may be the most equitable.

Selling Your Stock in a Public Offering

This is without a doubt the route that has made more millionaires out of entrepreneurs than any other. Subject to timing in the business cycle and other factors, the public has historically been willing to pay more for stock in a growing company than anybody. While an acquiring corporation might be willing to pay ten times earnings, or perhaps its own price earnings ratio, the public may pay 50 times, 100 times, or maybe infinity times earnings. There is no guarantee of this, however, and there are many more risks and hazards than in private acquisition. For example, if your initial public offering (in which you cannot sell any of your personal stock) comes out at 20, and the market promptly takes a nose dive, leaving you at 10, it may be all but impossible to get a secondary offering out. Too many people have already lost money on your stock. Your ability to pull off a satisfactory secondary offering may also be related to the investment banker who handles your offerings. Assuming that company performance is satisfactory, your secondary offering success may depend upon who your investment banker sold the initial offering to, at what price, and how much support (i.e., buying for his or her own account in times of market weakness) he or she has given the stock. If your stock price has risen a bit and held up well, you're golden. If it's fallen a bit and stuck there, you're in for a long wait.

Selection of an investment banker deserves about the same amount of energy as selection of a corporate partner since, in the best case, this person is a corporate partner. The worst kind takes a firm public, then disappears. The best hang on through good and bad, and try to ensure that each successful public offering sets the stage for the next.

In establishing your list of criteria for an investment banker, you may need a little help, since this is an area in which few entrepreneurs are familiar. You may wish to enlist your investors, lawyer, or accounting firm in the job. Among the criteria are:

1. Familiarity and comfort with initial offerings of smaller companies. The largest, most prestigious house may strike out completely in this department.
2. Success with small-company offerings. Their score is a matter of public record. Moreover, presidents of their client firms are readily identified for further checks. Look at the record. What happened to their deal?

3. Research capability. In every market and technology, there are one or two securities analysts considered to be the experts. Their firm is probably where you should be, because the periodic reports of this analyst on the progress of your company will do more to support the after market than anything you could do.

4. "General reputation" in the financial community. This is a vague parameter, but one which will affect profoundly their ability syndicate and sell out your issue quickly. Ask several people, including your lawyer, and directors, to rank a list of twenty firms you give them. Try the same thing on your broker, your banker, and the entrepreneurs they have brought public. A pattern may begin to emerge.

5. Present types of issues. Just because they have done your kind of offering in the past is no guarantee they would do it or do it well today. Was there a specific champion in the house who is no longer there? Where did this person go?

6. Your intuitive reaction. Does the candidate come on like a big-time hustler, a degenerate aristocrat, or a reasonable businessperson with whom you can discuss your business problems? Be sure it's somebody you can personally like and trust.

The selection and dealing with investment bankers is a realm where war stories abound. It may be constructive to listen to a few, and there is no better source than an entrepreneur who has just gone through it. Seek out a couple and see what they have to say.

Initial offerings, except in the case of very strong issuing companies, are seldom underwritten; i.e., they are normally taken on in a best-efforts mode by the underwriter. If the underwriter is unable to sell an agreed-upon minimum (e.g., 80 percent of the issue), you and the investment banker both simply walk away from the agreement. Such an agreement usually involves a hefty fee for the investment banker, if successful (say, 10% of the offering), plus some warrants or cheap stock for his or her own portfolio. The latter is very important, since it creates an incentive for the banker to support your stock and also to promote favorable conditions for a secondary offering so that he or she can cash in.

When you and an investment banker have agreed to work together, there will ensue a negotiation of the different variables of the offering: percent of ownership, pricing, timing, compensation to investment banker, and other considerations. There will be the question of expenses to be picked up by each side of the retention of special counsel (often of the investment banker's choice) for SEC work, and many other considerations.

These are all very critical areas, which may have a profound effect on the company's fortunes and your personal net worth. Your attorney should, of course, be a party to this negotiation. Try to be cooperative without being a patsy. If you honestly feel that they are trying to dictate unreasonable terms, say so. There are other investment bankers; it isn't the end of the world if talks are terminated.

A note on expense is in order. In addition to the investment banker's commission, your company will be expected to pick up the bills for legal, audit, printing, and SEC work incident to the offering. For an offering of, say, $5 million, this could be as much as $250,000. This is bad enough if the offering goes well. It may be disaster for the company, however, if for some reason the offering doesn't sell. Thus, the public offering must be undertaken with an appreciation of this risk, and with a contingency plan of recovery if the worst happens. Do not let the euphoria of public issue and mushrooming paper net worth cause you to lose sight of this very real hazard.

A FINAL NOTE ON GETTING OUT

Your ten-year plan will give you some guidance as to whether, how fast, and how completely you should get out of your firm. Market conditions and the progress of the company itself will provide the constraints. However, some things must be experienced to be understood. This is particularly true of being at loose ends with a lot of money.

The folklore is full of stories about entrepreneurs who cashed out, intending to retire with a bundle, only to discover after six months of walking the beaches that they really only wanted to start another company. Many of these stories are probably true. The personality traits, drives, and abilities that made you an entrepreneur in the first place do not go away the day you cash out. They are part of your permanent psychological equipment. Therefore, don't be surprised if your game plan to retire at forty must be extensively revised when you reach your goal. This will be a happy result for everyone if it happens, because it means that a decision has been reached to put back in use one of society's most valuable assets: a successful entrepreneur!

CONVENTIONAL WISDOM: When you finally make your million, you retire to clip coupons in Boca Raton.

REALITY: When you finally make your million, you'll have learned that starting companies is a lot more fun than retirement.

REFERENCES

1. Buskirk, Richard H.; Vaughn, Percy J. *Managing New Enterprises.* St. Paul, Minn.: West Publishing Co., 1976.
   See especially Section VIII, "Terminating the Enterprise."

2. Strange, M., ed. *Acquisition and Merger Strategy.* New York: Hawthorne Books Inc., 1971.
   Written from the viewpoint of the acquiring firm, this book will offer you some insights on how to be acquired on the most advantageous terms.

3. Liles, Patrick R. *New Business Ventures and the Entrepreneur.* Homewood, Ill.: Irwin, 1974.
   See section on evaluating a going company.

4. Vesper, Karl. *New Venture Strategies.* Englewood Cliffs, N.J.: Prentice Hall, 1980.
   See Sec. 10, "Acquisition Dealing."

5. O'Neal, F. H. *Expulsion or Oppression of Business Associates—Squeeze-outs in Small Enterprises.* Durham, N.C.: Duke University Press, 1961.
   Reviews virtually all squeeze-out techniques in general use, and examines some of the remedies of the squeezer.

Index

Epilogue

The New Economy and Other Myths

It rains upon the just and the unjust alike....St. Matthew

The movement of the Internet from the realm of scientists, academics, and government agencies into a public information infrastructure has brought as much change to business creation and growth as it has to any other segment of daily life that one might imagine. The Internet's impact extends well beyond the fortunes made and lost during the dotcom equity boom of the late 1990s. The Internet has and is fundamentally changing how commerce is realized. It has proven to be a great equalizer between established and emerging voices and ideas. Likewise, in many respects the Internet has leveled the playing field among newly created and established businesses. As we examine later, the equalizing properties of the Internet are a two-edged sword and present their unique challenges for the modern entrepreneur. The dotcom rise and subsequent fall remind entrepreneurs and investors that business fundamentals remain important – *perhaps especially so* – in the dotcom world.

It is also a true and equally important observation that in the wake of the dotcom bubble, venture capital financing has been sharply curtailed compared with 1999 and 2000. The curtailment was both because venture investors were more careful and because the dotcom bubble put many investors themselves out of business. However, this does not mean that venture capital is unavailable. Yes, venture financing is tougher to get than it was, but its demise has been greatly exaggerated.

THE GOOD NEWS

The Internet is a resource that enables entrepreneurs to overcome a number of important barriers in launching and running a new venture. It provides entrepreneurs (indeed all business people) faster, cheaper, and more effective access to important information and communication resources that would otherwise be prohibitively costly and/or complicated to use by non-Internet means. Over time, this should translate into better business plans, better execution, and better decision making.

Perhaps the most important property of the Internet is that it facilitates the flow of information—and information is one of the most valuable weapons in the entrepreneur's arsenal The entrepreneur can gain access to many kinds of market information and raw data more cheaply and with greater effectiveness than ever before. He or she can identify customers, competitors, supply sources, industry trends, and market pricing and obtain tidbits of market research. Such data points, by themselves, may or may not seem very meaningful but when analyzed in concert form a powerful insight on the addressable market.

The impact on communication probably ranks right behind information as a value of the Internet to the entrepreneur. E-mail has become as indispensable to the entrepreneur as the telephone and mailbox. E-mail and, to a lesser extent, instant messaging have become so important that a virtual dialect of the English language has grown around it. It has led to its own rules of etiquette (e.g., TYP-ING IN CAPS IS CONSIDERED SHOUTING).

The explosion of E-mail use is easy to understand. It enables the sender to convey written information without the formality of a paper letter. It allows the transmission of data and documents such as contracts, proposals, sales literature, and support information almost instantly between any two or more points in the world *virtually without cost*. It enables efficient collaboration among colleagues as well as effective communication between vendors and customers.

The Internet also offers the potential to raise managerial effectiveness by enabling managers and company representatives to travel to customers and partners while remaining in closer contact with the office, other partners, and other customers. Whether accessing your E-mail through your hotel room, sending a large file through a hotel's broadband connection, or managing E-mail and instant messages through a wireless device (which are continuously upgrading their speed capabilities), the Internet has played a key role (although not the only one) in enabling managers, representatives, and professionals to be more mobile, more responsive, and more in touch than ever before.

While some may debate the inherent quality-of-life issues that arise with such "road warrior" capabilities, there is no denying the fact that those individuals and companies that are willing and able to take advantage of the communication abilities that the Internet provides enjoy a tangible competitive advantage over those who do not. The blunt fact of the matter is that the only reason a manager is not in contact with the rest of the world at any given point in time is because she or he does not want to be reached.

The communication boon that the Internet offers transcends text messaging in its various formats. Secure "extranets" through virtual private networks enable offices to share files with each other and with customers and partners for collaboration. The Internet also offers an expanded talent pool to the new and growing business. With carefuland creative management, a company in Boston can hire a key executive in Seattle without having to pay for relocation or the salary pre-

mium to entice that person to move to Boston and get the same value
as if he were a local hire.

The Internet promises to offer cheaper and better
videoconferencing capability by a factor of 100, thus possibly saving
some executives' need to travel at all. At present, videoconferencing
of the quality necessary to carry on a serious business meeting is available only at exorbitant expense. Over time, the Internet will make
videoconferencing as casual and accessible as teleconferencing. Ultimately, casual videoconferencing access will reduce travel time and
expenses—which is much more important to the smaller company than
it is to the large one.

The Internet, through videoconferencing capabilities and other
services, is making it possible to collaborate with other managers and
customers on projects in real time and without travel. Travel wastes
time and energy, and it always is expensive. To the extent that your
company can use communication technology (including the Internet) to
facilitate collaboration to draw on geographically far-flung resources, it
will be better off. You may be able to cut consulting costs. Managing
on-line collaboration is one of the great managerial challenges of the
early 21st century. There is a real opportunity for you to gain a competitive advantage by being ahead of the competition in meeting the
challenge and embracing the benefits on-line collaboration offers.

The Internet has also become an important sales, marketing,
and distribution channel, although companies are still figuring out how
to use the new channel profitably. Although the loss carry-forwards
from investments in advertising-driven dotcom companies by individual
and institutional investors (including, notably, venture capitalists) will be
reducing their tax liabilities for years to come, the Internet reaches too
many potential customers to be cast aside as a marketing and sales
medium. Advertising can be as simple as an informational Web site, or
it can include pop-up ads, mass direct E-mail distribution (known in
many circles derogatorily as "spam"), banner ads, or even paid search
prioritization. Despite the dotcom crash, many companies still feel
that advertising on the Internet is a good idea, and a robust corporate
Web site is still considered to be a necessity for any serious company.

THE UNFULFILLED PROMISE OF INTERNET ADVERTISING

We now explore some of the factors that drove the dotcom advertising boom and subsequent bust. Dotcom advertising's initial attractiveness arose from two key properties: It could be made more interesting (interactive) to the consumer and therefore be more effective, and it could somehow be individually targeted specifically to customers who were the most promising prospects, thanks to information mined from the Internet users themselves. The latter was a particularly enticing proposition as it would bring greater financial efficiency to the advertising activity; one ultimately would spend advertising dollars only on those who were most likely to be motivated to purchase. The famous advertising adage, "I know half of my advertising expenditures are wasted; I just don't know which half," was considered to be obsolete.

Those assumptions turned out to be flat-out mistaken. Internet-driven ads turned out to be even easier to ignore than their printed counterparts—and software soon popped up that allowed users to block such ads before they even reached the user. The "microtargeting" of advertisements proved to yield disappointing results as well. Data mining methods proved to be far less than perfect. On-line shopping took hold more slowly than expected. Further complicating the approach were successful efforts by privacy advocates to convince the government to mandate obtaining user permission before obtaining the very data that would make the advertisements so valuable. Regulations also compelled advertisers to allow customers to opt out of advertising lists. The universe with whom on-line advertising would be effective grew ever smaller, even as Internet penetration grew steadily.

In a last-ditch attempt to validate the Internet advertising promise, on-line advertising companies began to offer (they were really compelled to do so by advertisers) "click through" models and "bounty models."

Under the former approach, advertisers paid only for ads that resulted in a link to their site, which indicated they were at least considering a purchase. Later, much of advertising moved to the bounty approach, where advertising agencies received a portion of the proceeds from each sale that was attributable to an ad that the agency sold. That model proved to be mostly unsustainable, and the industry found itself in a struggle for survival.

Perhaps paradoxically, it should not be concluded from the first go-round of the Internet advertising business that the Internet is not an important resource for sales and marketing. The Internet is an important advertising medium, particularly for businesses that operate largely through the Internet. However, the successful advertising model proves elusive. The best advice on this topic is to be very critical of your projected sales that arise as a result of the Web site and allocate resources accordingly. In other words, treat Internet advertising decisions like any other advertising decisions. You are probably still going to waste half your advertising dollars spent on the Internet and not know which half – but even being cognizant of and accepting this fact will help you make good decisions on how to use the Internet as a marketing resource.

COMMUNICATING WITH YOUR CUSTOMERS WITH THE INTERNET

One critical capability that the Internet opens to small companies is the capability to post product specifications, prices, and applications on-line—both on your own Web site and in on-line trade directories such as the on-line versions of Sweet's *Catalog* or Thomas' *Register.* Your customers will more than likely be conducting most, if not all, of their purchasing research on the Internet. Make sure your information is easily available to them. It also means you won't have to wait for the next print publication to be issued before you are available to readers of those catalogs. Instant gratification is one of the great attractions of the Internet. Gratify your customers instantly when you can.

One of the most exciting and tangible impacts of the advent of the Internet is that on distribution and delivery of products and services to customers. Already, the Internet represents a key infrastructure for moving products between vendors and customers. The benefits of using the Internet as a distribution channel are clear: It enables instant satisfaction of the customer's wants by offering real-time downloading of content. Furthermore, the product delivery process is almost completely automated. Once you pay for bandwidth, server capacity, and placement of the hardware, the marginal cost of delivery is practically negligible. Delivery costs, customer care costs (at least during the sale), packaging costs, and storage costs are all eliminated.

The result has been that a great many products and services are obtainable via the Internet. Most publications are available both in print and on-line. The on-line business models may be purchase (one-time payment) or recurring (subscription). Software is increasingly widely distributed over the Internet; this will become more common as broadband connections are more widely available. E-learning (taking classes remotely via the Internet) is a fascinating concept whose market viability has yet to be proven. The (legitimate) distribution of music and movies to customers via the Internet is likely to take hold in the marketplace in the next couple of years; the key issue to be resolved there is how production firms prevent the rampant redistribution (piracy) of their products to nonpaying users. Note that the distribution of content via the Internet has been pioneered in large part by the adult entertainment industry. They were the early adopters of secure on-line credit card processing technology, and they also distribute a tremendous amount of product (e.g., photos) over the Internet and have been doing so longer than most other industries. Putting aside the morality issues involved, the fact remains that the adult entertainment industry is one of the few early commercial success stories on the Internet.

WHAT'S THE CATCH ?

The case is fairly straightforward that the Internet has changed and continues to change the way business is conducted—and for the most part it is for the better. However, so many businesses that relied on the Internet to execute their business plans failed, and did so spectacularly, destroying billions of dollars of capital and often bankrupting their investors and vendors in the process.

The catch of the Internet is very simple, but it is a fact that many very intelligent investors, journalists, and businesspeople overlooked. The Internet levels the playing field for *everyone*. Absent a novel technology, the Internet provides the same opportunities to your competitors as it does to you.

Whatever efficiencies you can realize from using the Internet, new or existing competitors can do the same. Your business plan should reflect that fact in terms of smaller margins, higher advertising expenses, shorter innovation cycles, and (possibly) lower costs over time that enable you to continue competing in the mosh pit of Internet business. Competition is increased by the fact that barriers to entry in establishing yourself on the Internet are so low as to be practically nonexistent. Start-up costs are typically very low (many businesses are run right out of people's apartments), ramp-up time is very quick, geography is far less relevant, and there are few practical regulations that would present a meaningful obstacle to horning in on your business.

Adding to the competitive intensity is the availability of information on the Internet. Customers can price shop without ever leaving their chair. Indeed, a number of sites are available which will allow the user to enter a product, and the site's technology will gather prices from numerous vendors across the Internet. You are not going to receive a substantial premium for convenience if you sell on the Internet.

Just as you are able to gather intelligence on your competitors via the Internet, so can they on you. Skilled searchers can easily find most articles, user group reports, credit profiles, public filings, investor reports, or press releases pertaining to you or your firm. You will also want to publish some information about your company on the Internet. Bear in mind that it will be read by customers and competitors alike.

As if the competitive situation were not intimidating enough, use of the Internet for business is complicated by the fact that most Internet users are still used to the "free" Internet. Potential customers have developed an entitlement mentality that only now is starting to slowly change. Such is the psychology connected to the Internet that consumers who would never consider duplicating their software and distributing them to their friends because of their attitudes toward piracy don't think twice about ripping songs from their CDs and making them available for free to millions of users through Gnutella or some other peer-to-peer network. The lesson to take away from this discussion is that if you plan to use the Internet as a key part of your business model, your expectations for growth should take consumers' "entitlement mentality" into account. The mentality is less prevalent for professional products and services (e.g., market studies and specialized publications), but it is a major stumbling block for companies attempting to sell consumer products and services over the Internet.

Another challenge that the Internet provides to the entrepreneur is the issue of information security. If your company is connected to the Internet, then it is vulnerable to unwanted access by unwelcome visitors. Information security is no longer an optional expense or one that is reserved for large corporations. Information security is an expense that is as important and demanding as electric bills and meeting payrolls. Depending on the nature of your business, you may need anything from a very simple security system (such as an automatic fire wall and data backup tapes) to something more elaborate, such as a virtual private network, data encryption, and off-site data storage.

It is only a matter of time until a virtual intruder will attempt to access your network. That intruder may be fairly benign—just trying to hack in to your system to prove he can do it. He may be a vandal; someone who just likes to make other people's lives difficult by erasing or altering crucial data. Or she or he may be a competitor who wants to gain in-depth intelligence about you or your customers. Loss of data or even lack of data security can be a company-killing event. If word ever got out that someone hacked into your system and harvested credit card information, you could probably start filing for Chapter 7 the next day. Between the lawsuits that would come and the loss of business that would result, you would be history. Treat information security like your business's livelihood and your own personal financial security depend on it. They do.

It may strike you as funny that for all the hype of the Internet, for all the indications that more and more people are logging on every day, for all the money that has been made (and lost) through the Internet, and for all the real promise the Internet offers, it has proven very difficult to make money with.

Over time, two issues have emerged that are at the core of the challenge. First is that for some kinds of businesses, moving on-line does not offer the kind of cost savings that had been hoped for. This proved especially true for E-tailing (E-retailing) businesses, which learned that the cost of operating a mail distribution and shipping system could be at least as expensive as having to maintain retail space. It also turned out that many people were not all that anxious to or even comfortable with eliminating the middleman; he has been proven to be vital in many industries.

Second, the revenue streams have proven to be far less certain than was thought to be the case. As alluded to before, advertising-based revenue models have proven to be nonviable, and convincing customers to pay for the convenience offered by Internet commerce has proven more challenging than predicted. Convincing customers to pay for uniquely Internet-based content (specialty interest Web sites, on-line publications, service-based sites) has also proven very difficult.

Even on-line advertising and marketing methodologies are poorly understood. People view the Internet differently than any other communication medium. They are accustomed to commercials on TV and the radio. They are used to magazines whose content is half advertising. They are not used to banners popping up in the middle of what they are trying to read or having their E-mail boxes flooded with junk mail from advertisers. What's more, there are technologies out there that customers can use to actively oppose your attempt to advertise to them. Regulation of Internet advertising remains in a very nascent stage of development.

The Internet itself is changing rapidly, which makes understanding how to leverage it even more difficult. In addition to evolving regulations, technology is arriving almost daily that will change the nature of information and content being delivered over the Internet. It is widely accepted that at some point in time, the distinction between Internet and television will blur. How to use and leverage such a converged medium will offer its own challenges. It is unclear whether convergence will lead to a life-or-death struggle between television and the Internet for supremacy of the living room.

The entrepreneur needs to recognize that although the Internet offers great opportunities for the new business, maximizing the value it adds to *your* business will require great skill, ingenuity, and planning on your part. If the Internet is a key factor in the ultimate success of your business, then you must very carefully plan the business, taking great care not to overestimate the benefits using the Internet will bring you. It is imperative that you are highly critical of your assumptions and err strongly on the side of being conservative. Most businesses are much better off having too little capacity rather than too much. Challenge your business model. Think to yourself, "What lessons have I learned from prior attempts (by myself or others) to make money through the Internet so that I can succeed where others failed?" What is my business model (i.e., how do I generate revenue and profit)?

TEN TIPS FOR START-UPS—EXPLOITING THE INTERNET

1.   *Your Web site deserves as much attention as your other marketing literature, if not more.* It gives you a chance to "look big" and give customers confidence. Plan to spend some time and money making it look great and keeping it that way.

2.   *"Do it yourself" Web sites are a bad idea if your web site is intended to be a serious commercial asset.* Just as creating good brochures and catalogs requires a professional skill set, so does Web publishing and maintenance.

3.   *Don't pinch pennies on providing bandwidth for your employees.* DSL is cheap enough that you should be able to provide broadband access to your employees. Broadband access improves productivity. It will pay for itself many times over, and enables you to leverage some premium services such as on-line collaboration, videoconferencing, or Internet telephony.

4.   *Understand the limits of E-mail.* As convenient as E-mail is, it should be a supplement to your other communication means. You still need to talk to customers and suppliers on the phone, and you still need to see them in person when time and resources permit.

5.   *You can set yourself apart by making your Web site very user-friendly.* Most commercial Web sites still frustrate as many potential customers as they help. If your site is well designed and helpful, visitors will remember. Make your customers jump through as few hoops as possible to get what they want from you.

6.   *Integrate your Internet strategy into the whole corporate strategy.* Your Internet activities should be planned and executed in concert with your off-line operations. Your on-line presence should be treated explicitly in your business plan.

7.   *"Borrow" ideas from other sites.* If you like something another company has done to make their Internet presence more effective, use their ideas to inspire your own Internet development. If all your competitors have a similar site format and functionality, there is perhaps a sound reason why that is the case.

8.   *Make sure your on-line presence becomes reality as soon as or very shortly after your off-line presence does.* It is much easier to build your on-line presence alongside your growing business

than it is to have your on-line presence "play catch up."

9.   *Be highly skeptical of adopting new technologies or applications for your Internet presence.* Your small venture already has enough risks without assuming additional technology risk.

10.   *Recognize that the Internet is a means to an end— not an end unto itself.* Your Internet presence needs to generate revenue or cut costs measurably for your venture. If your Internet presence fails to tangibly improve your bottom line, then you need to change what you are doing and how you are doing it. It is a good idea to have a separate business plan for your Internet presence so that you can constantly review and improve its performance.

THE DOTCOM BUBBLE AND ITS IMPACT ON FINANCING YOUR BUSINESS

In the first years of the 21st century, raising capital is a lot tougher than it has been for recent memory. The tightness of the private capital market will not deter the dedicated entrepreneur. Good deals still get funded–albeit much more slowly and at much lower valuations than was the case during the late 1990s. The eventual (and inevitable) end of the dotcom run is healthy for the venture investing industry and, ultimately, healthy for entrepreneurship. Once again, the industry has become the brutal meritocracy that is an integral contributor to the success of the industry as a whole. You will have to work harder, and your faith in your opportunity and capabilities will be very sorely tested to raise venture capital for your business. Rarely are visits to a venture capital firm a self-esteem-building experience. However, in spite of these tough conditions, you as the entrepreneur should keep the fact in mind that if you have a good deal, with a sensible business model, a clearly defined and verifiable opportunity, and some track record that indicates that you are capable of converting plans into results, you have a realistic chance of convincing a venture capital investor to invest in your business. Investors are continuing to fund deals at historically highrates. The deals are out there—you just have to work harder and smarter.

FIVE TYPES OF INTERNET-DEPENDENT COMPANIES LIKELY TO SUCCEED IN THE POST-DOTCOM ECONOMY (AND ANY OTHER)

1.   Companies in more traditional industries that leverage the Internet to improve their business processes have a good chance at being successful.

2.   Companies that offer a unique and compelling value proposition are likely to succeed in any economy. The ONLY way to define a unique and compelling value proposition is to demonstrate that customers are willing to pay more for the product than it costs to produce it and are willing to buy enough of the product so that you and your investors are rewarded for the risk of bringing your product to the market in the first place.

3.   Internet-dependent companies that project slow, organic growth are more likely to succeed than those which attempt to achieve explosive growth. You are often better off missing a couple of short-term sales than you are investing to prepare for demand that fails to materialize.

4.   Companies that draw revenues from both its on-line and off-line presences (clicks and mortar companies) are more likely to be successful than pure on-line companies.

5.   Companies that offer incremental product improvements may be more likely to succeed than companies attempting to promote a revolution in their markets. The economy is still digesting the recent explosion in commercial and consumer innovation that arose from the last business cycle, and many consumers, businesses, and investors are still stinging from bets they placed on revolutionary technologies that never panned out commercially.

It may be helpful to review the present state of the venture financing market and learn the cause–effect relationships that have led the market to its present condition. Once you understand the investment environment from the viewpoint of the investor, you can understand investors' appetite for opportunities—including yours.

The causes of the dotcom bubble can be traced to a loss of sight on the basics of business. They lie in poor management, poor oversight, unchecked naivete, and poor judgment. Even only a couple of years after the dotcom craze ended, the fundamental decision-making flaws are so starkly revealed that one is left wondering how such an environment could even be created.

At the root of the problem was the fact that inexperienced managers were given responsibility that should have gone to people perhaps 10 or more years older in most cases. You don't need to have a Harvard MBA to see the strangeness in giving a 21-year- old full responsibility for a company that has raised a quarter of a billion dollars in capital. However, that is precisely what investors did. They decided to forsake hard business experience and acumen for the vitality and creativity of youth (and the mirage of easy money in the public markets). In retrospect, the results were predictable. The inexperienced executives solved efficiency problems by hiring more people rather than analyzing process. Capital spending included in-house gyms and pools. Most entrepreneur–managers were financially illiterate and poorly equipped for resolving personal and resource conflicts. When cash continued to pour in from investors even when it was practically absent from customers, there was very little accountability for decision-making and resource allocation. Everything had to be done in "Internet time." There was no time for due diligence, no time for team building, no time to talk to customers to find out if the dogs would eat the dog food.

Investors enabled their portfolio companies to lose sight of the fundamentals. Whereas before 1995, investment firms would be very open to making investing in a company contingent on replacing the non-managerial innovator with a professional executive, many investors suddenly lost their nerve. To the contrary, investors were so desperate not to be left behind in the dotcom boom that they became beholden to the young innovators. Shopping a deal to other investors became a very real threat. Another reason investors lost control of their portfolios is that the external investors provided almost all of the capital for these dotcom businesses. So while the investors were financially committed to their portfolio companies to such a degree that the failure of one or two investments might bankrupt them (or at least cause them to fall far short of the returns they promised their own investors), the innovators at any time could simply walk away and go to college and keep the Ferraris they bought with their bonus money. In the end, investors were competing for deals–completely upending the more natural state where projects should compete for capital. The result: the inmates were running the asylum.

The willingness to ignore hard performance metrics contributed to and in turn fueled the poor management that led to the failure of many dotcom investments. Revenues and EBITDA (Earnings Before Interest, Taxes, Depreciation, and Amortization – a rough proxy of cash flow from operations) were replaced with "eyeballs" (number of people seeing a site) and "click-throughs" (number of people actually clicking an advertisement with their mouse to learn more). It was assumed the eyeballs and clicks were assets that could be "monetized" (i.e.,become money). But, the cost of monetizing them mounted and mounted, with the pot of gold seemingly just at the end of the rainbow. Companies kept growing and growing—at least in terms of capitalization and annual budgets. It was on this basis that the term "new economy" was coined. The implication of the new economy was that a new kind of management was dawning on the economy and that the business cycle was pronounced dead.

After months and even years of predictions of doom from the market pundits, April 2000 was the month that reality finally beset the market, and it experienced a sharp, painful downward correction. Almost as if investors snapped out of a mass psychosis, they seemingly abandoned the whole dotcom sector, and they did it very suddenly and quickly. The appetite for initial public offerings seemed to vanish overnight. The natural exit, as well as a vital source of cash for so many venture investments, disappeared. Investors and executives learned the harsh lesson that it is far easier to manage a company with lots of cash than in an environment where cash is actually a resource in limited supply.

The business cycle had risen from the dead, and suddenly, things like revenues, earnings, and sustainable business models mattered. And the executive–entrepreneurs were, for the most part, nowhere near adequately equipped to meet the new demands that the vengeful old economy was placing on them. Thousands of jobs disappeared, including for many very capable people, and businesses closed left and right. Investors were left with very bad-looking portfolios, and some followed their investments into bankruptcy. Venture capital as an industry experienced its worst performing year ever, losing 21.4% of its value between Q3 2000 and Q3 2001. (By contrast the NASDAQ lost 64.4%

in the same period.)[1] Indeed, the dotcom closure story became so commonplace that it was a major contributor to the sharp slowdown of the national economy in 2001–2002. The image of the venture capitalist went from dotcom rock star to stodgy, brick-and-mortar curmudgeon almost overnight. Basic economics dictated as such.

By necessity, the venture investor's focus changed from expansion to survival. The first order of business was to decide which businesses were worth supporting and which ones needed to be left on their own. Investors diverted cash from new investments into keeping existing ones afloat until they could be brought public or sold privately. New opportunities looked less attractive without the lucrative public offering exit route. Privately held companies that planned to turn to the public markets found themselves forced to once again approach the same universe of private investors, not to raise capital for growth, but to give themselves a chance at survival. Some private equity firms saw their own investors (limited partners) become less enthusiastic about investing in private equity firms, thus choking their own supply of capital.

Amid the doom and gloom that the industry's statistics offer, the ray of sunshine is the fact that there is a lot of venture capital out there to be invested. Venture capital continues to be invested at historically very high levels. In fact, due to the perceived lack of quality deals available to venture investors, investment firms have actually been returning cash to their own investors. In spite of this, the pace of investment has slowed dramatically because investors are planning for a 3-5-year incubation period for their investments (which is in line with historical patterns), rather than the 12-18-month flip strategy that was more commonplace in 1999–2000.

Furthermore, despite the evaporation of the IPO (Initial Public Offering) market, an exit still exists through merger and/or acquisition. Historically, M&A deals tend to be smaller than IPOs, and M&A deals indeed tend to raise less capital and yield lower valuations than a public offering. However, in a tight exit market, beggars can't be choosers, and entrepreneurs who have exited via the M&A have financially done very nicely, thank you.

---

[1] www.ventureeconomics.com, "Private equity performance continued downward trend in Q3 2001." February 19, 2002.

The deal pendulum has swung and remains sharply in favor of the investors, who must make decisions about how to allocate capital among a huge number of opportunities. It is a great challenge again to raise venture capital financing. *In other words, the venture financing industry has returned to normal.* That is not a bad thing. You should bear in mind that the pre-dotcom years (pre-1996) also were years when the venture landscape was filled with such brick-and-mortar curmudgeons. Those years were also profitable ones. Deals got done, people got rich, and some other people went broke. But the deals were fewer and of higher quality—largely because they fell under far greater scrutiny.

Venture capitalists typically have very acute and long memories. Those venture capital firms that survived the crash have returned to relying on "old-school" business fundamentals. You as the entrepreneur must recognize that risk aversion is high among venture investors and that your business plan and model must be rock solid to obtain funding.

This is a positive development for both entrepreneurs and investors. You will get better managerial coaching and support from your investors if you find venture financing than you would have in the late 1990s, and investors will have better portfolios over time. Better returns will encourage more capital to be made available for venture deals in the future. Maybe that capital will be intended for a follow-on round for your present company or maybe for the new company you start.

There are a number of lessons that you as the entrepreneur can take away from the Internet craze of the 1990s.

1.   The Internet bubble served to underscore the need for business fundamentals. The most important lesson to be learned is that the same formulas for success for a brick-and-mortar business apply to online businesses as well. In fact, because of the competition-enhancing nature of the Internet, the basics of business are even *more* important. The market will punish executives for managerial errors more swiftly and severely than ever.

2. The nature of the Internet as a business opportunity is poorly understood. It is widely assumed that the Internet represents a great business opportunity, and billions of dollars have been made thanks to the Internet. However, harnessing the value of the Internet has proven to be a great deal more challenging than was previously believed. The

Internet does not make money for its own sake, and there will likely be no such thing as an "Internet company." Instead, all or most companies will use the Internet as a means of conducting their ordinary business—just as the telephone and the computer were adopted in the past. You still need a business model that convincingly demonstrates who pays for your product or service, why people will pay for it, how you generate a profit, and why someone else cannot replicate your business plan and thus impede your profit potential.

3.   Investors became reacquainted with due diligence. The era of the two-week (or less!) venture deal is over. Expect to spend months in meetings and conversations with investors, possibly traveling thousands of miles making pitches, and spending lots of time fulfilling investors' requests for information. If you expect anything better, you will die of frustration. Expect rejection and be pleasantly surprised if you get positive responses. Investors are not making you run just for laughs. They are upholding their fiduciary responsibility to their own investors by gathering all the relevant facts about your investment opportunity before reaching a decision to commit funds and principals' time.

4.   The need for building startups at "Internet speed" has been completely discredited. As proof, simply reference the nearly total disappearance of so-called Internet incubators. Ask yourself if you are really a "first mover" or simply a lead lemming. The keys to building a successful business remain assembling solid management teams, developing robust products with a clear value proposition to customers, having strong boards, and creating a supportive infrastructure, and they cannot be accomplished overnight. Attempting to outsource these ingredients is an even worse idea.

When it rains, we all get wet. The excesses of the dotcom bubble resulted in a huge loss of faith in the entrepreneurial model, and in a large backlog of bad venture capital deals. Both made it difficult (and very costly) to raise capital for *any* deal, whether Internet-dependent or not. At the time of this writing, the venture capital industry is just starting to recover from an 18-month shortage of venture capital. These are tough times to be an entrepreneur, but not impossible. By learning and embracing the lessons offered by the dotcom frenzy, you will give yourself and your business a real advantage not just in raising capital, but in succeeding in the market.

Printed in the United States
52106LVS00004B/164